STAKEHOLDER CAPITALISM

Stakeholder Capitalism

Edited by

Gavin Kelly
Political Economy Research Centre
University of Sheffield

Dominic Kelly
Political Economy Research Centre
University of Sheffield

and

Andrew Gamble
Professor of Politics
University of Sheffield

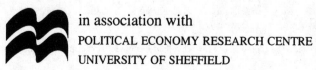

in association with
POLITICAL ECONOMY RESEARCH CENTRE
UNIVERSITY OF SHEFFIELD

First published in Great Britain 1997 by
MACMILLAN PRESS LTD
Houndmills, Basingstoke, Hampshire RG21 6XS and London
Companies and representatives throughout the world

A catalogue record for this book is available from the British Library.

ISBN 0–333–68773–6 hardcover
ISBN 0–333–68774–4 paperback

First published in the United States of America 1997 by
ST. MARTIN'S PRESS, INC.,
Scholarly and Reference Division,
175 Fifth Avenue, New York, N.Y. 10010

ISBN 0–312–17346–6

Library of Congress Cataloging-in-Publication Data
Stakeholder capitalism / edited by Gavin Kelly, Dominic Kelly and
Andrew Gamble.
p. cm.
Includes papers originally presented at an international
conference sponsored by the Political Economy Research Centre at the
University of Sheffield in March 1996.
Includes bibliographical references (p.   ) and index.
ISBN 0–312–17346–6 (cloth)
1. Industries—Social aspects—Congresses. 2. Industrial
management—Congresses. I. Kelly, Gavin, 1970– II. Kelly,
Dominic, 1965– III. Gamble, Andrew.
HD60.S678   1997
302.3'5—dc21   96–29602
                                                        CIP

This book is printed on paper suitable for recycling and made from fully managed and
sustained forest sources.

10   9   8   7   6   5   4   3   2   1
06   05   04   03   02   01   00   99   98   97

Printed in Great Britain by
The Ipswich Book Company Ltd
Ipswich, Suffolk

Contents

Foreword

This book constitutes one of the products of the wide-ranging research programme initiated by the Political Economy Research Centre (PERC) at the University of Sheffield since its establishment in late 1993. PERC itself was created in the belief that the perspectives of the past cannot address the problems posed by the world-wide economic and political transformations of the last decade. Its mission has thus been to explore the new issues in political economy from an interdisciplinary standpoint. In this spirit PERC held a major international conference in March 1996 devoted to a critical examination of the emerging concept of 'stakeholder capitalism'. The conference attracted over 350 participants who came from all parts of Britain and from several other countries, including the USA, Russia, Germany, Norway and Poland. The event was spread over one and a half days and involved a number of workshops and plenary sessions. By common account it was a great success. This book, which has been jointly edited by three members of PERC, Gavin Kelly, Dominic Kelly and Andrew Gamble, takes forward the debate about stakeholder capitalism initiated by that conference. It is not, however, the conventional conference volume. Although some of the chapters do draw upon presentations made in Sheffield in March 1996, several others have been specifically written for the book by eminent political economists and political thinkers who wanted urgently to join the debate about 'stakeholding'. As a result the book offers an invaluable, contemporary account of what is meant by stakeholder capitalism.

Anthony Payne
Director of PERC
Sheffield

Preface

This book has its origins in the conference on 'Stakeholder Capitalism: Blind Alley or Best Hope?' held at the Political Economy Research Centre (PERC) on 28 and 29 March 1996. Revised versions of some of the papers presented at the conference are reproduced here, along with other contributions which have appeared previously elsewhere but which seemed to us to be of particular relevance to the contemporary debate. The majority of the contributions, however, have been specially commissioned for the book and appear here for the first time. The contributors are drawn from a range of backgrounds – policy researchers, MPs, journalists and academics. The aim of the book has been to represent the many different perspectives and approaches to the idea of stakeholding in the hope that this will stimulate further debate and exploration of the principles underlying it.

This book has been prepared in a very short time and the editors would like to express their thanks to all the contributors for writing their chapters and responding to queries so promptly, and also to Tony Payne (Director of PERC), Sylvia McColm (PERC Administrator *extraordinaire*), Natalie Wood (PERC Secretary) and Sunder Katwala (Macmillan) for their help, encouragement and support. Nourishment provided by the Balti King the Mangla and the South Sea has also been indispensable to the completion of the project.

Gavin Kelly
Dominic Kelly
Andrew Gamble

PERC
University of Sheffield
September 1996

Acknowledgements

The editors would like to thank the following for permission to reprint material in which they hold the copyright.

Political Quarterly for Harold Perkin, Chapter 5, 'The Third Revolution'.
New Political Economy for Meghnad Desai, Chapter 17, 'It's Profitability, Stupid'.
Prospect for David Soskice, Chapter 18, 'Stakeholding Yes; the German Model No'.

Notes on Contributors

Anthony Barnett is Director of Charter 88 and has written widely on different aspects of constitutional reform.

Dan Corry is Senior Economist at the Institute for Public Policy Research and the founding editor of IPPR's journal of economic policy *New Economy*. He is currently editing a major book on public expenditure for release in early 1997.

Alistair Darling is shadow Chief Secretary to the Treasury and has been the MP for Edinburgh Central since 1987.

Meghnad Desai is Professor of Economics at the London School of Economics, and Director of the Centre for the Study of Global Governance. He is also a Labour peer in the House of Lords.

Andrew Gamble is Professor of Politics at the University of Sheffield and a member of the Political Economy Research Centre. He is on the editorial board of *New Political Economy* and is joint editor of *Political Quarterly*.

Paul Hirst is Professor of Social Theory at Birkbeck College, University of London. He is a member of the editorial board of *Political Quarterly* and an executive of Charter 88. He is the author of a number of books including *Associative Democracy* (1994) and (with Grahame Thompson) *Globalisation in Question* (1996).

Will Hutton is editor of the *Observer*. He is the author of *The Revolution That Never Was* and *The State We're In*. He is on the advisory board of the Political Economy Research Centre.

John Kay is Director of London Economics and Professor of Economics at the London Business School.

Dominic Kelly is researching into East Asian political economy and forms of governance at the Political Economy Research Centre.

Gavin Kelly is a Research Officer at the Political Economy Research Centre and is working on a project on corporate governance and regulation.

Robert Kuttner is co-editor of the *American Propect*, and columnist for the *Washington Post* and *Business Week*.

Ruth Lister is Professor of Social Policy at Loughborough University. She is a former Director of the Child Poverty Action Group and sat on the Commission on Social Justice. She has published widely on issues around poverty, income maintenance and citizenship, and is currently writing a book on feminist perspectives on citizenship for Macmillan.

James McCormick joined the IPPR in 1993 and worked as a Research Fellow with the Commission on Social Justice. He coordinated the work of the Commission's Services and Communities policy panel, publishing *Citizens' Service*.

John Parkinson is a Professor of Law at the University of Bristol. His book *Corporate Power and Responsibility* contains a detailed analysis and critique of the British system of corporate governance and an examination of the concept of corporate social responsibility.

Andrew Pendleton is a lecturer in Industrial Relations at the University of Bradford. He has written extensively on different aspects of employee share ownership.

Harold Perkin is Professor of History at Northwestern University, USA, and author of *The Rise of Professional Society* and *The Third Revolution: International Professional Elites Since 1945*.

Jonathan Perraton is Baring Fellow in the Political Economy Research Centre and Lecturer in Economics at the University of Sheffield. He is author, with David Goldblatt, David Held and Anthony McGrew, of *Global Flows, Global Transformations: Concepts, Evidence and Arguments* (forthcoming).

Michael Rustin is Professor of Sociology at the University of East London, and co-editor of the journal *Soundings*.

David Soskice is Director of the Institute for Employment and Economic Change at the Wissenschaftszentrum fur Sozialforschung, Berlin. He is also Emeritus Fellow in Economics at University College, Oxford.

David Willetts is Conservative MP for Havant. He has been closely associated with the development of Conservative policy over the past decade and has written widely on economic and social issues. His publications include *Modern Conservatism* (1992), *Civic Conservatism* (1994) and *Happy Families* (1991). He has served in the government whips office and was Paymaster General in 1996 until his resignation.

Janet Williamson is a Policy Officer at the TUC in the Economic and Social Affairs Department. She has been a member of the TUC Stakeholder Task Group since its inception in the autumn of 1995.

Part I

Perspectives

1 An Overview of Stakeholding
Will Hutton

It is currently rather fashionable to say 'I don't know what stakeholding means'. Like all political ideas it has many different meanings, and it has sparked a lively debate on the left between advocates and detractors. There is nothing surprising in this. The right has its internal debates as well. Yet although there are many shades of Conservative opinion few people do not know what the right stands for. One purpose of a book such as this should be to puncture the claim that stakeholding has no clear meaning once and for all. In this chapter I shall first set out what I see as the political economy of stakeholding, then indicate some areas of policy where I think it could be developed, and finish by trying to rebut some of the criticisms that are laid against it.

What underpins the fundamental idea of stakeholding is that social and economic inclusion, rather than equality, should be the overriding objective for the contemporary left. Inclusion implies membership; you cannot be included if you are not a member. But membership entails obligations as well as rights. So a stakeholder society and a stakeholder economy exist where there is a mutuality of rights and obligations constructed around the notion of economic, social and political inclusion. What stakeholder capitalism does is to apply those principles to the operation of free market capitalism and by doing so it places limits on the operation of unfettered markets.

In exploring the notion of stakeholder capitalism we have to address such vexed questions as where the market should end and where relationships of inclusion should begin, and how the flexibility and autonomy associated with market relationships can be combined with the inclusion and solidarity associated with relationships of inclusion. Although these are difficult questions that does not mean that the search for answers makes no sense. But if we are to devise convincing answers then we must first recognise the interconnections between the social, economic and political systems: economic events do not occur in isolation, they arise out of particular social and political contexts. In short we need to develop an analytical approach which recognises these interconnections. For this we should turn to the traditions of political economy.

THE POLITICAL ECONOMY OF STAKEHOLDING

Some critics, including many who would class themselves as advocates of stakeholder capitalism, have rejected political economy as being an approach dominated either by Marxists or by the New Right. This view is mistaken. Political economy is an attempt to broaden the basic concepts and insights of economics by understanding economic behaviour in the particular political and social contexts in which it arises. It seeks to understand the dynamics of whole social systems and the interrelationship of economics, politics and culture.

How can we understand the current model of political economy within the UK? We should start from the proposition that in market capitalism there will always be a constant tension between relationships of commitment and relationships of flexibility; between market contracts and non-market contracts. My central argument is that many of the present instabilities within society are the result of the balance being tilted too far in favour of an emphasis on free markets. This creates an environment which is so unstable, and which leads to such exclusion and polarisation, that it actually destroys the social habitat within which a successful regulated market system needs to be embedded. This pattern is particularly clear in the US where you see atomistic markets throwing up, for example, an excessively large financial services industry as people try desperately to protect themselves against unquantifiable and unmeasurable degrees of risk. Simultaneously 2 per cent of the black population of America are incarcerated for turning to crime due to their exclusion from the labour market.

To understand the cause of this instability we need to consider the fulcrum on which capitalism turns: the drive for profit. In Britain this takes the form of the pursuit of abnormally high rates of return. Of course, in any capitalist society there will be profit, it is the juice on which the economy runs. What we need to unpack are the ways in which we think about profit. What are the time horizons over which profit is made and what are the benchmarks used to appraise investment proposals? What is a reasonable level of profit?

In Britain we face a particular intersection of two factors which together bring about the drive for these high returns. First, we have a very diffused ownership structure – in which a hundred insurance companies and sixty pension funds own 70 per cent of the shares in British companies – and a highly liquid capital market. When this is combined with our nineteenth-century conceptions of corporate governance – in which shareholder interests rule supreme – it sets in train the search for exceptionally high financial returns and exceptionally short payback periods. This is reflected in the way corporations conduct their policies and set their strategic objectives. Hence the spiral of corporate downsizing and delayering, and the displacement of risk onto labour forces which are increasingly unprotected due to the deregulation of the labour market and the attack on trade unions. The emasculation of labour can be seen as a direct result both of the way the macroeconomy has been run – which has led to the creation of a large pool of unemployed and economically inactive individuals – and in the stripping away from trade unions of rights to representation and recognition.

The linkages are clear. Liquid capital markets, the pattern of ownership, and unregulated market processes all feed straight through to the labour market and result in what I call the 'thirty/thirty/forty society'. These percentages represent the structural fissures in today's labour market. Thirty per cent of the workforce are economically excluded from work through unemployment (whether officially counted or otherwise) or through being economically inactive. This is the domain of social dislocation and endemic poverty. The next 30 per cent are the newly marginalised and insecure. These are the workers on short contracts, part-timers, the recently self-employed and others with little or no security of tenure. This leaves a privileged 40 per cent who are in the comfortable possession of a secure full-time job, or who have remained self-employed or in the same part-time job for a number of years. Of course living standards within this group vary but taken as a whole these are the winners in the post-1979 period. The economic forces behind these disturbing labour market trends are central to the way we live our lives. Their effects shape our capacity to perform the most vital tasks in our society: our ability to parent, or the amount of time we have to participate in voluntary organisations.

These domestic patterns are part of the wider global picture. The analysis is familiar by now: free and excessively volatile capital flows; the onslaught of globalisation; the rise of the multinational. Again the uncertainty thrown up by these international trends is reinforced by another factor – the increasing technological change that we are currently experiencing (although we should be careful not to overstate this trend). Put these trends together and I think we have a convincing story about why our society is fracturing and Balkanising in the way that it is. It also provides us with an account of why our economy is not performing as well as it should and could.

Is there an alternative political economy? I believe that there is, and that the way to address these issues and begin the fight back should focus on five distinct clusters of proposals.

POLICY PROPOSALS

Cluster One concerns the relationship of the financial system to business. Essentially I advocate a much more committed ownership of productive assets. This entails shifting the legal and regulatory framework to one which actually encourages owners to be more committed to the underlying assets which they are responsible for. This should help lower the desired rate of return and lengthen the payback period of return, which would in turn afford more scope to corporations to act as responsible corporate citizens.

The second cluster of proposals surrounds workplace relations. Here I have argued that we should see workers as members of a social organisation – the firm. If we are to reach the point at which we can conceive of the firm as a living social organisation (rather than as nothing more than a bundle of legal contracts), then we must rethink the role of key actors within it. For instance, in my conception of a corporation a director is not someone who aims to maximise profits within a given trading period; rather he or she is a trustee who must ensure the responsible use of the firm's assets on behalf of the different stakeholders who constitute the social organisation. Employees will obviously be one of the key constituents within this conception of the firm.

Cluster Three is a series of proposals which centre around the welfare state and the benefit system. A stakeholder society has to have a strong universal welfare state to which everyone contributes and from which everyone benefits. It is one of the essential institutions of a civilised society. In particular the benefit system must become more proactive. It should not be constructed merely as a support mechanism which offers people income when they are out of work. Instead a reformed welfare state must have the objective of trying to include people in the world of work. This will mean major changes in the way the benefit system is organised.

Cluster Four, and I make no apology for this, betrays my roots as a passionately committed Keynesian economist. In essence this means that we must be willing to challenge the monetarist orthodoxy about the supremacy of market forces and the restrictive rules of sound finance. I believe that a market economy, if it is to be successful, requires coordination between savers and investors which is not done best by unregulated markets. This means that we must be willing to have an expansionary bias in macroeconomic policy which creates the expectation of steady increases in demand. Consequently I am a critic of economic policies which are too oriented around financial targets – be it inflation or one measure of the money supply – or which seek stability at all costs.

Cluster Five of these proposals is the reconstruction and reform of the British political system. Discretionary executive government precludes rather than facilitates the achievement of genuine representative democracy and is, therefore, an instrument of political exclusion. Unfortunately, the same essentially undemocratic principles which lie at the heart of this form of government are mirrored in the organisation of civil society – as evidenced by the way we run both our companies and our welfare system. Surely quinquennial elections in which we confer extraordinary and unlimited powers on the executive, legitimised by an increasingly dog-eared House of Windsor is no way to run a political system in the 1990s. It needs to be recast and thoroughly democratised.

REBUTTING THE CRITICS

The proposals within each of these clusters should not be considered independently of the others, for the economic, social and political case for reform go hand in hand. Every element in these five clusters will be required, and will be reinforced by the others. Some key questions remain, however. First, is stakeholding too contradictory for it to be able to make any kind of sense? The simple answer is that the current situation is full of contradictions. Put differently, I do not believe that the status quo is so devoid of contradictions that it is worth retaining; and indeed in my judgement any kind of society has contradictions within it. Furthermore, I think the bad society is the one in which you have a single hierarchically-imposed social and economic order. This seems to me to be an unworkable principle on which to build sensible rules for economic and social organisation.

Second, is it a return to corporatism? Absolutely not. A stakeholder society would certainly mean a stronger or different role for trade unions than we have currently in Britain. But I am not an advocate of either industry-wide collective bargaining or the antagonistic relations between capital and labour which tend to characterise British thinking about industrial relations. Instead I conceive of the workforce as, in European terms, a social partner who will bargain and operate at the level of the firm and the industry. This is not a return to old-style corporatism.

Third, is it capitalism with a human face? Just being nice to people? Again, absolutely not. In order to make these things happen in the way I have outlined there needs to be a substantial body of legislative change, a change in the way in which the economy is managed, and a change in values. This is a substantive reform programme and should be understood as such.

Fourth, does globalisation mean that a stakeholder economy is impossible? While I accept that the world in which one is trying to build stakeholder capitalism is changing and that internationalisation grows apace, I am also a bit of a sceptic where some of the more extreme claims of some protagonists of the globalisation thesis are concerned. The world is not *that* global. Careful note should be taken of the fact that multinationals are refocusing their operations in regions rather than operating globally. But to the extent that globalisation is occurring, those advocating stakeholder capitalism must be concerned with reforming international economic institutions. We should not be thinking about trying to establish it in one country alone. Therefore it is important that we consider other similar initiatives in countries such as the US, where the Democrats have quite advanced proposals on how to implement stakeholder type ideas, for example ACORP – the Alliance Corporation between capital and labour. This is similar to the situation in Germany, where even though there is a widespread recognition of the need for economic reform, there is also an acceptance shared by left and right alike that the fundamental principles of stakeholder capitalism should be upheld. These are crucial models in helping to construct a stakeholder UK. The countries in which they are being developed also represent future political partners in the movement to create a more rule-bound international economic framework which spans the international financial system, the trading order and the regulation of labour standards.

Finally, will Mr Blair and the New Labour Party pull any of this off? Here I think that the jury is still out, but I think one should be positive rather than negative. Mr Blair has chosen to use the concept of stakeholding with all its radical connotations, and he has stood by it. Many elements in his programme and in New Labour's programme correspond closely to those five clusters in which I group my own thinking. And indeed in some of them, such as in the proposals for reforming the political system, I do not think you could ask more of a political party than New Labour is currently delivering. That said, in other areas I think they have been overcautious and in some areas tepid. But this is an inclusive debate. If we can get the arguments right and find a vernacular in which they can be sold to the British electorate I think politicians will pick up these arguments and run with them. There is clearly a huge interest in trying to construct a way in which a moral community can coexist with a successful capitalism; in building economic institutions which are based on a mutuality of obligation within civil society, rather than on the principles of slash and burn. I think that everyone is aware that our country is becoming less of a good place in which to live; that the social capital which we all rely on to build well-being and the good life is diminishing. When Dunblane happened I doubt that there was a man or woman in the country who did not think that there are likely to be more rather than less of these events in the future, because the way our society is ordered produces deranged people who are disconnected from, and incapable of, empathising with their victims. So I think the time is right for these kinds of ideas to have a more positive reception: intellectuals, journalists, academics, policy wonks, politicians, businessmen, trade unionists and civil society at large are beginning to engage in a rich dialogue which is also taking place in other countries such as the US. The debate is growing and so is popular support for change. Of course there are all kinds of trade-offs between one element of the programme and another which need to be thoroughly explored and thrashed out. Given the costs of failure we have no choice but to ensure that a new stakeholder capitalism is built on solid ground.

2 A Political Perspective
Alistair Darling

Stakeholding is a straightforward political concept. It is also a matter of common sense. As a political idea, it addresses the two dominant facts of the age: a feeling of alienation from the political process and a growing sense of economic insecurity. That insecurity comes at a time when the world economies are being transformed by another fact: globalisation. Globalisation may be seen to bring wealth, but it also brings uncertainty, and for many that means insecurity; the fear that world markets are overarching, powerful forces which override all sense of control over the individual's ability to influence the life they may want to create for themselves and their families.

THE STAKEHOLDER PHILOSOPHY AND GOVERNMENT

Of course we may not perceive insecurity in terms of the global economy. We may feel ourselves instead to be buffeted by forces beyond us and unable to control those forces. We may even therefore feel ourselves to be rootless and on our own. The philosophy of stakeholding describes how, contrary to that feeling of insecurity, we are rooted in society, and aims to show how individuals working together can affect the forces that shape society.

Every individual ought to have a stake in the future of their country. Individuals should have the opportunity to contribute, to be allowed to do the best they can for themselves and their families. To have such a stake is good for the individual and therefore good for society. It is a measure of the Conservatives rightward drift that such a proposition is so fiercely contested by them.

It has become a truism that this country is divided, that the divisions have widened and that the decay is deepening. There is no doubt that there are fears about a generation which is disillusioned, disaffected and increasingly feels itself to be without a place in society. There is concern too that a second generation has grown up without work, unemployed people who feel alienated and apart from the rest of society. They have no experience of work or the work ethic. Few would disagree that it is vital for good social and economic reasons for there to be a sense of cohesion in any society. They look to government to provide the opportunities to enable individuals to have a stake in society by building and maintaining the appropriate economic and social framework. Openness on the part of government and decentralisation of power is an essential part of that process.

There is something of a contract between the individual and the government he or she elects. We elect a government to do those things we cannot do alone. Individuals are entitled to believe they have a stake in their government – that is an essential part of the stakeholder society.

But having recognised the importance of individuals within society, the question must be, how can the appropriate economic circumstances be maintained to allow individuals the opportunity to make a stakeholder society a reality rather than a theoretical possibility? And in that context, what is the role of a modern government?

PUBLIC AND PRIVATE: BEYOND THE OLD ARGUMENTS ABOUT OWNERSHIP

In medieval times people looked to the King to defend them. Later they looked to the state to protect their property rights and to construct a framework within which they could live. Today it is the government's job to maintain an economic and social framework that will give individuals the opportunity to succeed.

There is an important point here. We look to the government to do those things we cannot do ourselves, but the government itself does not always have to provide the services, or the delivery mechanisms. Public provision is effective in some cases, in others it is less so. For example, the government has a duty to maintain a publicly funded network of schools. The private sector, on the other hand, is best placed to operate airlines within the country and beyond. But training, for example, can and should be provided by public and private sector together as appropriate. Increasingly joint provision between public and private sector will become commonplace. Indeed, the old arguments which have so dogged British politics as to whether public provision was always best or whether privatisation was the only answer, are increasingly anachronistic.

There are some things which the private sector does best and others where the public sector is appropriate. In many more cases a combination of both public and private sector provision is necessary. Look, for example, at pension provision. Britain has one of the most sophisticated financial services industries in the world. It already offers numerous savings options for the short, medium and long term. However, only the state can determine the overall framework against which people can plan. When the state determines

how much the pension will be, people can determine how much they want
to save towards their old age or other eventualities and the industry will then
respond to that. Only government, however, can put in place a regulatory
regime that commands the confidence of both the public and the industry.
It is not a conflict between public and private; both government and private
sector have different roles to play; indeed they are dependent on each other;
there is a partnership between them. And of course there are also many people
who have insufficient means to meet their current obligations, let alone save
for the future. The government has a clear obligation here. The idea that such
provision will be 'minimalist' or 'nugatory' is wrong.

It is important that the decision as to whether public or private provision
is appropriate is taken on a practical and reasonable basis. For the
Conservatives it is increasingly a matter of dogma. They believe that
privatisation is always best and persistently denigrate public provision and
indeed public service. In fact the public sector can provide high-quality
service. The National Health Service is a classic example of where it is more
efficient, cheaper and more effective for us all to contribute to it rather than
attempt to make provision for ourselves on an individual basis. Not only is
it socially just and fair, but it is also efficient and effective.

So the recognition of this interrelationship between public and private is
an essential part of the new realism in our political and economic approach.
Classically, the mixed economy was one in which a certain percentage of
the economy was in private hands, the rest being in public ownership. That
is changing. Joint public or private partnerships can help to rebuild the
country's infrastructure; sharing of provision will become commonplace, as
appropriate. Again, however, it is for the government to determine the
overall framework against which business and individuals can plan. It has
to take a lead. Without this, progress will inevitably be difficult. Moreover,
the government's power to influence this change of culture should not be
underestimated.

Let us be clear, however, about the market in the stakeholder economy.
The market economy can be efficient and effective. Not unfettered, not
unqualified, but it is a useful starting point. Of course if the market does not
work, governments should not be afraid to take action; for example, by
operating an effective competition or regulatory regime to prevent markets
from being anti-competitive. In short the traditional hostility or ambivalence
to the market by some on the left is misplaced – as is the opposite devotion
and almost deification of the market by the right. Both are wrong.

Indeed, the Conservatives' obsession with the market mechanism has led
them to try to create markets where none naturally exist. That has caused
far greater problems than it has resolved. For example, it is not possible to

convert the health service into a factory production line. The public will judge provision by the results achieved. Most people take the commonsense approach: to them the question that matters is 'which system works best?' Accordingly we should be concerned first and foremost about the consumers of goods and services.

WHAT WE SHOULD EXPECT FROM GOVERNMENT

What is the role of government in terms of creating a stakeholder economy? As we have seen, the role of government is more limited than it was in the past but it remains nonetheless crucial. There is a new realism about what can be done. There is no wish to return to what was referred to as 'interventionism' or the 'corporatism' of the 1970s. But governments still have a crucial role in helping both individuals and businesses.

As a starting point governments have to recognise that the economic world is changing rapidly. Globalisation means that no country can go it alone in economic terms. That should be seen not as a threat, as something to be feared, but as a fact of life which can provide opportunities. Similarly, businesses have had to evolve; many have done so already with great success. The objective must be to make this sort of success the norm, not the exception.

It is also clear that where British companies are competing well, they are doing so on quality and excellence. Britain's future lies in competing with the rest of the world by producing goods and services of high quality. There is no future in trying to succeed through the vain attempt to undercut the Far East, or anywhere else, on low wages and skills. Protectionism, either total or partial, has also to be rejected. The key to our survival is our ability to compete by offering high-quality, high value-added goods and services.

Britain and the rest of Europe will have to compete in an increasingly international marketplace, not just with the US and Japan, but with the new and fast-growing economies of the Far East and elsewhere in Asia. Although there are hard questions to be asked about the direction and pace of further European integration, in a generation's time Europe will be overtaken by Asia unless it develops its own entirely new economic approach.

The philosophy of stakeholding therefore must have a wider economic application in order to give it some reality. Thus the stakeholder economy must provide opportunities for individuals and therefore the country as a whole.

What macroeconomic framework is necessary to enable businesses, and therefore individuals, to prosper? What is the role of government in creating economic opportunity?

Long-termism Through Stability

Business needs stability. Without stability, Britain will continue to pay a premium on the cost of borrowing, and individuals and businesses will be reluctant to invest for the future. It is not possible to eliminate all the fluctuations of the economic cycle, but getting the overall framework of fiscal and monetary policy right, and ending the series of booms and busts that have characterised the British economy, is probably the best thing that any government can do to encourage investment. So too is the commitment to maintain a low inflation environment: a stable platform on which to build.

Much of the 1990s has seen a debate about alleged short-termism of investors in British businesses. But it is important to note that there are many examples in Britain and elsewhere of far-sighted investment decisions as well as examples of damaging short-termism. It is a mistake to make generalised assumptions in this field. More tellingly, before politicians begin to blame others, they should look to themselves. Much of Britain's short-term culture comes in effect from government. For far too many politicians, long term is the next general election. If we want to create an environment where businesses and individuals look ahead, five, ten or fifteen years, then a different approach is essential. A stable economic environment with low inflation is an essential part of that.

Stability is also important to changing the saving patterns of individuals. If we want to encourage a culture where people save and invest, then they must be confident that their savings will not be eroded by inflation. There is compelling evidence that countries which save and invest a higher proportion of their national output tend to grow faster and have a greater increase in real wages and living standards, so stability is, first and foremost, essential. But government has other responsibilities which are just as important.

Investing in Skills

The government has a duty to ensure that people have access to the best possible education. Without that access, it will be difficult for people to cope with the changes that will take place in the labour market over the next few decades. High-quality education and training are essential, not just at the start of life, but throughout life. An ability to adapt and to maintain skills is essential. People will have to be familiar with the new technology. In a world where capital is completely mobile, one of the things that will mark Britain out as a place to invest are the skills and training available in this country.

Modernising Welfare

Of course, to give people a stake in the country, they need a job and the means with which to participate fully, so getting people back into work and helping those who are unemployed back into work are essential. Here again there is a contract, or understanding, between the individual and the government: the individual will expect the government to put in place a framework and the opportunities for education; in turn, they have a responsibility to take up that assistance and to make the most of those opportunities. It is, thus, a partnership between individuals and the government they elect.

The government therefore has an obligation to modernise the welfare state. If everyone is to have a stake in the economy and to share in prosperity, the welfare state has to move towards offering a means to equip people to succeed. Today's demands and changed lifestyles require a more active conception of welfare based on services as well as money, child care as well as child benefit, training as well as unemployment benefit. In Britain in the 1990s one-sixth of the population relies on means-tested benefit. Too many children grow up in poverty. Over eight million people have had a spell of unemployment since 1992 and one in five households of working age has no one earning a wage. There is a second generation of people with no experience of work or the work ethic who have little sense of contributing individually and socially. The implications are clear: getting people into work makes both social and economic sense.

Helping Business

The government clearly has other responsibilities on behalf of individuals and business; for example, in the maintenance of the country's infrastructure and the operation of a competition and regulatory policy. It should promote open markets throughout Europe and the world and operate the appropriate tax regime to encourage investment. There is also an obligation to help small and growing businesses and to ensure balanced regional development.

Overall, government has to create the climate in which individuals and businesses have the opportunity to prosper in a modern economy; not running individual businesses, but providing a framework which enables them to succeed.

CORPORATE STAKEHOLDING

Having looked at the role of government in general economic terms, let us see how the concept of stakeholding may be applied to companies and in the workplace. There are two important preliminary points to be made here. First, we must make the distinction between the political concept of stakeholding and the conventional corporate sense of the term. Stakeholding is a general philosophy or concept. Whilst corporate governance, for example, is an important part of that, it is not at the heart of the philosophy. The corporate concept of stakeholding is very important, but it is a distinct part of what is an overall economic approach.

Second, creating a stakeholder economy is very much about creating a change of culture in the country. It does not rely on new rules or regulations or new acts of Parliament. These are not the essence of achieving real change, rather the stakeholding philosophy should be about changing the way people think. Of course there will always be a need to review and improve legislation to improve the existing body of corporate law. And, equally, government can influence that change in culture; for example, in its fiscal and regulatory approach or in ensuring minimum standards at work, but much of this is good business sense as well. For example, health and safety rules should complement good business practice as well as ensuring standards of fundamental decency at work. Essentially, however, we are considering a change of culture. We cannot create a stakeholder economy by regulation: government has its part to play but it cannot legislate for business flair, entrepreneurial spirit, or common sense.

Looking at the corporate sector, what does stakeholding mean? Specifically, what could it mean in Britain? Comparisons are sometimes made between the German and Japanese models of ownership and those of the Anglo-American tradition. We should accept that there is good and bad in both. We should also accept that it is impossible to import German and Japanese patterns of ownership even if we wanted to do so. That does not mean we cannot learn something from their culture and, in particular, their propensity to take a long-term view. But the fact is that German and Japanese models are very different for historical and other reasons. Rather than waste any more time on that point let us see what needs to be done in this country building on our own traditions.

We have to be clear about how government should approach corporate stakeholding and, in particular, in which areas it can or should seek to influence. Its responsibilities are quite different from that of management or investors: business and government have different spheres of interest. They should be complementary but they are distinct.

WHO ARE THE STAKEHOLDERS?

It is also essential to be careful about generalised definitions of the term 'stakeholder'. For example, if a customer goes into the supermarket and buys a can of baked beans, that does not make him or her a stakeholder in either company. And if the same individual lives on Teesside, for example, that does not make him or her a stakeholder in ICI which operates there. Equally, the fact that the Standard Life Assurance Company is in Edinburgh does not make its citizens stakeholders in that institution. They clearly have an interest in the success of these companies but they do not necessarily have a direct stake in them.

This distinction is important in policy terms. There is the interest of the primary stakeholder who has a real interest in the company that is direct and tangible – the investor, the employee or the management, for example – and there are the interests of others who have a more remote or indirect interest – the secondary stakeholders, the suppliers, the customers, or perhaps a neighbour. Who is or is not a stakeholder will vary from business to business. We must be careful not to make generalised assumptions or, even worse, impose generalised requirements on people whose interest in the company is temporary, remote, or at arm's length, often for very good reasons. These relationships with the secondary stakeholders are usually a matter for business judgements. We may want to encourage them but governments cannot legislate for such links.

Clearly governments should not attempt to run individual businesses. It is not their job to sit in the boardrooms and to second-guess management. However, a government has a quite legitimate interest in influencing the culture and general climate of thinking; indeed, it should do so in the interests of the country: for example, in the way that owners of British companies regard their investments.

FOSTERING ACTIVE OWNERSHIP

To build the stakeholder economy, it is necessary to foster the kind of environment in which business and companies are likely to prosper. Amongst other things, that means fostering a long-term commitment on the part of owners of business. Here the role of institutional investors is important. What they do will not only govern whether an individual company prospers or fails, but will influence the success of the economy as a whole, so it is important to foster the culture of constructive ownership.

There are two different approaches towards ownership in the UK. Some institutional investors take an active role as owners; they are prepared to do so for the greater good of their investment. The alternative view is that the investor simply looks at his or her return and if the return isn't appropriate, the investment can, at least in theory, be transferred elsewhere.

The approach will vary depending on the size and nature of the investment, but we should encourage investors to act as constructive owners because the spread of that culture is of the utmost importance to the economy. There are encouraging signs that the culture is changing.

Despite the dominance of institutional investors, individual share ownership is also important, but for different reasons. Such ownership is a good way of saving and investing and should be encouraged, but it is also important to recognise its limitations. The over-optimistic and sometimes cynical rhetoric of the Conservative Party in the 1980s about the 'great share owning democracy' was misplaced.

Before leaving this point, it is important to remember that not all of British industry is dominated by large institutions – by size, yes, but numerically there are many more small businesses employing almost half the population. Stakeholding has relevance here as well, especially in the way that management, who are often the owners of the business, cooperate with the whole workforce. There is clearly a role for government in this area. Helping small and medium-sized business is important; government can provide that help itself: for example, creating a climate where research and development can be promoted. Again there is scope for government and private sector to work as partners in this regard. And government can and should influence the climate in the workplace. That is part of the stakeholder culture.

A STAKE IN THE WORKPLACE

The importance of securing participation by the workforce, by providing proper motivation to get improved performance, and therefore success, is a major part of the philosophy of stakeholding. It is crucial that individuals who work in a business have a stake in its future so that they feel committed and identify with the enterprise with which they are involved. Successful companies see their employees as a resource not just of production but often as a source of creative innovation. They work with them as partners, consulting and listening, both sides aware that partnership is a two-way process. None of this necessarily needs more laws, rules and regulations. Many firms and

the editorial chair of the *Observer*. It would be good if he did
tton could match his view of commercial potential against others
d be tested against results. Indeed, arguments like Hutton's are
y by people in the City trying to sell their preferred investment,
have spotted that ten-dollar opportunity. It is how markets work.
r is that the Huttonists, impatient with having to operate in a
like everyone else, try to get the politicians on their side and
taxpayers' money should be invested in their chosen projects
islative favours given to them. It is then that the real mischief
e seem to fall for it every time. It is disconcerting that Hutton
d put even more money into the old British Leyland. Britain's
omic policy is littered with failed schemes aimed at plugging
ancing gaps for investment. They always fail because political
investment decisions are far more irrational than the City could

RMISM

s that such government intervention is necessary because the
ermist, but 'short-termism' is a very slippery concept indeed.
embodies all known information about the performance of a
ill move around very rapidly as information comes in. This is
n', it is an immediate response to information which may have
nificance. There is nothing specific to the City of London in
r. I remember visiting the Tokyo stock exchange during the final
Emperor Hirohito. Many shares were marked lower but one
ing well. The explanation was that they were shares in printing
the Emperor died, many Japanese calendars and guides would
rinted so those firms would enjoy more revenues. Every event,
h of a monarch, is subject to rational economic calculation.
e moves around day to day does not mean that it is somehow
e account of information with long-term significance. The
n studies of financial markets is that if a firm announces an
capital investment programme or in research and development
share price tends to rise. One of the most exciting industries of
iotechnology. When you invest in biotechnology there is often
all, merely a research team which is trying to develop one. One
rgest companies, close to the top 100 on the stock exchange,
ct: it is purely R&D stock. The only significant sources of

individuals understand and practise stakeholding already. It is essentially a matter of cultural change, but government can encourage that development.

Employee share ownership, for example, can play a major role in providing motivation and incentives to individuals to work. It should be seen as something that is the norm in a dynamic economy; not just in the boardroom but also on the shop floor. Specific measures to promote the wider take-up of employee share ownership schemes should therefore be considered.

The days of 'them and us' need to be put behind us. Businesses will only succeed where there is both a common endeavour and a common purpose. The central point is that partnership at work is a far more productive and profitable relationship than adversarial workplace relations. Indeed, whether it is at work, or in society as a whole, the stakeholder philosophy is very much about using the talents of everyone. In that way business is strengthened and so too is the whole economy.

CONCLUSION

Stakeholding is about cultural change. It is a way of thinking which offers insights as to how the economy can be organised so as to benefit business, individuals, and therefore society as a whole. It also demands a reappraisal of the role of government. Government has the capability of being the engine of economic and social change. It should not be afraid to act when that is appropriate, but it must know its limitations. It cannot attempt to stand in the shoes of individuals or make judgements for them. Government's job is to enable, to act in partnership between individuals and businesses, to do things that individuals cannot do in isolation. But it is inevitable that in the increasingly global economy a modern government's role will be more limited than it was in earlier days when national economies were more autonomous than they are now. But that does not mean governments are powerless, far from it. Government can and should achieve a great deal.

Stakeholding is not just a philosophy of government. It is an individual philosophy and an approach that can be applied at work, in business, as well as in the way that people regard themselves and those that live around them. It is a philosophy that recognises the importance of social and economic cohesion. Indeed, the neglect of it makes for economic inefficiency, insecurity and failure. Stakeholding recognises the individual as its starting point, but it also recognises that those individuals expect government to act on their behalf: a genuine partnership between individuals and the government they elect.

3 The Poverty of Stakeholding

David Willetts

Will Hutton's book, *The State We're In*[1] is readable, accessible and dangerous. It is not a synthesis of modern economic thinking but an attack on it. It is an exercise in anti-economics. Hutton takes several long-standing lines of criticism of British political economy and mixes them together in a heady brew.

First is the 'deindustrialisation' thesis which was developed in the 1960s. The argument is that Britain's industrial base is too small as a result of decades of underinvestment. More investment and more manufacturing are what we are supposed to need. Second, add a dash of social history. Hutton argues that industry does not have social prestige in the British class system. As soon as people make any money from commerce they start pretending to be country gentlemen, and the learned professions have always regarded themselves as superior to people who actually make things. The most elegant exposition of this argument is Martin Weiner's book *English Culture and the Decline of the Industrial Spirit*, published fifteen years ago.[2] Third, there is a hefty slice of political analysis. Hutton believes that government here is unconstrained and that the law is simply what a majority in Parliament says it is (he does not appear to recognise the existence of either judicial review or the constraints of the European Court of Justice). By giving such power to the governing majority, this system, Hutton believes, also gives particular power to individual departments of state, notably the Treasury which comes particularly high in his demonology. Another of his demons is the Conservative Party which he sees as 'finding Middle-England's centre of gravity and ensuring that no other party endangers Middle-England's pleasures and privileges'.[3]

Then he needs something to bring these economic, cultural and political ingredients together. The City provides that binding. It is the financial system which deprives British industry, Hutton argues, of the stable long-term finance enjoyed in our main industrial competitors. The City is the one area where British culture allows a gentleman to work in commerce and thus enables the upper classes to make their money whilst looking down on industry. And the City, he believes, has a potent hold on British government through its social connections with the Conservative Party.

Although these arguments appear to be fashionable now, they are really very old indeed. Hutton's book is a classic text for 1965. It is a mixture of

Nicholas Kaldor, *That Was The Week T[...]* and angry young men. The way to s[...] identify sounds new, however – it is b[...] 'Stakeholders in British society' are to[...] national political constitution and the c[...] wants big changes in the way that we[...] central role of the House of Commons.[...] rights which have sustained our indust[...]

HUTTON'S ANTI-ECONOMICS

Hutton goes straight to the heart of the[...] and says that it is the source of the p[...] failing to recognise the true value of l[...] boldness of his argument is that he a[...] rational capitalist appraisal of investr[...] books tell us is its *raison d'être*. And[...] hope is there for the rest of the British[...] which sets him against mainstream ec[...]

Let us explain the free market posi[...] economists are walking down the stre[...] the pavement and points it out to his cc[...] be. If there were somebody would [...] believe that by and large capitalist s[...] possibilities and seize them. Hutton's a[...] more absurd proposition from that of t[...] that British industry leaves a host of[...] which the City systematically fails to[...] successful investment opportunities in[...] a good flow of future profits but whi[...] City does not recognise their value. A[...] – it is a persistent problem caused by[...]

If Hutton believes that, then he kr[...] indeed. He should set up the William[...] and invite the people who bought his[...] They could then finance these investr[...] their reward by building up a fund v[...] managed in the City. In a free econc[...] rather more difficult than it may ap[...]

Guardian c[...] have a go. H[...] and they co[...] used every [...] claiming the[...]

The dang[...] free market[...] demand tha[...] or special l[...] starts – and[...] wishes we h[...] postwar ecc[...] imaginary f[...] pressures o[...] ever be.

SHORT-TE[...]

Hutton clair[...] City is shor[...] A share pri[...] company. It[...] not 'short te[...] long-term s[...] this behavio[...] illness of th[...] group was d[...] companies:[...] have to be re[...] even the de[...]

That a sh[...] failing to ta[...] evidence fr[...] increase in i[...] spending, it[...] the future is[...] no product a[...] of Britain's[...] has no proc[...]

commercial funds for biotechnology come from Wall Street and the City of London – citadels of 'short-termist' Anglo-American capitalism.

Of course some people are stupid some of the time and mistakes are made. But Hutton's view has exactly the same arrogance as J.K. Galbraith. Hutton believes that people are systematically and predictably stupid – and in one of the most sophisticated financial markets of them all. There is no evidence to support that view. This is not to say that British industry does not have its problems. It may well have been the case that because of the poor performance of British industry since the war there has been a shortage of good investment opportunities in which a rational person would wish to sink their savings. The only way to deal with that problem is through a rigorous supply-side reform of the sort the government has been pursuing since 1979. But Hutton wants something else, as we shall see – a fundamental change in the way in which British industry is run and financed.

British industry does indeed have an unusual pattern of financing. There is relatively little long-term fixed interest debt. Instead British industry is heavily dependent on variable rate overdraft and equity finance. This is a direct consequence of our suffering from high and variable rates of inflation. We now have in place the institutional arrangements to deliver low and stable inflation, the best possible environment to encourage the sort of long-term fixed interest lending which Hutton claims he wants to see. There is no need for heavy-handed changes in the structure of British companies as well. As Sir Geoffrey Owen, former editor of the *Financial Times* and now at the London School of Economics, observes: 'The danger with this book is that it will reinforce existing misconceptions on the Left about the City and tempt a future Labour government to tinker with the financial system as unproductively as its predecessors did in the 1960s and 1970s.'[4]

THE STAKEHOLDER COMPANY

A company's profitability depends on its relationships with a variety of groups – consumers, investors, workers and suppliers being the most obvious ones. That is uncontroversial, even banal. The stakeholder agenda goes further than this, however, in its claim that there needs to be a change in the composition of company boards and the legal framework within which they operate, so that all these different groups are properly represented on the body which governs the company.

There are several problems with stakeholder corporate governance. There is no reason why the interests of these groups should all coincide, certainly not in the short term. Indeed, they may be interests of a fundamentally different type – a supplier's interest in continuing to have a remunerative contract is different from a consumer's interest which may be in a cheaper or more innovative product. The stakeholder agenda does not explain how these different claims are to be balanced. What other criteria are supposed to be used to enable boards to reach their decisions, other than the traditional one of long-term profit maximisation? And if we are told that the ultimate aim is still profit maximisation then the grandiose rhetoric of stakeholders has not got us beyond conventional capitalism at all. As Sir Samuel Brittan has shrewdly remarked:

> There is also a deliberate ambiguity about the pronouncements of stakeholder theorists. Such theorists say that managements should look beyond the bottom line and mere financial return. On the other hand, they are quick to tell their opponents that companies which adopt the practices of which they approve will also be more prosperous. It is like the old Welsh preacher who waxed eloquent about the moral virtues of honesty, adding just before he left the pulpit that it also paid.[5]

The different claims of the different interest groups involved with the company may best be registered in different ways. As one expert sympathetic to 'stakeholding' has put it, 'Given the different types of relationship that different categories of stakeholder have with the company, it is likely that different mechanisms for protecting their interests will be appropriate.'[6] Representing all these different interests on the board could well make it more difficult for a company to respond to changing circumstances. There is no advantage for British industry, as they seek the best possible suppliers, if their old-established suppliers are legally entitled to seats on the board. Nor would we be able to preserve the industrial relations successes of the past fifteen years if we shifted towards giving trade unions legal representation on the board.

After changing the structure of company boards, the next part of the stakeholder agenda is to try to cut back on distribution of dividends. This attack on dividend distribution fails to distinguish between gross distributions by individual companies and net distributions out of the commercial sector as a whole. When companies pay out dividends, the money is not all spent on candy floss and foreign holidays. Much of it goes to institutions, or even individuals, who reinvest the funds. So the money may well go to investment, but instead of that process being internalised within one business which retains its earnings, it is done via the capital market which allocates the flow of dividend income to new investments which it thinks have the best long-term potential. This is the classic account of the role of the capital market and contributes to the distinctive character of Anglo-American capitalism.

We are also told that Britain needs to discourage takeovers so as to encourage long-termism. The best explanation of the usefulness of the takeover threat was put not by some Friedmanite fanatic but by Paul Samuelson in his classic textbook on economics: 'Take-overs, like bankruptcy, represent one of Nature's methods of eliminating dead wood in the struggle for survival. A more open and efficiently responsive corporate society can result.'[7] Of course, a dozy management might wish to make takeovers more difficult, but there is nothing in it for the rest of us. On the Continent there are other types of pressures for improved performance by failing companies. Hutton admires, for example, the role of long-term bank lenders in gingering-up weak management. But it is difficult to see how this would be compatible with Britain's rigorous law on insider trading – introduced under pressure from some of the very leftwing critics who now want new long-term relations between banks and the firms they lend to. The danger is that we would end up abandoning the pressure which the Anglo-American system exerts on poorly-performing companies without substituting any other new disciplines in their place. We would end up with the worst of all possible worlds.

The overall effect of this agenda – giving stakeholders legal representation on boards, encouraging companies to retain more of their earnings rather than to distribute it to the capital markets, and making takeovers more difficult – is to make economic change more difficult. It is seriously misguided at a time when the Rhineland economies are looking enviously at our flexibility, our ability to respond more rapidly to economic change.

Many firms proudly regard themselves as stakeholder companies. It has become part of their corporate culture. If it makes sense for them, then so be it. The language of the stakeholder has become almost a cliché in corporate strategy. But it moves from a cliché into a dangerous piece of industrial inter-ventionism if it is transposed from the individual company to the economy as a whole. Individual companies can develop their own styles of management but there is no need for the government to step in with more intrusive legislation so as to require by law a new uniform pattern of corporate behaviour. It is a great strength of the British business scene that we have Lord Hansen and Anita Roddick, BP and JCB. A more prescriptive pattern of corporate law that tried to oblige them all to run their affairs in the same way, would be a threat to British firms' ability to change and experiment.

There is a dangerous intolerance in Hutton's stakeholder approach. Genuine free marketeers are happy to allow a diversity of corporate cultures, and if an individual company wishes to be a stakeholder company, then so be it. Our market changes have made that more possible. British Telecom now calls itself a stakeholder company: one of the many benefits of privatisation. Indeed, our liberal regime can make it easier for stakeholder companies to flourish here than on the Continent. There was a fascinating letter in the *Financial Times* from Robert Bischof, chairman of the Boss Group. He defended the German model of corporate governance, but went on at the end of his letter to make the following remarks:

> The problem with Germany's system is not its basic principle but that it has been perverted by a mass of legal and institutional red tape. It is also true that it has led some German management boards to be too preoccupied with seeking consensus and with pursuing long-term strategies, where tough decisions were needed ...
>
> In Boss, like in most Continental and Japanese owned companies, we have of course the best of both worlds: we practice our stakeholder culture and are not restricted by the paraphernalia of an institutionalised framework. Hence it's such a joy to run companies in Britain.[8]

A BLOCKED SOCIETY?

Hutton's attack on economic policy is tied in with a social critique. He attacks a 'network of City institutions, public schools, regiments, landed estates, and boardrooms' which he believes stops any genuine 'economic citizenship' being spread across the country. It is a picture of a country of gentlemanly capitalists coming from a socially-privileged class keeping out fresh blood and unable to compete on the world stage. There are a series of misconceptions as well as simple factual mistakes which lie behind these claims.

Let us start with those criticisms of 'gentlemanly capitalism'. It is an example of the worst sort of intellectual snobbery to imagine that somehow industrial success is incompatible with distinction in the more rarefied areas of academic study. At the very same time in the late nineteenth century when German industry was overtaking British industry, German classical scholars and critical historians were overtaking us academically as well. Hume was much wiser than some of today's fashionable critics when he wrote:

> The same age which produces great philosophers and politicians, renowned generals and poets, usually abounds with skilful weavers and ships-carpenters. We cannot reasonably expect that a piece of woollen cloth will be wrought to perfection in a nation which is ignorant of astronomy or where ethics are neglected. The spirit of the age affects all the arts, and

the minds of men being once roused from their lethargy, and put into a fermentation, turn themselves on all sides, and carry improvements into every art and science.[9]

Moreover, Hutton appears to have been taken in by the surface show of City rituals. One of the features of capitalism (which some of its Marxist critics recognise) is that it can 'commodify' old-fashioned arrangements and bring them into the market economy. Even if City financiers are off for a weekend's shooting it is unlikely to be because they are hereditary members of the aristocracy and much more likely to be because they are successful traders or businessmen enjoying corporate hospitality. The social rituals which still seem strangely to rile critics such as Hutton are now almost entirely open to money or to people who have achieved some sort of public position – such as being editor of the *Observer* – presumably to some degree or other on merit. People are not excluded from them because of where they were born or who they were born to.

The Institute of Fiscal Studies (IFS) has added some empirical evidence with a ground-breaking study: *Two Nations? The Inheritance of Poverty and Affluence*, by Paul Johnson and Howard Reid, published in January 1996.[10] The story is a complicated one: how one interprets a piece of evidence such as the following is perhaps a measure of one's political views. They have taken sons who ended up in the top quintile of the income distribution and investigated where their fathers were in the income distribution. In a totally mobile society with no social barriers (and no inheritance of aptitudes either), the sons in the top 20 per cent would have fathers equally distributed across the entire income range, so that 20 per cent of their fathers would have been in the top quintile, down to 20 per cent in the bottom quintile. The IFS further calculates that 10 per cent of sons in the top quintile had fathers with incomes in the bottom quintile compared with 34 per cent of sons in the top quintile who had fathers whose incomes were in the top quintile. Interpretations of this data will vary of course, but I personally find evidence of quite an encouraging degree of mobility. It is far from the closed and blocked society in the lurid imaginations of some social critics.

CAPITALISM AGAINST CAPITALISM

The time was right for books like Hutton's. The collapse of command economy socialism has ended the harsh ideological battle between Marxism and capitalism. What it has revealed instead is a more intricate and complicated argument about what kind of market economy we wish to live in. Free marketeers now need to confront not old-fashioned common economy socialists, but Confucians, Orientalists, Francophiles and Continental social democrats with a taste for industrial (and constitutional) interventionism. Their common thread is a dislike of Anglo-American capitalism.

There comes a point, admittedly difficult to identify in such a theoretical argument, at which it becomes perverse to separate Western capitalism from its roots in liberal individualism. We may perhaps be seeing in parts of the Far East models of capitalism very different from those that have thrived in Western Europe and America. But that is not our experience of capitalism and certainly not how it arose in this country. It is the individual, his protection under law, his ability to make his own way in the world, which matters to us in the West. In France a similar book to Hutton's has had a comparable impact. Michel Albert's *Capitalism against Capitalism* argues that the ideological battle is now between what he calls the Anglo-American model of capitalism and the Rhineland/Alpine model.[11] Albert's book shares Hutton's belief in the superiority of Rhineland capitalism and mounts similar arguments for it. But what is most significant about his book is that he clearly believes that the Anglo-American model is winning. There has been a collapse in confidence in the old Continental model. They increasingly look enviously at our record of privatisation, deregulation and the achievement of a more flexible labour market. They believe that the Anglo-American model of capitalism is going to triumph, and I believe they are right.

NOTES

1. Will Hutton, *The State We're In* (London: Jonathan Cape, 1995).
2. Martin Weiner, *English Culture and the Decline of the Industrial Spirit* (Cambridge: Cambridge University Press, 1981), which has been brilliantly rebutted recently by W.D. Rubenstein in *Capitalism, Culture and Decline in Britain 1750–1990* (London: Routledge, 1993).
3. *The State We're In*, p. 42.
4. *Sunday Telegraph*, 15 January 1995.
5. *Financial Times*, 1 February 1996.
6. John Parkinson, *Employment Policy Institute Economic Report*, Vol. 10, No. 2.
7. Paul Samuelson, *Economics* (London: McGraw-Hill, 1995), 15th edition.
8. *Financial Times*, 7 February 1996.
9. David Hume, 'Of Refinement in the Arts', in *Essays Moral, Political and Literary* (London: Grant Richards, 1903).
10. Paul Johnson and Howard Reid, *Two Nations? The Inheritance of Poverty and Affluence* (London: Institute of Fiscal Studies, 1996).
11. Michel Albert, *Capitalism against Capitalism*, (London: Whurr, 1993).

4 An American Perspective
Robert Kuttner

The interesting question within this debate is whether the culture of a country is for sale or whether there are some things that are simply not for sale under any circumstances. That is the great difference between the right and the modern left. In times gone past the right very firmly believed that culture was *not* for sale, although it anchored this in tradition rather than in the market. On both sides of the Atlantic it is almost axiomatic that people tend to romanticise and envy each other's countries. Unfortunately, at one and the same time that Americans are envying the stability and the social security of Europe, and many Europeans are envying the dynamism of America, the UK is invariably caught somewhere in between – often feeling that it has the worst of both worlds.

There is an interesting contrast between the situation of the moderate left in both the United States and the United Kingdom, in that the US seems to have the economic space in which to design its own version of stakeholder capitalism. It is a big enough country that it is not so subject to global capital and trade that it could actually design something approaching a stakeholder society and make it stick. But the fact is that political insitutions in the US are so weak and divided that the ability to govern has been lost. Even with a legislative majority it is difficult, if not impossible, to govern, except at very unusual periods of crisis, because it requires a 'super-majority' in the states. In the mid-1990s the country has entered one of those periods where there is absolute deadlock between the Republican and Democratic Parties. Under such circumstances any kind of expansive vision is precluded, with the result that the existing frustration on the part of the electorate only deepens and the search for extremist solutions grows more perilous.

By contrast, the nature of government in the United Kingdom makes it possible to govern for precisely some of the reasons that Will Hutton decries: the centralism in Westminster makes government possible. But as a medium-sized country heavily dependent on trade, prisoner to some extent to the dictates of the global markets, there is very little running room; the result being that proposals for the creation of a stakeholder society are aimed at the level of the enterprise and to some extent at the level of the structure of the financial markets. Two questions immediately suggest themselves in this regard. First, is this the right way to proceed? Or in other words, is it realistic, would it work if you could impose it? Second, is this a genuinely new phenomenon or does it relate to something older? To take the second question first, in my opinion I think we are talking about something that is around a century old. It is the project of house-breaking capitalism. Stakeholding is not an attempt to supplant capitalism with socialism. Rather, the project of the moderate left – namely, making the free market system socially bearable – has been around for about a century: inventing and reinventing a social market economy, which after all is an oxymoron. In a market economy by definition prices capture everything of value and everything is for sale. In a social market economy, however, some limits must be placed on the operation of markets; some things are simply not for sale. So I take the project of stakeholder capitalism as being yet another attempt at creating a social market democracy, one version of which was put in place after the war. Capitalism is intensely powerful and dynamic, however, which has meant that the nature of the beast has changed almost beyond recognition in the intervening years. To make it socially bearable in the contemporary era we will have to be at least as daring as the postwar reformers because the environment of the present is so much more hostile.

STAKEHOLDING IN THE UNITED STATES?

Let me briefly turn the discussion towards a consideration of the United States. This is the best of times and the worst of times for America. On the one hand there is a great deal of dynamism in high-tech industry, but on the other the country is overcome by social division. The fact that productivity growth is outstripping wage growth is a sure sign that labour has lost bargaining power, because if it had not, then wage growth would be keeping up with productivity growth as it did during the postwar boom. All the institutions that used to make it possible for wage growth to keep up with productivity growth have been weakened. To all intents and purposes this was an enterprise-based social market economy – one in which large employers treated their people decently, and did not lay them off precipitously even when they thought they could raise the share price by doing so. This was possible for four reasons: first, there was a great deal of regulation in the basic industries, the AT&Ts, that were essentially regulated monopolies; second, the economy also featured a large number of oligopolies who did not fight too hard for a market share; third, the union movement was strong; and fourth, there was a low level of international competition. As a result of these basic characteristics a certain set of norms were injected into the labour market which included the norm that business did not precipitously lay people off simply because there was someone on the pavement who would do the job for less. In the contemporary era that implicit social compact has disappeared. There is no sector of the economy – with the possible exception of tenured university professors – where there is real job security. Incredibly, this is celebrated as a *virtue*. From this perspective the ideal corporation has one entrepreneur while the rest of the employees are on short-term contracts. When AT&T laid off 30,000 workers under the chairmanship of Bob Allen, the joke was that AT&T stood for 'Allen and Two Temps'. All this is based on the notion that there is a company called 'You, Incorporated'. It is you against the world: you are your own vice-president for marketing, you are your own vice-president for training and social capital – if you are not Bill Gates, that is your problem. The implication of all this being that, whatever the outcomes, they are inherently just.

Where in Britain the talk is of a meritocratic society, in the United States the fashionable term is 'meritocratic inequality' – thirty years and more ahead of Michael Young's schedule. By definition, therefore, since all market outcomes are 'natural', economic failure must be equated with personal failure. Under these circumstances it is an easy task for the right to put the left on the defensive, because a political movement which is seen constantly to take the side of the 'loser' can be portrayed as being either overly pessimistic or on the wrong side of history. To talk, as Will Hutton does, of the costs of remedying these problems is to be a realist not a pessimist, but to talk only about a society in which a handful of people are winners and everyone else is a loser is unquestionably to be a dour fatalist.

In any case, in the United States there is a rather timid version of this debate, which involves an interesting split between President Clinton and the Democrats in Congress. Clinton came into office as a rather bold left-of-centre figure, promising to invest a lot of money in training and education, and to put a public infrastructure programme before the deficit. Remarkably, he also planned to expand the welfare state by embracing universal health insurance. There was more promise in this than delivery, however, because by the time he was about six months into his term of office Clinton had abandoned almost all of these proposals except for universal health insurance, an initiative which, even though it was designed in accordance with market principles, was still not enough to satisfy the requirements of the insurance industry and so eventually went the same way as the rest. Worse was to come when he lost his majority in Congress and became even more conservative – to the extent that he is now in favour of balancing the budget, in theory at least, although he keeps ducking the particulars. All of which effectively adds up to the fact that there is no money to spend on anything. Which implies that the 'politics' of the 1996 election are that the moderate left voted for Clinton because not to do so would be to face something even worse – the inescapable conclusion being that any real change is foreclosed.

Now, interestingly enough, the exception to this is that the Democratic leadership in Congress has embraced something very much like Hutton's stakeholder capitalism. The Democratic leadership of both the House and the Senate have proposed a bill that was initially drafted by Jeff Bingaman, a senator from New Mexico. In essence the bill defines a stakeholder corporation, one that would receive certain tax and regulatory advantages if it behaved as a good corporate citizen. In the American context this is defined as having a certain degree of investment in the training and education of its workforce, demonstrating a long-term commitment to its employees, having an anti-layoff plan, having health insurance (since we continue to provide this intermittently at the company level), a decent pension plan and several other benefits. This legislation also includes a so-called 'Tobin tax', which is a tax on short-term gains from financial trading in an effort to slow down the financially-driven trading economy. This is probably the most radical initiative that the mainstream of the Democratic Party has come up with in thirty years. That they have done it at all is testament to the fact that there is a high and growing level of anxiety and apprehension over the cavalier attitude that corporations have adopted towards the workforce. In just ten years the old idea that the corporation owed something to the employee has simply disappeared, and as we have noted before, far from being decried this is actually celebrated. So we do have the beginnings of a debate over stakeholding in America, although not one confronted by the President of the United States, even though he is a Democrat.

STAKEHOLDING IN BRITAIN?

Now, let me turn to Will Hutton's programme. In the context of the UK I think it is rather sensible politics because it is forward looking, because it seizes a moral high ground, because it is not syndicalist in the sense that the old Labour Party was, and because it is not corporatist in the sense that a lot of the experiments of the 1970s tried and failed to be. Rather, it splits the difference between the new individualism of the 1990s and the need for a more inclusionary or collectivist society. On the one hand that means defining a stakeholder society rather in the way of 'You, Incorporated', where 'You' the individual become a stakeholder by paying attention to your own human capital, by paying attention to your own retirement planning, and so on, which implies that you become a stakeholder to the extent that you are a successful individual. Alternatively, a stakeholder society could be seen as one that is more collective and inclusive – one that defines membership in a community and that relies on the welfare state. I think Hutton is being quite sensible in trying to marry the fashionable rhetoric of the former with the practical politics of the latter.

Turning to particular aspects of the programme, I do think that the criticism of British and American financial markets as being excessively traders' markets and being driven by short-run returns is a fair one, and I think it makes sense to address the issue. The same can be said with regard to the adversarial character of labour relations. The pity is that labour unions in the US – and to some extent in the UK – are quite ready to accept that relations between themselves and employers have in some mutually acceptable way to be made less adversarial, but too few enterprises are either willing or able to meet them half way. This is one of the difficulties of a stakeholder model that is primarily based on the enterprise, because the supreme characteristic of the global economy of the 1990s is that the enterprise does not stay put. The global corporation has become 'footloose' to the extent that geographic location no longer matters to the extent that it once did. Thus it may well have been possible to bring about the kind of stakeholder relationship that we have been envisaging in the 1950s and 1960s, when enterprises had more durability and when a particular enterprise could reasonably be expected to be around in twenty years' time. But in a world of outsourcing and downsizing in 'virtual' corporations, it is awfully hard even for the most conscientious of corporations to reciprocate the loyalty that is tendered by the employee, because the entrepreneur does not know what the order book is going to look like; does not know what the competition is going to look like a year from now, or even a month from now, and is all too tempted to solve his competitiveness problems, or to solve the demands of the financial markets for higher returns by adopting the strategy of the casualisation of labour.

There has been much debate about whether the trend towards the casualisation of labour is a good thing or a bad thing, but the United Kingdom is the only country in which I have ever heard anyone deny that it is actually taking place. I do not know whether it is taking place in the UK, but I do know for certain that it is taking place in the United States. Lester Thurow has highlighted the fact that if you measure unemployment in the same way that it is measured in Europe, the real unemployment rate in the US is somewhere in the mid-teens. Problems of measurement do exist, and they come from several sources including immigration, the existence of a large underground economy, people who are out of the labour force and who are not measured at all, and independent contractors who have been laid off but are too proud to say so and who are working part time. If we include these people in estimates of unemployment then the real unemployment rate is at least 14 per cent – the statistical proof of this being the fact that wages are lagging so far behind productivity. As noted above, if labour had any bargaining power – which it does when labour markets are tight – wages would not be lagging behind productivity. In the state of Nebraska, where, for a number of reasons the unemployment rate is 2.8 per cent, McDonald's has to pay $8 an hour, even though it pays $5 an hour elsewhere. That is what happens when labour markets are tight.

Which brings me back to full employment. I think those of us – and I count myself to some extent, along with Will Hutton – who stress human capital, the welfare state, reform of financial markets and all the other putative ingredients of stakeholder capitalism, must keep the need for full employment at the absolute centre of our thoughts and actions. In situations where full employment has been lost, no amount of money directed towards the improvement of the stock of human capital will make a meaningful difference: instead of being simply frustrated, workers will be educated to the point where they can give voice to their frustration but can do nothing concrete about it. Conversely, in the context of full employment all kinds of miracles take place because people can learn things on the job. Too little attention is paid to the relationship between the slow growth regime that results from the globalisation of capital and the hegemony of the central bankers, and the difficulty of maintaining any kind of a social contract. Whether it be German-style, Japanese-style, French-style, Swedish-style, let alone Anglo-Saxon-style capitalism, it will not succeed while 12 per cent of the workforce remain unemployed. It simply does not work. Too much money is paid to sustain people in idleness – the result being the division of society into a privileged third, a middle third, and a forgotten third; and in countries that have unfortunate traditions of turning ugly, such a situation can turn ugly very, very quickly. So in any consideration or formulation of a stakeholder society, full employment must feature as a primary policy objective.

5 The Third Revolution[1]
Harold Perkin

The modern world is the world of the professional expert. Just as pre-industrial society was dominated by landlords and industrial society by capitalists, so post-industrial society is dominated by professionals. Pre-industrial landlords controlled the scarce resource of land for agriculture; capitalists controlled the scarce resource of physical capital in machinery and factories or the financial capital that lay behind it; professionals in today's society control the scarce resource of human capital, the capitalised value of their education, training and experience. Human capital is not limited like land or material capital but is expansible as far down society as talent and training can make it go. Like the landed and capitalist elites before them, the professional elites, notably the corporate managers and bureaucrats at the head of the system, control the flows of income and strive to steer more and more of it to themselves. Thus a society designed to produce far more sophisticated goods and services for everyone than ever before is in danger of being corrupted for the benefit of the few.

THE THREE REVOLUTIONS

Professional society is the product of the third great social revolution in the history of mankind. The first world-transforming revolution was the Neolithic Revolution which, by inaugurating settled agriculture, raised living standards for a much larger population and enabled a majority of food producers to support a minority of craftsmen, warriors, priests and rulers. These created the first cities and thus civilisation, invented writing and thus history, and initiated all the organized arts and sciences, literature and drama, political and social structures. Warriors and priests forced or seduced the peasants to give them the land, and so enabled the elite to extract a major share of the produce (in crops, labour services or rent) to support the activities of government, warfare and/or religious ritual. The gains were dearly bought for the peasant – 'In the sweat of thy brow shalt thou eat bread' – and he had to carry the whole weight of ruler, landlord, warrior and priest on his back. Although this system of extraction was efficient and long-lived, the landed elites were tempted from time to time to extract too much and

7. The associated expansion of the welfare state, a necessary safety net in an insecure world – now under attack by the right wing but hotly defended by middle-class beneficiaries of state education, health services and pensions.
8. The expansion of higher education, the chief creator of human capital, to embrace an unprecedented proportion of the relevant age group.
9. The rise of the giant business corporation, now the dominant force in national and international economies, which preaches the free market but does not practise it.
10. The globalisation of the economy, in which a few hundred transnational corporations (TNCs), most of them based in Western countries, are wealthier than most members of the United Nations.

These ten major trends operate unequally in different countries, and are handled with differential success and benefit to their populations by their elites, who exploit them with varying scales of intensity.

THE GREAT ARCH

The seven countries, like all their fellows in the developed world, lie on a great arch, stretching from the classic free market economy – strictly, the corporate managerial – to the extreme command economy – strictly, the state bureaucratic. Their position reflects their elites' method of extraction of income from their society and their commitment to creative social cohesion or to dysfunctional self-indulgence.

Britain is, or was, the keystone of the arch: a mixed economy with a pioneering welfare state and, until the Thatcherite privatisations, one of the largest nationalised sectors in the West. Industrial concentration has gone further there than elsewhere and it was one of the nurseries of the multinational corporation. It has suffered from a more intense rivalry than most between the public and private sector professionals, who continually squabble over the distribution of resources, rather than cooperate to increase them like the Germans or the Japanese. In consequence, Britain is the least successful of the major post-industrial societies, and the advanced country most vulnerable to the crises of the global economy. Unfortunately, the Thatcherite backlash against state intervention has brought the country nearer to the American version of the free market but without the American safeguards against monopoly and extreme exploitation (themselves under threat from the current Gingrichite backlash), so that the supports for a stakeholder society have been undermined by an increasingly irresponsible right wing.

France and Germany have avoided Britain's mistakes. Each has a long history of collaboration between government and business and, paradoxically from an Anglo-American point of view, a conservative tradition of state welfare going back to Bismarck and Napoleon III for the sake of national unity in the face of hostile neighbours. Both are meritocracies, the French deliberately so through the *grandes ecoles* and the civil service *grands corps*, which have increasingly come to provide the leaders both in government and the major corporations; the Germans less formally but just as elitist in practice, with top positions recruited through selective secondary schools and state universities. Both have developed different forms of stakeholder capitalism which give some degree of partnership in corporate governance to workers and creditors.

The United States and the defunct Soviet Union (with its former satellite East Germany) form opposite pillars of the arch, the most triumphantly free market and dogmatically state-centralised versions of post-industrial society. Neither is, or was, quite as extreme as it claimed. The United States has a close rapport between government and big business, symbolised by the revolving door through which corporate executives go in and out of government, and fuelled by huge streams of cash flowing in both directions, from corporations to Political Action Committees and from government to corporations in contracts, subsidies and bail-outs. The current backlash by Gingrich, Dole and the Republican Congress against taxing and spending is very selective, and targets welfare for the poor and health care for the elderly but not tax breaks for the rich, subsidies for agriculture, and oil exploration, timber felling and mining in the national parks, and certainly not defence spending in, say, Newt Gingrich's own constituency. Wrapping themselves in the American flag comes ill from politicians and businessmen who export jobs and capital, not to say pollution and dangerous occupations, to Third World countries with no social overheads using low-wage and child, prison and forced labour. 'Engineering the corporation', a euphemism for firing workers including once-safe middle managers and replacing them with insecure and part-time 'consultants', is undermining the social contract on which the American dream was built, with disastrous consequences for social cohesion and the country's future. The decline of American hegemony, disguised by military posturing – cf. its inability to finance the Gulf War by itself – and the unprecedented budget and trading deficits, threaten the demise of the United States as world superpower. As some of them are beginning to realise, the greed and selfishness of the business and political elites and their repudiation of responsibility for other stakeholders in their crumbling society threaten the unity which has been the nation's boast since the American Revolution.

The late Soviet Union was the prototype of the centralised command economy, with an egalitarian ideal of care and support for every member of society. It inherited a strong bureaucratic state from the Tsarist regime and turned it into a ruthless meritocracy, with merit defined in terms of political loyalty rather than competence. The Communist Party became the profession at the head of all the professions, a sort of church which blessed and exploited the faithful as long as they believed and contributed their tithes, but hunted out heretics with the zeal of the Spanish Inquisition or New England witchfinders.[4] Unfortunately, the *nomenklatura*, the higher clergy as it were, succumbed to the temptation of extracting more of the surplus than the system could stand. The 'contradictions of communism' became more destructive than Marx's 'contradictions of capitalism', and the elite squeezed the proletariat, the putative ruling class and intended beneficiary, to the point of exhaustion. The producers could no longer afford to buy the products of their own labour, and the economy imploded. The workers and peasants complained, 'They pretend to pay us, so we pretend to work.'[5] The Party became a kind of mafia, a protection racket that extended upwards as far as Brezhnev's son-in-law, Yuri Churbanov, if not to Brezhnev himself, with brown bag 'gifts' of roubles and secret incomes in cash and kind, and caches of roubles, gold and jewellery stashed away by the satraps of government in every Soviet republic.[6] The working class for whom the system existed had no say in its control, and the malaise proved to be self-destructive. It was corruption rather than ideology that destroyed the Soviet Union.

The same can be said for the most prosperous and economically successful of the communist satellites, East Germany. Despite its egalitarian ideology, the same hidden flows of income went to the high Socialist Unity Party officials and industrial managers, and the same deprivations were imposed on the working population. A comparative analysis of rates of extraction by Jaroslav Krejci in 1976 showed that the intensity of exploitation was greater in the East than in West Germany, and was increasing at a more rapid rate.[7] Through their access to Western television the East Germans had greater knowledge of Western affluence than the Russians, and began to vote with their feet as soon as *perestroika* lowered the barriers to emigration via Hungary and Austria. The East German economy, already weakened by inequality and exploitation, began to bleed to death even before the Berlin Wall came down. The refusal of Gorbachev to prop up the corrupt puppet regime of Honecker brought it tumbling down.

Japan is the exception to every rule and stands at both ends of the great arch, or rather floats above it in a sphere all its own. It is ostensibly a classic free market economy on the American model, with giant corporations dominating the domestic economy and investing huge trade surpluses in

Europe, America and east Asia. Yet alongside a weak and corrupt political system it has a powerful government bureaucracy that controls economic policy and steers 'Japan Inc.' towards perpetual growth and new sunrise industries. With a more concentrated meritocracy even than France and a cultural tradition of group loyalty and social harmony, it would seem to be the ideal version of professional society. There are of course social costs, in the exploitation of workers in the subcontracting sector, the subordination of women, and the harsh treatment of minorities like the Koreans and the *burakumin* (the pariah caste of 'hamlet people').[8] Western economists frequently forecast, and the Japanese themselves are apprehensive, that the 'Japanese miracle' will shortly end, but every forecast so far has been premature and Japan has bounced back stronger than ever. Its success can be traced to a peculiar version of stakeholding, which through the Confucian tradition of group loyalty operates upwards from the family or household to the workshop, the corporation and the nation itself. This has made Japan one of the models, along with the German-inspired European one, for the stakeholder society world-wide.

Stakeholding is the key to the high trust and willing cooperation between executives and workers, government and citizens, that is the secret of enduring success and survival in post-industrial society. Unfortunately, some elites seem not to be aware of its inexorable necessity, and if they do not learn it in the very near future they are likely to suffer the same fate, social malaise, economic implosion and political collapse, as the Soviet Union and its satellites.

THREE VERSIONS OF CAPITALISM

What is to be done if the free market economies are to avoid the fate of the Soviet Union and East Germany? Professional society is the most productive and potentially beneficial system ever attained in the history of mankind, but like all earlier systems it is vulnerable to the greed and selfishness of its elites. The problem goes far deeper than at first appears, because it is embedded in the very structure of the societies and in their implicit definitions of property. Above all, it is inherent in the nature of the business corporation, whether private or state-owned, which operates very differently in the different countries. This determines the structure of rewards to the competing stakeholders and therefore the willingness with which they cooperate for the success of the enterprise. The Soviet Union collapsed because the professionals who ran the government and the state corporations were paid in such a way that they were tempted to seek their rewards in corrupt and secret ways while the ordinary workers were reduced almost to subsistence and despaired of being rewarded for their efforts. As the controllers of the flows of income from the system, the *nomenklatura* were in effect the 'owners' of the state's capital, but owners who had to hide their property behind a false egalitarian ideology. In consequence they put all their effort into cheating the system, while the ordinary workers put all theirs into 'playing ca'canny', malingering, absenteeism, alcoholism on the job, and avoiding work by whatever means they could. A system that pays people to cheat and shirk rather than to work constructively to increase production and productivity is a formula for disaster. System collapse was the inexorable result.

The free market economies at first sight seem to be very much alike, with large corporations run increasingly by professional managers dominating each national economy and sharing out the global economy between them. The corporate executives control the major flows of income to all the rest of the stakeholders and are under temptation to steer more and more of it to themselves. Corruption seems to operate everywhere, from American Congressmen funded by big business to Japanese 'money politics' where members of the Diet are expected to distribute 'presents' – supplied by the *keiretsu* – to their constituents, from British ex-Cabinet ministers and civil servants who take their deferred rewards in (perfectly legal) corporate appointments, to French and German politicians who accept enormous party contributions from business supporters. The major scandals, from the Recruit and Lockheed affairs in Japan to the Savings and Loans collapse in the United States, are too well known to need recounting here; they differ only in the extent to which they are illegal and condemned or are part of the quasi-legal 'structural corruption' in the relations between government and business throughout the developed – and indeed the developing – world.[9]

On further analysis, however, it appears that the structure of rewards to the various stakeholders is very disparate in different countries, with diverse effects on public morale and on economic growth and company survival. The difference can be traced to the structure of the corporation and who owns it, or can claim a share in the profits and the decisions which determine its future. In Britain and the United States the company, although in law an artificial person owning itself, has come in common usage to be owned solely by the shareholders, who can do with it what they like: sell it, break it up, fire any or all the employees, export its operations to Third World countries, or run it into bankruptcy and liquidation. In practice, since the shareholders are ephemeral partners with no commitment to the company beyond the next balance sheet, this means that the shareholders' proxies, the directors, have complete control over the company and its assets, and as long as they can keep the dividends high enough to stave off raiding predators they can do whatever they like. What they like, of course, is to pay themselves enormous salaries, 'perks' in kind like luxury cars, expense accounts and unlimited travel, pension rights, stock options, 'golden handshakes' when they leave, and so on. Meanwhile, they can treat all the other stakeholders, notably the employees, subcontractors, creditors and customers, with scant respect, or even contempt.

Britain and the United States, once the most successful economies in the world, are now in steep decline, with record trade deficits and enormous public debts. Depression does not stop at the economy but affects the whole of society: inequality and poverty have increased, crime and drugs are at unprecedented levels, and the sense of insecurity and fear of falling have extended upwards from the blue-collar workers to the middle managers and professional classes. Malaise has spread to all levels of society below the very rich, whose greed and selfishness are its main cause.

Fortunately, there are two other versions of free market capitalism based on different conceptions of the corporation which, while run by professional executives just as self-interested, are structured in such a way that it pays them to pursue enlightened self-interest. They distribute the profits not only more equitably between all the stakeholders but with more positive effects on economic growth and the survival of the enterprise. These are the German-inspired European social market economy and the Japanese-inspired East Asian familistic version of capitalism. Unlike the Anglo-American free market, which stems from a deep-rooted belief in individual ownership going back beyond Adam Smith to the early modern transition from feudal lordship to absolute property,[10] their inheritance of community spirit and social responsibility embodies traditions of Catholic corporatism and Protestant altruism in the one case and of Confucian harmony and self-restraint in the other. Their commitment to stakeholder capitalism reflects their concept of property, their social ideals and values, and their structure of human relationships.

THE CONTINENTAL SOCIAL MARKET ECONOMY

As befits the heirs of the Western tradition of rationality and legalism, the Continental Europeans have encapsulated their version of professional society in an explicit framework of law. The leading model is the German social market economy, a combination of regulated capitalist market with generous social welfare which aims at high productivity based on social cohesion. It rests on a structure of company law that guarantees the interests of all stakeholders, not merely the shareholders and directors but the employees, the bankers and other creditors, and indirectly even the suppliers, subcontractors, franchisees and consultants. Co-determination (*Mitbestimmung*) ensures the involvement of all partners in the enterprise in decision making, thus engaging them in the long-term survival and profitability of the firm. The self-interest of all parties, not just quick windfalls for the few, is thus harnessed to the common benefit of all. Long-term investment, research and development, and the training of managers and workers to create human capital, are given priority over instant returns to the shareholders, and a fair share-out of rewards between shareholders, executives, managers, creditors and employees is ensured by involving all of them in the oversight of the company. The two-tier structure of the firm has a supervisory board (*Aufsichsrat*) on which workers are represented alongside shareholders, management, and major creditors, including the banks which provide more capital than the stockholders, which oversees the managerial executive (*Vorstand*) responsible for day-to-day operations. This makes the survival of the firm and its long-term profitability the aim of all the partners and guards against quick raids by outsiders and snatched windfalls by opportunist shareholders and directors.[11]

The French corporation has less formal safeguards but still ensures that employees and creditors are not bypassed and outmanoeuvred. The French PDG (*président-directeur-général*) of a large corporation can be a 'little Napoleon' over his directors but he operates within an environment that restricts his initiative far more than the Anglo-American CEO (Chief Executive Officer). The institutional investors form a hard kernel (*noyau dur*) of professional watchdogs, two-thirds of whom must be non-executive directors owing allegiance to their institutions rather than to the company, who maintain a permanent interest and can dismiss the PDG if they so wish. And he has to deal with a *comité d'entreprise* including workers and trade unions who send observers to the main board and have the right of access to accounts and policy decisions, which at least makes the management think twice before it overrides their interests.[12]

The German system, with French and other member countries' backing, is now being extended to the rest of the European Union. The Social Chapter of the Maastricht Treaty of 1994 underwrites the interests of all members of the stakeholder society, including citizens' rights to welfare and workers' trade union rights, except of course in 'opt-out' Britain. By September 1996 every large multinational corporation which operates in more than one member country will have to appoint a works council with the right to be consulted over all aspects of company policy, including pay and conditions for executives as well as workers, investment, research and development, relocation abroad, and so on.[13] The European social market economy upholds capitalism without undermining the social contract on which a civilised society is based.

EAST ASIAN CONFUCIAN CAPITALISM

The East Asian version of professional society does not stem from a tradition of rational law but from a different inheritance, an implicit belief in social balance. The Japanese call this *wa*, harmony or domestic peace, which derives from the Confucian belief in social congruity and the golden mean. Since *wa* starts from the needs of the social whole rather than the autonomous individual, it does not embody itself in individual rights or concrete rational law. From the individual's point of view it is an emotional attachment to the group – the family, household, working team, firm, nation – and an expectation that effort, cooperation and loyalty will be rewarded by the group's permanent concern for one's welfare. It is not a matter of universal human rights but of the warm embrace of belongingness.

The downside is that non-members are outsiders, to be bargained or competed with but not accorded the same claims or privileges. Foreigners and pariah groups like the *burakumin* are totally excluded. Even inside the group there are differences of status and belongingness, and differences too between nearer and wider groups, family, firm and nation, which sit within each other like Russian dolls. At each level all insiders have preferential claims over all outsiders. Western universalising objectivity has no place, and the Kantian categorical imperative – do unto *all* others as you would be done by – is not a meaningful concept.

Such an outlook – it is too diffuse to be called an ideology – can be infuriating to rational Westerners, with their demand for objectivity, equal treatment for all, and a 'level playing field'. It makes doing business between East and West extremely frustrating and leads to misunderstandings, recriminations and accusations of bad faith. But in Japan and other nations in the Confucian tradition it makes very good sense. The working team, and the firm itself, becomes a quasi-family in which each member has a role, can contribute to the success of the whole, and be rewarded in proportion to his or her status. The 'three sacred treasures' of the Japanese *kaisha,* lifelong employment, rising wage scales and promotion by seniority, and the company union, are based on the mutual trust arising from *shudan shugi* (team work), and without it the 'treasures' are meaningless or counterproductive, as they would be in the West.[14]

It is easy for Westerners to see the flaws in this system, which is unfair as between insiders and outsiders, operates unequally between the large companies and the majority of small subcontractors, and without legal safeguards is vulnerable to erosion in hard times. Yet it has survived the world crises of the last twenty-three years better than its Western competitors, has produced rates of economic growth more than twice as high as theirs, and given the Japanese massive trade surpluses which are the mirror image of Western indebtedness.[15] The East Asian version of stakeholder capitalism – 'individualism in the arms of collectivism', rewards for the individual through cooperation within the group – has proved to be far the most successful of the three.

ARE CAPITALISMS CONVERGING?

Michel Albert, the French businessman and economic philosopher who coined the idea of Rhine capitalism versus neo-American, fears that the three capitalisms may be converging. This, he worries, may not be on the more moral, productive and progressive European and Japanese models but on the more seductive and instantly gratifying neo-American model.[16] This is because the professionals who run the corporations in all three systems are under the same temptation to pursue their immediate self-interest to the neglect of the other stakeholders. Competition for world markets, the use of cheap labour in countries without social welfare, trade unions, or pollution controls, and the fear of takeover by American and British asset-strippers with no interest in long-term survival or profitability, are forcing corporate executives everywhere to look graspingly at the high social costs of mutuality between stakeholders. Welfare, whether public or corporate, is under pressure from the rightwing backlash spreading outwards from post-Reaganite America and post-Thatcherite Britain. Corporate executives everywhere see that they could make an instant killing by stripping the other stakeholders, whatever the consequences for tomorrow's prosperity. The future may take its revenge, but as Keynes said, in the long run we are all dead. The temptation to eat the seed corn now, like their American and British competitors, is very powerful.

Albert may be right, but there are signs that even British and American executives are beginning to see that the siren songs of the free market economists and politicians are an invitation to self-destruction. The director-general of the Confederation of British Industry, Adair Taylor, has warned that a low-wage economy is bad for business and that high wages linked to productivity and performance, together with employee share ownership, are the way to break the cycle of economic decline.[17] In the United States, big business men like Richard J. Franke have called for a more responsible approach to democracy by business, 'to counter the excesses of greed and unfair advantage that threaten our concept of the just society' by means of 'a modern social contract' guaranteeing a fair and open system with 'a sense of general proportion between the haves and have-nots'.[18] Tony Blair's call for a stakeholder society is catching an opportune tide that is beginning to flow around the world, which even British and American businessmen are more aware of than their obsolescent politicians.

More significantly, perhaps, the transnational corporations that now dominate the world economy have begun to issue codes of conduct for their overseas operations which offer a global ray of hope. Even here, the Anglo-American TNCs differ from their European and Japanese counterparts by emphasising the primary rights of shareholders over other stakeholders. While a typical American corporation begins: 'The overall purpose of Caterpillar is to enhance the long-term interest of those who own the business – the stockholders', a typical Japanese one does not even mention the shareholders but states: 'Toyota has always been a company devoted to enhancing the quality of life for people around the world by providing useful and appealing products.' Both codes are of course public relations exercises, but one puts profits first and moral responsibility second, while the other puts service first and expects that profits will follow.[19] Nonetheless, the bow to public opinion shows that businessmen at the highest level, unlike their rightwing political friends, recognise that mutual trust and a fair distribution of rewards between all stakeholders are the best way to guarantee their own future.

If convergence of capitalisms is the alternative to collapse, it will have to be convergence on European and East Asian terms rather than Anglo-American. The world after all belongs to the whole human race, not just to those who claim to own or control the means of production, and to the vast diversity of species that support human life. Each generation only borrows it for a while, and if they exploit it beyond reason they can destroy themselves along with a large part of the biosphere. The third great social revolution in the history of mankind, the revolution of the professionals, has enabled us to attain a higher plane of existence, with knowledge and power, health and longevity, the sheer ease and abundance of life – for those in the developed world at least – beyond the dreams of previous generations. It would be a pity if the professional elites who control it, in their greed and selfishness, should throw it all away and lead us and themselves down the primrose path to the everlasting bonfire.

NOTES

1. This article is based on the author's book *The Third Revolution: Professional Elites in the Modern World since 1945* (London: Routledge, 1996).
2. Cf. Harold Perkin, *The Origins of Modern English Society* (London: Routledge, 1969), ch. 9.
3. Perkin, *The Rise of Professional Society: England since 1980* (London: Routledge, 1989).
4. Cf. Alex Simirenko, *The Professionalization of Soviet Society* (New Brunswick: Transaction Books, 1992).
5. Cf, Tatyana Zaslavskaya, *The Second Socialist Revolution* (London: Tauris, 1990).
6. Arkady Vaksberg, *The Soviet Mafia* (New York: St. Martin's Press, 1988).
7. Jaroslav Krejci, *The Social Structure of Divided Germany* (London: Croom Helm, 1976).
8. Misiko Hane, *Peasants, Rebels, and Outcasts: The Underside of Modern Japan* (New York: Pantheon, 1982).
9. Cf. Chalmers Johnson, 'Tanaka Kakuei, Structural Corruption, and the Advent of Machine Politics in Japan', *Journal of Japanese Studies*, Vol. 12, 1986, p. 1.
10. See Perkin, *Origins*, pp. 51–6.
11. Jonathan Charkham, *Keeping Good Company: A Study of Corporate Governance in Five Countries* (Oxford: Clarendon Press, 1994), ch. 2.
12. *Ibid.*, ch. 4.
13. *Guardian*, 18 February 1995.
14. Cf. Ronald Dore, *Taking Japan Seriously: A Confucian Perspective on Leading Economic Issues* (Stanford: Stanford University Press, 1987); Tadashi Fukutake, *Japanese Social Structure* (Tokyo: Tokyo University Press, 1983); Chie Nakane, *Japanese Society* (London: Penguin, 1973).
15. Average percentage annual rates of manufacturing growth 1964–92: Japan 6.6; USA 3.9; France 2.9; West Germany 2.7; UK 1.5 (Michael Kitson and Jonathan Michie of Cambridge University, in *Observer*, 21 January 1996); the United States' cumulative trading deficit in 1983–92 was $762 billion (US Department of Commerce, *Statistical Abstract of the US, 1994*, p. 806); Britain's in 1988–92 was $117 billion (*Britain: A Handbook*, HMSO, 1994, p. 122).
16. Michel Albert, *Capitalism against Capitalism* (London: Whurr, 1993).
17. Adair Taylor, Speech to Institute of Personnel and Development, reported in *Guardian*, 25 January 1996, and his letter, *ibid.*, 27 January 1996.
18. Richard J. Franke, *A Business Man's View of Responsible Participation in Democracy* (Chicago: John Nuveen and Co., 1989).
19. UNCTAD, *World Development Report* (United Nations, 1994), pp. 319, 323.

6 An International Perspective[1]
Dominic Kelly

Within the first few pages of *The State We're In* Will Hutton tells us that 'the behaviour of the economy can only be understood in terms of the whole of each country's social and political system and where it stands in the global order'.[2] If we make explicit what is implicit in this and add the historical dimension then we can readily agree with him: capitalism is not simply and exclusively an economic system but a socio-political system whose content and structure is formed and moulded by its history. In relation to the debate over the creation of 'stakeholder capitalism' in Britain this understanding raises some interesting questions, for if the British economy needs a fundamental overhaul in order to make it more competitive in the global marketplace then by implication there will have to be some fundamental social and political changes also. Conversely, if we are to overhaul the social and political structure then we can expect major upheavals in the economy. Creating stakeholder capitalism in Britain, or even drawing up the plans for its creation, must take this fully into account. Unfortunately, this does not seem to be happening within at least some of the policy making circles of the Labour Party, which in their pursuit of the holy grail of electoral victory appear to have been blinded (temporarily, one hopes) by the perceived benefits of Japanese long-termism, the German structure of corporate governance and the Singaporean welfare system.[3] But as we all know to our cost, the importation of ideas, practices and policies from abroad can be disastrous: witness the devastation wrought by 'supply-side economics' and the ideas underpinning it as they moved from Reagan's America to Thatcher's Britain. How much more costly then might the structural changes in the British economy implied by the importation for example of Japanese long-termism be, and how would these affect the social structure of Britain?

It is impossible to predict what the outcome of such a transformation might be. We can, however, usefully explore some of the issues that contemplation of such a transformation raises by posing a number of questions. Is it possible to fundamentally transform a society in the absence of war or other major upheaval? Can one (or more) sets of societal arrangements, practices and policies be successfully transplanted from one country into another? What are the dangers and costs associated with such an attempt? In our search for satisfactory answers to these questions we will find that history still matters and that what happens beyond our shores in the 'global political economy' will loom ever larger, not only over the domestic political debate but over the everyday lives of individual people.

These questions have been asked before in relation to the stakeholding debate (and herein lies the importance of *The State We're In*), but with the exception of Will Hutton they have been asked half-heartedly and in such a way as to suggest that they are peripheral, that they get in the way of discussion of the detailed specifics of policy making. But Hutton fails to see the possible costs involved in looking abroad for solutions to Britain's domestic problems; and while there is nothing wrong in concentrating on specific policies it is my contention that these wider questions must be confronted head-on: if they are not then the public's understanding of the nature, origins and ramifications of the debate and the possible consequences of transforming it from political rhetoric into concrete reality – in terms of the hurdles that must be overcome, the costs to be borne, and the opportunities that may arise – will be severely impaired. That is why in this chapter I will avoid discussion of particular policies and policy changes associated with stakeholding – many of which are addressed elsewhere in this book – and concentrate instead on the broader questions outlined above.

GLOBALISATION, THE END OF HISTORY AND THE POST-COLD WAR WORLD

The stakeholder debate is only one facet of a wider debate concerning the future shape of the global political economy. It reflects on the one hand the uncertainties that have arisen with the ending of the Cold War between the two opposing ideological camps led by the United States and the Soviet Union, and on the other, the uncertainties that have arisen in the wake of the globalisation of economic activity. Let us briefly consider how each of these impinges on the stakeholder debate and on the future of Britain.

Globalisation and the End of History

Several years ago Francis Fukuyama published a book entitled *The End of History and the Last Man*,[4] in which he argued that the settling of the ideological dispute between the capitalist 'West' and the communist 'East' – signified most dramatically by the dissolution of the Soviet Union – was a precursor to the universal acceptance of a set of ideas about how economy and society could best be organised within nation states. Exhausted and moribund, communism was no longer seen as a viable alternative to free market capitalism and liberal democracy – even by that other communist giant the People's Republic of China (PRC), whose seemingly irreversible turn to the market began in the early 1980s. A few smaller states – North Korea and perhaps Cuba – did seem to be holding on to the old beliefs but it was regarded as only a matter of time before they too would come to their senses. In the absence of this ideological struggle, Fukuyama argued, and with the universal acceptance of free market principles and their political counterpart liberal democracy, the foreseeable future of the world would be one characterised by increasing peace and prosperity.[5]

At roughly the same time that Fukuyama's influential book appeared, a rash of books and articles focusing on the phenomenon of 'globalisation' was also beginning to emerge,[6] all broadly arguing that three interrelated currents – the rapid pace of technological innovation (particularly in the area of communications technology), the globalisation of production (including the shifting centre of gravity of world manufacturing production from North America and Western Europe towards Japan and the Pacific), and the increasing mobility and power of transnational capital – were acting as midwives at the birth of a truly 'global' economy: one in which national boundaries, and therefore domestic strategies of national economic management, would become obsolete.[7] Far from living Fukuyama's life of peace and prosperity, therefore, we seemed to be faced with a situation wherein the feelings of vulnerability and uncertainty engendered by the nuclear confrontation between the superpowers had been replaced by an entirely different (but not exactly new) set of circumstances in which the uncertainties surrounding 'globalisation' and the volatility of the market predominate. But in contrast to the Cold War confrontation where there was an element of choice (however unpalatable) of political destiny for the major states – joining the 'West' or the 'East', or remaining 'non-aligned' – the triumph of capitalism appeared to have been so overwhelming that socialism was no longer seen as a viable alternative: the only conceivable path to development, the only possible route to economic prosperity was a capitalist one. In such a world, so the argument goes, all national institutions will come to resemble each other, and so too will all government policies.

If these separate but related lines of argument are correct, then it would appear that either stakeholding represents the future not just of Britain but of all other countries as well, which seems unlikely, or that stakeholding is doomed to failure in the face of competition from other countries less caring or more efficient than our own. Both lines of argument – that we have reached the 'end' of history and that globalisation is leading inexorably to a borderless world – have, however, been seriously questioned: by events in the 'real' world (of which the resurgence of communist/socialist sentiment in some of the former Eastern bloc countries is the most obvious example),[8] and by theoretical arguments noting the persistence of national political economy in an era of global markets and casting doubt on the extent to which the process of globalisation has actually occurred.[9] It would seem, therefore, that there is at least *some* remaining space for national economic policy making in a more global but still *international* economy even if capitalism has become the only viable path of economic development for the industrialised as well as the industrialisng world.

The United States in the Post-Cold War World

Freed from the constraining influence of its Cold War competition with the Soviet Union the US has in recent years – with major exceptions such as the Gulf War – turned its attention inwards in an attempt to solve some of its pressing domestic problems, of which the trade deficit is the most relevant here. Unlike the case of the budget deficit which is seen largely as a domestic problem, the blame for the trade deficit can be laid elsewhere: here there are identifiable rivals situated outside the United States, partly in Europe but primarily in the countries of North and Southeast Asia; starting with Japan, but increasingly involving other countries in the region – South Korea, the 'Three Chinas' (the PRC, Taiwan and Hong Kong), the Philippines, Singapore, Malaysia, Indonesia and Thailand.

The economic challenge that these 'producer' economies represent to the US is formidable, for the simple reason that they are able to produce all kinds of top-quality goods that Americans want (for example, cars, electronic goods, textiles) at lower prices than their home-grown counterparts, even given the higher transport costs involved. Bringing the trade deficit down to manageable levels means exporting more American-made goods and importing fewer goods from abroad. Simple. The problem was, or so the Americans argued in the 1960s, 1970s and 1980s, that the countries which had the largest trade surpluses with the US also tended to have the most restricted domestic markets: the solution, therefore, seemed to require persuading or forcing these countries to open their economies to the rigours of global competition and open trade. This policy has not worked, even though some of America's major competitors, Japan for example, now have the most 'open' markets in the world. As a result attention has turned to so-called 'structural' differences between other economies and the American ideal. It is from these structural differences in the economic and social organisation of individual countries that the notion of different forms of capitalism – Anglo-Saxon, Confucian, Rhenish, (Stakeholder?) – comes. It would appear that there are alternatives to socialism after all: different forms of capitalism. The contemporary economic struggle is cast less in terms of competition between individual states and more in terms of competition between varieties of capitalism; it is a struggle for the right to define the framework of rules and norms within which economic competition takes place, and it is a struggle that the US is determined to win.

One of the most distinctive alternatives to the US model of capitalism is Confucian capitalism, whose main exemplar is the chief economic rival to the US – Japan. But as we shall see from the discussion that follows, different forms of capitalism can be shaped and altered by international as well as domestic forces.

Since its defeat in the Pacific war in 1945 Japan has lived under the shadow of the United States. During the period of Occupation that lasted until 1952 the Americans thoroughly 'democratised' the Japanese economy and society through a series of reforms which saw the dissolution of the armed forces, major land and tax reform, the breakup of the large business conglomerates, and the purge and prosecution of many of those deemed responsible for leading Japan down the path of imperialism. In its place was put an elected legislature, a free market economy, and a 'Peace' constitution guaranteeing democratic rights for the Japanese people and renouncing forever the use of war as an instrument of foreign policy. At least that is what the Americans started to do before the Cold War came to Asia in the form of the Korean war, which led Washington to declare that keeping Japan safe from the clutches of communism was 'vital to the interests of the United States'. Naturally, since the US needed a strong and prosperous Japan as its leading ally in the Pacific, this entailed halting the democratisation process and even reversing some of the reforms – which is why Japan is one of the top two or three spenders on military arms and technology in the world today despite having a constitution banning possession of any 'offensive' military capability. The democratisation process and its reversal have thus had a profound and lasting effect on how the modern Japanese economy and society is organised. Many of these effects have been positive – economic success and parliamentary democracy being the most obvious – but many have not: the overriding pursuit of rapid economic growth meant putting the interests of big business before social security, before the environment, and before the well-being of the population, measured by such indicators as having little access to public amenities, such as a decent sewage system for example, or having to live in cramped houses in narrow streets, or being able to spend little time together as families. Much the same can be said in the political sphere, where freedom of expression took a back seat to reconstruction of the economy – the nascent socialist and communist movements of the early postwar years being ruthlessly suppressed by the Japanese leadership, with tacit support from the American occupying forces.

Protected by the American nuclear umbrella and sustained by American money the Japanese people were able to rebuild their war-torn country free from fear of communist invasion from without or of communist subversion from within. Under these circumstances it took the addition of only two more ingredients – ready access to the US market, and freedom, at least in the early crucial years, from the costs of military production – to complete Japan's 'miraculous' rise from the ashes of defeat; a miracle that was completed by the mid-1960s. Ironically, it is these same two ingredients of the Japanese success story that have been the cause of so much of the anger directed by Americans towards Japan from the 1970s onwards; and now that the US no longer has to worry about protecting its ally and rival from a hostile Soviet invasion Americans are determined to do something about it.[10]

STAKEHOLDER BRITAIN

So, we have three interrelated strands to consider. The first is the notion that national economic policy making is still possible even in a 'globalised' world but that it is more difficult than it was previously. The second is that there are distinct forms of capitalism which provide different routes to economic prosperity and social well-being. The third is that the world's most powerful state, the United States, is pushing more strongly than ever before for the kind of global economy in which it believes it can prosper – a 'level playing field' free from non-tariff barriers such as impenetrable distribution networks, rule-bending for domestic firms and the like: in effect a global economy which conforms as closely as possible to the idealised American economy. Putting these three strands together – as so few people seem willing to do – leads to the inevitable conclusion that achieving stakeholder capitalism in Britain is not only about the reorientation of the economy and society in the domestic context of what is acceptable socially and politically to the British people. It involves and will require understanding and combating forces beyond our borders and over which we have little or no control. These forces will include pressure from other states to conform to acceptable 'norms' of behaviour in the economic sphere; and processes of social, economic, technological and even environmental interaction for which national borders simply do not exist. Creating stakeholder capitalism in Britain will be exciting, challenging and most of all difficult because it cannot be done without reference to the world beyond our shores.

It will also be difficult for an entirely different reason, because interfering with the socioeconomic structure of the country to the extent that people like Will Hutton suggest is necessary to bring about a stakeholder society in Britain will require at the very least a speeding-up of the slow process of historical evolution of our society, and more likely very profound changes in some of the institutions that are most valued, in relationships that have been forged over centuries, and in the values and perceptions that the British have about themselves and their country. It will not be a return to 1970s corporatism because this is simply not possible: and even if it were, there would still remain a society presided over by an hereditary monarchy whose very existence casts doubt over the validity of British 'democracy'. The House of Lords too, would still be there, as would other anachronisms. My point is not that trying to build a stakeholder society in Britain is inherently wrong or 'bad' and thus should not be attempted: on the contrary, there is a powerful case that deep-rooted change is vital. But creating a stakeholder society in anything more than name means going beyond the patchwork of quick-fix policies normally associated with electoral politics: stitching such policies together – whether they originate in Britain or in other countries – will not do the job. It also means going beyond policies which promote stakeholding but which do not address the larger issues – on their own they cannot do the job either. A stakeholder society that really means something requires the tearing down of centuries-old structures such as the monarchy, it requires the tearing up of deeply rooted and entrenched relationships (Church and state, class barriers, even old-school-tie networks), and the creation of new structures, new relationships, new perceptions and values. All this must be acceptable to and welcomed by the majority of individual people at a level that goes beyond electoral politics, and must therefore appeal to their minds and hearts as much as to their pockets.

History Matters

The particular form and structure of contemporary British society – the monarchy, Parliament, the electoral system, the unwritten constitution, the place and role of the Church of England, the centrality of the City, the Commonwealth – has been shaped and moulded by centuries of historical experience: of war and revolution, of technological innovation, of social upheaval and of peaceful 'progress'. And although most other countries have also experienced war and revolution, and have had their share of successful innovation and dreadful social upheaval, none has experienced these same events in quite the same way: they had different causes and different consequences. Britain is unique, but then so is every other country.[11]

Essentially, it is from this understanding that the notion of 'forms' or (ideal) types of capitalism emerges; and it is from here that another set of major problems seem to emerge when we envisage the creation of a stakeholder society. Take, for example, the highly individualistic 'Anglo-Saxon' variety of capitalism, which is characterised by high levels of competition in all areas and at all levels of social life, be it between individual people or individual firms. A dramatic retelling of the historical development of this form of capitalism would surely point to the analogy between the self-reliant frontiersman staking his claim to a piece of virgin Californian land, drawing on his own resources in its cultivation and defence with little or no recourse to the law or to the sheriff, and the vast American corporations of today which establish themselves, grow and prosper (or wither and die) in the hazardous but fertile soil of an economy characterised by little interference from government and therefore maximum competition. It is romanticised comparisons such as this that apparently leads so many Americans to the conclusion that because this type of 'free competition' made America great, then free competition in any form must be good.

This description may be a caricature but it does at least draw attention to the fact that the workings of the economy cannot be permanently abstracted from the wider socio-political environment which gives them substance. To take just one example, when the American leadership publicly criticise the Japanese over restrictive trading practices they seldom draw on 'rational' analyses of the situation: they draw instead on emotive images of what free trade means to them. These images come straight from the collective American memory of the 'good old days' of the frontiersman boldly going where no one had gone before. As such they have been the cause of many a misunderstanding between the two sides for the simple reason that because Japanese history differs so dramatically from the American experience, the socio-political structure of Japan is radically different also, and as a consequence the Japanese draw on different images and understandings of what free trade is really all about. The result is that more often than not the two sides to the dispute end up talking past rather than to each other.

History matters then because it determines what values and perceptions become embedded within a particular society; what constitutes acceptable behaviour. It can therefore be the source of fundamental misunderstandings between countries which have different value structures but who use a common vocabulary (free trade being the obvious example). History matters also because it sets limits on what can and cannot be changed in a society – the type of institutions that can be introduced and the values that they express, for example – and at what speed. Certainly, even centuries-old institutions can be changed, and very deeply held beliefs and values transformed. But this usually takes a great deal of time, or it happens because of some major catastrophe or shock such as revolution or defeat in war, as suffered by Japan in 1945. Even after sweeping changes had been imposed in every area of Japanese social, economic and political life, however, much of the pre-war structure survived – most noticeably the Imperial family, the ultimate symbol of Japanese militarism. Ironically, the most deeply rooted and 'genuine' change that took place in the aftermath of the war – the rejection by the bulk of the Japanese population of the utility of war as an instrument of foreign policy – was never given the opportunity that it should have had to flourish and prosper, because the very people who wanted to change Japan – the Americans – needed a re-armed ally to side with them against the forces of communism.

STAKEHOLDER CAPITALISM OR 'MECCANO' CAPITALISM?

In their pursuit of a better future for Britain both the Conservative Party and New Labour draw upon images of the past, whether these be of the 'buccaneer nation'[12] sailing the seven seas of economic success, or of the kinder, more inclusive society of the 1940s, where the welfare state was strong and where working-class people had some say in the decisions taken about their economic future. Whether these images are accurate or just the rosy glow left behind by passing memories does not really matter: they are aspirations, visions of the type of society that each side of the political debate would like to see realised once more – the Conservatives by tearing us away from the restrictions of Europe and the Social Chapter; Labour by creating the type of 'inclusive' society that cares about the sick, the unemployed, the poor, the uneducated – all those who have traditionally been excluded by accident of birth or by social circumstance. Both claim, then, to be drawing upon those elements which represent the best in us, those human charcteristics which combine to make Britain a 'good' society.

Clearly the Conservative vision is not working and has not done so for some time. British society is riddled with inequality, poverty and various forms of injustice – such as persistent and widespread homelessness – about which successive Tory governments have done little or nothing. The time is right to pursue the ideas that underpin New Labour's vision of a stakeholder society and to turn them into the sort of concrete policies which have been outlined elsewhere in this book. The message of this chapter, however, is that there are other constraints to be overcome besides political opposition from the right and from other domestic groups. One set of problems emerges

from the globalisation of economic activity and the consequent stretching
of economic relationships beyond national boundaries. Another set has its
roots in the history of Britain, in the difficulties associated with undermining
and eventually ridding society of unelected and unaccountable institutions
(and the network of relationships underpinning them) that stand in the way
of the stakeholder society, and which in any case have no place in a modern
democratic state. A third set of problems is associated with the adoption of
other forms of capitalism or of the policies that sustain them. There is
nothing wrong with learning from abroad and from the experiences of
others – after all the Japanese did this themselves when the Meiji leadership
toured the United States, Europe and Russia in the late nineteenth century
in search of ideas and inspiration for the first phase of Japan's own
modernisation process. Problems arise (as they did in Meiji Japan) when
the importation of different ideas or policies clashes with the interests of
established groups within society but outside of government. Violent reaction
can often follow. This is far from likely in stakeholder Britain, but at the
very least piecemeal adoption of new ideas from varying sources will entail
the bearing of new costs by new and different social groups. Great care must
be taken over their selection.

NOTES

1. I would like to thank Gavin Kelly and Andrew Gamble for their comments on
   an earlier draft of this chapter.
2. Will Hutton, *The State We're In* (London: Jonathan Cape, 1995), p. 20.
3. David Willetts has made these criticisms and others in his pamphlet, *Blair's
   Gurus: An Examination of Labour's Rhetoric* (London: Centre for Policy Studies,
   1996).
4. Francis Fukuyama, *The End of History and the Last Man* (London: Hamish
   Hamilton, 1992).
5. Sam Huntington has suggested one other fault-line along which the global order
   might fracture: a clash between three civilisations – Christianity, Confucianism
   and Islam. S.P. Huntington, 'The Clash of Civilizations?', *Foreign Affairs*, Vol.
   72, No. 3, 1993, pp. 22–49. For an alternative view see Robert Cox, 'Civilisations
   in World Political Economy', *New Political Economy*, Vol. 1, No. 2, 1996,
   pp. 141–56.
6. See amongst others Peter Dicken, *Global Shift: The Internationalization of
   Economic Activity*, (London: The Guilford Press, 1992), 2nd edition; and R.J.
   Barry Jones, *Globalisation and Interdependence in the International Political
   Economy* (London: Pinter, 1995).

7. Robert Reich, *The Work of Nations: Preparing Ourselves for 21st Century Capitalism* (New York: Alfred A. Knopf, 1991); and Kenichi Ohmae, *The Borderless World* (London and New York: Collins, 1990).
8. The growing trend towards the regionalisation of the world economy being another: see Andrew Gamble and Anthony Payne (eds), *Regionalism and World Order* (London: Macmillan, 1996).
9. John Zysman, 'The Myth of a "Global Economy": Enduring National Foundations and Emerging Regional Realities', *New Political Economy*, Vol. 1, No. 2, 1996, pp. 157–84; and Paul Hirst and Grahame Thompson, *Globalization in Question* (Cambridge: Polity Press, 1996).
10. The US has also been steadily increasing the pressure on the Japanese (and the Europeans) to play a larger part in their own defence, but that is a story we cannot pursue in any detail here. See John Welfield, *An Empire in Eclipse: Japan in the Postwar American Alliance System* (London: The Athlone Press, 1988), and Glenn D. Hook, *Militarization and Demilitarization in Contemporary Japan* (London: The Nissan Institute/Routledge Japanese Studies Series, 1996).
11. I for one reject the brand of British 'exceptionalism' championed by some members of the Conservative Party: Britain may be unique but that does not make its economy, society or its inhabitants any 'better' or 'worse' than those of any other country.
12. David Willetts, 'A buccaneer nation dares to be different', *Sunday Times*, 25 August 1996.

Part II

The Stakeholder State

7 From the Economic to the Political
Paul Hirst

The idea of stakeholding originally developed in relation to the modern firm. At its simplest it consists in applying the principles of democracy to economic life. Firms are engaged in authority relations, not just market exchanges. Thus the principles of open competition, free exchange and fair contracts are no longer sufficient to govern an economy in which large firms predominate. The decisions of firms cannot just be internalised in markets as prices and products, hence other methods are needed to ensure that all actors have roughly equal chances in economic life.

The basic democratic principle is that the interests that are directly affected by the decisions of companies or under their authority should either have a proportionate voice in the making of those decisions or some other check upon the content and scope of such decisions. The range of interests directly affected by a company in ways that cannot simply be handled in market terms is very wide. Investors have an interest through the capital they have advanced and may lose if they are forced to sell their shares to challenge a bad decision. Employees have an interest because they earn their living through working for the firm and may not be able to find another job easily. Local residents have interests in avoiding obtrusive development and pollution, and also in preventing companies dumping social costs on localities if they leave. Consumers of monopoly or near-monopoly suppliers have a right to protection against such unavoidable market power. Suppliers or subcontractors in ongoing relationships and partnerships with firms have expectations that implicit loyalties beyond the formal terms of contracts be honoured.

THE PROTECTION OF INTERESTS

Stakeholding claims that these interests be incorporated in company governance, or protected through legal regulation, or secured through voluntary cooperation and negotiated governance. It implies a society that is neither based on unregulated markets nor on socialist attempts to replace markets with other methods of distribution. It empowers investors and employees, but denies that any given interest is paramount. It therefore rejects both exclusive control by capital and workers' control. The ways in which stakeholders' interests may be protected are various: from the right to elect members of the board, through rights of advocacy and arbitration, to national and local legal regulation over such issues as land use planning and pollution controls, and the informal but often effective sanctions imposed on those who break trust relationships.

The essence of democracy is thus that affected interests have the right to representation or to some other form of protection if representation is impractical. Economic democracy and political democracy are not that different, both imply voice in the pursuit of goals or rights for the protection of interests. Modern democracy began with the demand for voice and inclusion in the affairs of state by non-elite constituencies. If we need a starting date for modern democracy it may as well be 1776 and the claim by angry American merchants, artisans and farmers that there should be no taxation without representation. Democracy is a challenge to hierarchical authority – it denies the right to impose orders from above and without the possibility of legitimate challenge by those affected by them. Autocratic rule was rejected as inherently illegitimate by the American Revolution – power could only henceforth be justified by consent of the governed and exercised in order to benefit them.

Stakeholding extends the scope of democratic principles from the political sphere to the institutions of the wider society. It treats the members of such institutions as if they were citizens and includes those having affected interests within the scope of such membership. The effect of this is that while hierarchy may be technically necessary, orders may need to be transmitted from above and obeyed in order to get things done, such requirements for imperative control are never legitimate in and of themselves. Managerial control, the power to give orders, needs a legitimacy outside of itself, a justification which is in essence political. The things that hierarchies do when orders get passed down through them, ought not merely to benefit those administered but be accepted by them and be subject to the test of their satisfaction. The idea of an unchallenged 'power to manage', which many modern corporate executives believe is theirs by right of necessity, is thus quite contrary to the core values of our society. It is in essence the same claim as that made by enlightened autocrats in the eighteenth century and by advocates of guardianship down the ages. Such power without representative check is insufferable, and in the long run it cannot stand, it is illegitimate.

Managers claim the right to unquestioned power within the firm on the basis of technical efficiency, that it promotes the greatest possible wealth creation, and, to the extent that they seek legitimacy, because it is authorised by the shareholders. Managers believe shareholders are the sole interest justified to make political claims upon them and also that they expect the highest possible financial returns. Neither claim will withstand such examination. Uncontrolled power is not the most efficient route to wealth creation if it ignores the knowledge and experience of employees, and if it fails to motivate employees by not actively involving them. Shareholders are not the only interest affected, even if they are the only one formally represented, and, in practice, they either actually have little effective voice in the governing councils of firms or are uninterested in exercising it even if they could do so. To say that capitalism is about wealth creation and therefore managers should be subject to as little check as possible, is to legitimate authority by success. But capitalism is always a mixture of success and failure. Those who suffer from failure have interests and rights too. Wealth creation sounds fine if you have just picked up a big cheque from your unit trust or life insurance policy. It is less attractive is you are bankrupt or redundant and standing in the middle of a rustbelt.

Moreover, investors are often ill-served by managers. Stakeholders need greater protection, including investors. Where did the concept of stakeholding originate? In the aftermath of the Great Crash of 1929 in the United States. The core book about stakeholding is *The Modern Corporation and Private Property* by A.A. Berle and G.C. Means, first published in 1932. Berle and Means are famous for advancing the thesis of the divorce of ownership and control, that property rights and the means effectively to dispose of assets are not the same thing. They argued that inadequate regulation had left investors with precious few rights – the widows and orphans of Wall Street apologetics were being exploited by the robber-baron capitalists of the 1920s, along with mom and pop and most other small investors. Their shares typically conferred few rights, whereas insiders had superior classes of share with greater rights and fewer risks. The pyramidal structures of holding companies enabled those with relatively small amounts of the total equity to control businesses they didn't own as if they were feudal lords. Berle and Means proposed greater regulations and improved company governance – their work was directly influential in creating the Securities and Exchange Commission.

Berle and Means were radicals and sought to protect the savings and investments of the mass of ordinary Americans. Modern corporate capitalism is not owned by the very rich. It can't be – it's just too big. Thus protecting investors, ensuring their stake, is as 'popular' a cause as empowering employees. Most UK shares are held by financial institutions. This means that most of us are indirectly investors – we have financial assets like pension fund contributions or life insurance policies that are invested in equities. We have a stake in the capitalist system, but virtually no control. The current system in the UK is one in which unaccountable company directors (who are close to being a self-selecting oligarchy) preach the power to manage without check, and in which they are subject to the sanction of largely unaccountable fund managers in the investment companies shifting their resources between different companies' shares. Neither set of managers is subject to much democratic governance – by active shareholders in companies or pension fund trustees.

The results are highly problematic. Investor's interests are not effectively protected by our current system of corporate governance, and they might be better defended by a new system if a wider range of interests with active voice was introduced. Not least because investors and financial institutions would have to be concerned about what those holding the votes of other affected interests might do and thus become more actively involved. In a society in which most capital provision is driven by the assets of people saving for retirement or other contingencies, then those assets ought to be far better protected than they are. For example, the returns on different pension funds and insurance policies are dramatically different, some perform appallingly and in a way that is not acceptable. It is no use saying that capitalism is about risk taking. The average person is taking out a pension to avoid risks and simply doesn't have the information or the option to make an effective choice. It is not just a matter of better and worse performing funds. Fund managers are raiding assets through commissions and charges, and, at worst, off-loading onto funds bad paper from elsewhere. This has to stop – both through better market regulation and better company governance.

THE STAKEHOLDER STATE

A stakeholder system is thus first of all one that treats those involved in companies – investors and employees – as having genuine democratic rights. But what about the state? Surely the answer is easy: obviously we have a stakeholder state because we live in a democracy? If stakeholding is the application of democratic principles to economic life, then that's it. The state follows stakeholding principles, QED. One person, one vote – legislation by elected representatives. That's what they fought for at Lexington, isn't it?

But is that all there is to it? And do we have a modern and fair democracy in the UK? How much of a stake do many of the UK citizens have in the political system? How much influence do they have over government decisions? In practice far too little for us to be complacent and to put off the reform of our political institutions. Stakeholding means inclusion and our current political system is exclusionary. It ignores those who didn't vote for the ruling party, the majority, and also it ignores those who are not part of the charmed circle of Whitehall and Westminster, the media and the managerial elite. I will mention two writers, very different in character, each very English, neither easily dismissed as a disaffected member of the modern chattering classes.

In 1978 Lord Hailsham was terribly worried about the future of our democracy, so much so that he wrote a book about it – *The Dilemma of Democracy*. It is an accurate diagnosis of our constitutional crisis. Hailsham argued that the executive had become over-mighty in Britain – that it had too much power over Parliament and could use its dominance to exploit parliamentary sovereignty to force through unpopular legislation. The electoral system was unrepresentative, to the point where it might allow a government elected on a minority of the votes cast the power to push through partisan policies against the will of the people. Hailsham christened our system an 'elective dictatorship'. The party he feared, of course, was the Labour Party, and partisan politicians, the likes of Tony Benn rather than Michael Howard. Everything Hailsham said stands redoubled and reinforced after a long period in government by a party that promised to empower the individual against the state.

Our system is too close to an elective dictatorship for comfort. Close enough to drive through the Poll Tax in the face of almost total citizen hostility; not close enough to make it stick in a country where democratic public life remains strong. Legislation and government action have moved relentlessly against that broad-based and decentralised democracy in which power was local and widely diffused. Power has passed increasingly from elected to unelected officials. A long period of partisan but weakly legitimate government, sustained by our unfair electoral system, has allowed those at the centre to eliminate wherever possible other sources of voice or democratic governance. Our Conservative politicians came close to treating office as a kind of long leasehold property, subject to the inconvenience of periodic elections in which the people had to be given some influence, much like a periodic ground rent.

They simply don't trust us, our rulers – the elected politicians, the civil servants, and the whole stratum of quango bureaucrats. You will remember that it was said of George Orwell that he was a man who 'went native in his own country' – his essays excoriate undemocratic officialdom and present the lives of the excluded. Our politicians, civil servants and quangocrats have, on the contrary, gone district officer in their own country. They treat us like a colonial population, who have to be administered, an inconvenience who will occasionally protest or riot. Basically our concerns are simply secondary to their desire to get their own version of the business of governing done. If that involves lying to us and manipulating opinion through an endless diet of PR tosh, then so be it.

This may seem harsh. Of course there are people in politics and public administration who mean well and try to provide services, but basically even the best bureaucrats treat us as consumers, not as citizens. There is the beginnings of a collapse of trust between the official class and the people. This is in good measure due to the centralisation of decisions and the growth of managerial power, based on hierarchical control. Government has deliberately chosen and promoted the institutional forms and styles of control from the private sector that I earlier said enjoyed weak legitimacy and that created the need for the greater democratisation of economic life. The problems of corporate governance have been compounded by remodelling much of the state as if it were a company.

THE COSTS OF STASIS

As a constitutional reformer I believe our political system needs changing in order to make Britain a first class democracy again – one fit for the future rather than one liquidating the achievements of the past. Our problems cannot be blamed on Mrs Thatcher or John Major alone, they have been serious for some time, but the current drift towards remote and weakly accountable power has made change imperative. Moreover, our non-stakeholder political system has serious consequences for our economy too – and not just for economic democracy but also for economic efficiency and prosperity. The concentration of power in the executive and the ease with which laws can be changed because of the principle of parliamentary sovereignty have led to three major evils.

The first is macroeconomic adventurism. Britain has a record of spectacular economic policy failures and dramatic zig-zags in the methods and objectives of economic management, made easier by the concentration of the levers of power in Whitehall and especially in the Treasury. We may start this litany with Wilson's failed National Plan of 1964, passing on to the insane Barber Boom of the early 1970s, to the Thatcher experiment in monetarism, the Lawson Boom, and our idiotic attempt to join the ERM at an unsustainable exchange rate when our inflation rate was three times that of Germany. Two major recessions in the early 1980s and early 1990s were deepened and prolonged by incompetent and unpopular policies. This is a record of macroeconomic mismanagement almost without equal among major industrial countries.

The second evil is the failure to govern the economy through social cooperation at national and local levels. Thatcher deliberately dismantled the corporatist machinery of the 1970s. The unions contributed massively to its demise: they were undisciplined, stupid and short-sighted to a degree that now seems incredible. But Thatcher shut her ears to much of business too, 'metal bashing' was out of favour. No advanced industrial economy can be run well from the remote centres of Whitehall and top-down boardrooms. Cooperation is essential: between firms, who need to collaborate and not just compete, between labour and management in the firm, between business and local authorities, and between the major social interests and the national government. This cooperation and dialogue need not mean rigid corporatism, nor does it mean adopting the German model wholesale. But without cooperation industrial training cannot be improved, research and development cannot be furthered, and effective common services for industry cannot be funded and delivered.

The third evil is to promote concentration in the corporate sector and to neglect promoting diverse types and styles of enterprise. Big government feels easy with big business as a partner. Small and medium enterprises are less salient in the UK than in most other advanced economies. Local authorities have been excluded from active participation in economic governance – unlike countries as diverse as Germany, Italy or Denmark. The result is a monoculture of big high street and national firms, with few options for declining localities where those firms are reluctant to invest.

PROPOSALS FOR REFORM

Criticism is all very well, but the whole point of challenging institutions is to offer effective remedies. How could our system be improved to be more inclusive and responsive to affected interests without a thoroughgoing and simultaneous reform of all our institutions from Parliament, to the privatised utilities, to the stock exchange, and so on? The first remedy is to make our electoral system fairer and thus to introduce a system of proportional representation so that the votes cast are mirrored by seats in Parliament. At present the winner-takes-all system means that, if the Opposition fragments, a party can win an unassailable majority on less than 40 per cent of the vote – the Conservatives have never had more than 43 per cent. With a minority of the votes, the victors get complete executive and legislative control. Such an electoral system could only survive on two conditions – a high degree of cross-party consensus and a strong Opposition. These conditions have gone.

Since the early 1970s we have had restless and partisan governments committed to major change. The Tories may be about to find themselves as a weak and divided Opposition, they must pray that Labour uses the highly concentrated power of government less than they did.

Second, we need the decentralisation of government and as quickly as it can be achieved. In fact we need it in the economic sphere before major institutional reforms are likely to be effective – regional governments are not really on the political agenda in England yet and existing local authorities are too small for most purposes of local economic governance. The answer perhaps is to create 'virtual' regional institutions based on cooperation between local authorities, business and unions to promote economic objectives like training and reversing industrial decline within real economic regions rather than tidy administrative entities. Administration is the easy part, one can always find someone to manage a programme – the difficult bit is finding the right thing to do, sticking to it and monitoring the effectiveness of its delivery. There is no point in opening new offices, designing new logos, creating new ranks of expensive officials – the aim must be to make what is there work better and differently. It will need to involve the people by dialogue and cooperation between organised interests in the first instance – democracy through negotiation. To do this representative institutions like trade unions, trade associations and the voluntary sector need to be brought into the work of governance. Governing through and with the social interests must be the cheapest, but also the most democratic way forward; far more so than 'decentralising' to lesser authorities that would still be remote and bureaucratic to most citizens. From such genuine, if 'virtual', governance we can hope to begin to build the lasting institutions of a future settlement between the centre and the localities.

Finally, we have got to increase the degree of control by society over politicians – to make them listen to us, not just to the media or the think tanks. This needs to happen fast before a degree of apathy becomes established that finally destroys the trust between governors and governed. The situation is not beyond repair, if politicians recognise they must listen and get out of Whitehall and the *Today* studio. Britain is a country that still has a remarkable number of activists and doers. It has one of the strongest civil societies in the world and we should build on this asset rather than trying to copy some more institutionalised model, like that of Germany. People still volunteer, to run the Scouts, to stop the Newbury bypass, to help make schools work, and so on. That is why we are still a very democratic society, even if the state needs some repair. But the message from activists is uniformly critical of politicians, it is that they simply are out of touch and indifferent to the concerns of the public. This is true of both major parties.

We have to get our civil society back into synchronisation with the political system. Politicians have to stop treating the citizens as something to be controlled, to be 'run'. As G.K. Chesterton said of the Fabian administrative rationalism of the Webbs, people are not trams and they do not want to be 'run'. The public is not a nuisance, but our major resource in effective economic and democratic governance. This change of attitude will not be easy, everything conspires against it. But it is essential – without it institutional change will mean little. Politicians have to lead officials and quangocrats into a new style of dialogue and involvement, the best already do this with little lead or encouragement. Top-down authority treats us as objects of administration, a population to be 'managed' and, if we are lucky, kept contented. This mentality destroys democracy. It treats us as at best consumers, not active stakeholders. A stake implies a voice, and the right to voice implies the obligation to use it, to steward our own assets. In that sense the concept helps us to restore the robust democracy of free people governing themselves, a road that began in modern times at Lexington but that has no end.

8 Stakeholding and the Public Sector

Michael Rustin

Equalitarian values have been in political retreat for nearly two decades. But even though the sustained postwar move towards greater equality of wealth, incomes and life-chances has gone sharply into reverse, it is deemed politically impossible to refer to such facts of life as the grounds of a contemporary radical programme. And still less, to propose reforms, or significant changes in the tax and benefit system, which might bring a return to greater social justice.

Class has become another forbidden topic of political debate. Commonplaces of nineteenth-century Conservative and Liberal politics, that parties represented significantly different class interests, have become unmentionable. Yet how can one write a credible political history of the last two centuries that is not based on the struggle of the landed interest, the industrial middle class, and the challenges to them of Cobbett's agricultural labourers in the early part of the nineteenth century, and of the urban workers – as Chartists or trade unionists or the Labour Party – from the decades afterwards? The present all-but-complete triumph of capitalism as a hegemonic system seems to entail virtual political silence by the major parties about the structured inequalities it engenders. It seems possible to attack the power of large businesses from the radical right, as in Pat Buchanan's campaigns in the United States, but not from the moderate or scarcely any other significant left.

In this context, we should not be surprised that very old discourses have had to be reinvented and brushed up to make the case for justice and equality. One of these discourses is 'citizenship', developed in the 1980s as a language of civic rights against the authoritarian communist states of the East, but then finding some purchase in arguments against the only partially-democratised monarchical British state. The adoption of the name Charter 88 from the Czechoslovak Charter 77 acknowledged this political debt. The other is the idea of 'stakeholding'.

THE ORIGINS OF 'STAKEHOLDING'

It is worth recalling how limited the original claims of 'stakeholding' in British political theory were. Stakeholding was a concept which sought to tie the rights of political participation to the possession of property, in particular of landed property. It was radical in that it asserted claims of property (which could be acquired in land and commodity markets in a mercantile society) against the exclusive claims of aristocratic birth. It remained conservative in so far as it denied that political rights belonged to men (still less women) or to members of society as such. Gradually, as the argument for universal political rights developed, the concept and extent of the property required to justify the franchise became broadened, until eventually, well into the twentieth century, property and voting rights become wholly distinct from one another. The propertied interest, in both its landed and industrial forms, was eventually defeated, at least in its struggle to restrict political rights to itself, if not in other respects. Mrs Thatcher's poll tax was rightly perceived as having, and probably intending to have, the effects of a back-door property qualification, those unable or unwilling to pay tending to disappear from the electoral rolls. 'No taxation without representation' becoming 'no representation without taxation'.

The idea of universal rights of citizenship was an alternative to the restrictive idea that only those with a (propertied) stake in the country should share in its governance. Social democracy, as T.H. Marshall pointed out, was a programme which sought to challenge the claims of property, and balance them with a different array of institutional powers, derived from the ballot box and from political institutions. For many years after the Second World War, this 'balanced regime' or 'mixed economy' as it was called, worked tolerably well, generating improved living standards, slowly enhanced equality, and of course basic social and economic rights to work, health, social security and education.

On the left, there was an assumption that this equilibrium between capitalism and social democracy was not fixed, working in favour of what were thought of as democratic institutions and social rights. The high-water mark of this programme of social democratisation was the 'wage-earner fund' reforms of the Swedish socialists in the 1970s, and the related ideas for industrial democracy developed by the Labour government in the 1970s. These reforms represented an attempt to secure some measure of employee ownership and control of capital itself, initially on a modest 'minority stakeholder' basis, but clearly with a potential for a creeping expropriation or domination of private shareholders by shareholder representatives of employees and thus, in the main, citizens at large. The British industrial democracy proposals were dropped, however, as this social democratic high tide receded, and the Swedish one watered down and then rendered insignificant. Soon afterwards, the Labour Party and the Swedish Social Democrats lost power, and have been redefining their mission ever since.

Private Ownership and Stakeholding

The Thatcherite concept of a 'property owning democracy', and the drive
to create wider share ownership (in particular through privatisation of
publicly owned industries) and house ownership was probably a response
in part to the challenge of these more collectivistic challenges to economic
privilege. It was not of course absurd to suppose that capitalism would gain
in legitimacy, and indeed in its justifiability, if the rights of property ownership
were more widely dispersed. Indeed, analytical Marxists like John Roemer
were making the theoretical case at this time that it was inequality of
ownership of capital, not the relation between capital and labour as such,
which was the central issue of social justice. The central problem with this
programme was one of realism and practice, not theoretical justification. The
market economy, in its capitalist form, does not seem to generate universal
capital ownership as its natural consequence. The majority of employees do
not have an income surplus which enables them to acquire property assets
other than in the form of owner-occupied dwellings and pension entitlements,
and many are still excluded from these forms of property ownership. It has
even become a matter of concern how the present population of working age
is to be supported in its old age, a vision of prospective mass pauperism, not
of benign familial inheritance. Share ownership has not significantly widened.
Increased insecurity of employment may well be reducing rather than
enhancing the capacity of the majority of citizens to acquire assets.

Whilst the radical right have advocated the wider distribution of capital
for ideological reasons, the intensified struggle which it has unleashed to
realise surpluses on all assets, both private and public, has increased rather
than reduced the concentration of assets in the hands of a small minority.
The scandals accompanying privatisation, in which coteries of managers and
directors have become millionaires from profits made by laying off tens of
thousands of workers, are only the most well known instances of this process.
This has brought a response even from the super-cautious Labour Party.
Although legally many capital assets do belong to citizens of modest means,
through pension plans or insurance policies, there has been no support for
the idea of more collective and socially responsible representation of these
now dispersed interests, which might enable wider goals of employment, long-
term growth, community interests or economic sustainability to be taken into
consideration in investment decisions. As things stand, decisions taken by
pension funds to maximise their owners' interests can often be at the expense
of the jobs, communities, or indeed (in the case of tobacco shares, for
example) their health, without the 'stakeholders' in question knowing the
first thing about it.

The 'stakeholder debate' has been created in order to bring these issues into the public eye, and some of the above arguments are crucial to it. We should note, however, that its starting point has been the obsolescence or discrediting of the earlier programme for a 'mixed economy' and for a labour movement-led attempt to balance private power with enhanced public power. The earlier instruments for compensating for the power of private capitalist corporations through the creation of other non-private institutions have been quietly dropped. Among these seemingly extinct 'democratic' devices are, for example, nationalised corporations, or significantly expanded state-provided services and the enhancement of the power and rights of trade unions, seen in earlier times as a means to *de facto* co-determination via extended wage bargaining. It is a debatable point whether the loss of these potential agencies of 'balance' can be compensated by the new forms of regulation and representation proposed by the advocates of economic stakeholding. One wishes this programme well, but it is necessary to acknowledge the position of political weakness from which it has had to start, and the circumspection with which it has avoided anything that might seem like an 'Old Labour' challenge to the sovereignty of the market.

The problem with the idea of stakeholding (but also its postmodern charm) is that it leaves indeterminate a fundamental issue: who is entitled to what stake, and on what grounds? It is not only the political instruments of social democratic reformism which have been left behind, but also the certainty and simplicity of democratic socialist philosophy. In the old conception, everyone was theoretically entitled to an equal stake, as human beings or citizens, and the political problem was to bring the unequal realities of capitalism and inheritance more or less into line with this principle. It was never easy to see how this was to be done, of course, though its inspirational value and its bite as a critique of vast existing inequalities, was high.

Modern economies and societies are increasingly differentiated, have many roles and functions, and are exceptionally complex systems. For some time there has been an increasing strain between an adequate understanding of how such advanced systems work, and the moral norm of equality by which their radical critics judged them. Michael Walzer's distinction between 'complex' and 'simple' equality was one important attempt to take note of this difficulty, within a socialist ethic.[1] Of course as new forms of inequality and their contestation have come to the fore – with the emergence of different kinds of gendered, ethnic, and lifestyle politics – the problem of what 'equality' might in practice mean and how any approximation to it might be achieved has become more evident still.

In as much as the concept of 'stakeholding' requires the specification of the different 'stakes' (as employees, community members, future generations, former contributors and present dependants, risk takers and owners) it has the great advantage of realism. It allows the recognition of the real differences of position, interest and claim that have to be taken account of in any actual polity. 'Stakeholding' emerged as a political concept at a point when conflicts and differences of political interest and principle had to be recognised and negotiated. We are certainly in that position now, and it may be as well to have available a language within which conflicts can be explicitly formulated.

FROM THE PRIVATE TO THE PUBLIC

Most discussion of the stakeholding concept has been directed towards the private sector, where it now frames potential ways of making private capital accountable to the wider community. But the problems which have led to the emergence of the stakeholding discourse exist in the public sector as well. Stakeholding has its useful applications in the sphere of public as well as private accountability. It was the discrediting of simplistic ideas of equality, and the questioning of the self-evident superiority of public institutions over private ones, which undermined belief in the postwar democratic socialist vision. According to this, the values of both equality and democracy were to be served by the incremental increase in the power of government, as this was thought to advance the well-being of its citizens.[2]

What became evident throughout the sphere of the public sector, were the inequalities of power seemingly inherent in the institutions of the state, whether or not these institutions were notionally democratic. The institutions of government both national and local, were, from the point of view of administration and execution, bureaucratic hierarchies, not democracies. Even though ultimate decisions might be made formally by democratically elected members of Parliament, and by elected members of local councils, the practical realities were that these decisions were informed by administrative expertise, particularistic lobbies and interests, and bureaucratic inertia: ordinary citizens enjoyed little say in them.

Radical constitutional critics of British government, not least in Charter 88, pointed out how authoritarian British institutions have remained and how little the inherited monarchical regime had in fact changed in the course of its adjustment to an electoral democratic mandate. Social theorists like Ulrich Beck have generalised this insight, seeing the limited rights accorded to citizens in modern democratic states (and in other institutional spheres such as the workplace) as a stage of 'incomplete modernity'. Democratic rights, although celebrated by radicals, turn out to be little more than the legitimation by regular plebiscites of a system whose powers remain concentrated in highly durable and self-regarding elites, one part of which is sometimes referred to as 'the political class'.

Observers of the party political process also note how unrepresentative political representatives are of society. The process of selection and self-selection which leads to political office involves an unusual degree of tolerance of the time-consuming, unproductive and boring routines of maintaining a political party and its vote – the routine work of the 'political activists' from whom representatives are recruited. Many of those citizens with better things to do, in either the private or public domains, will avoid or will be unwilling to bear the opportunity costs of such activities. Although those mandated by these electoral processes claim legitimation from the ballot box, the fact is that they are often members of a specialist calling, whose primary resources are skills in manipulating ideology, and in acquiring and managing power itself. Competition between parties, and the need to recruit popular support in this competition does of course give some authenticity to the claims of politicians to be representatives of the people. But the procedures by which power is captured, and the pattern of selection involved in its capture, is a distinctive segment of institutional life, not a distillation or representation of society itself, as is widely recognised.

Politics Beyond Parties

The fact is that power is deployed in many different forms in modern societies, of which representation through political means is only one. The problem which political parties face in trying to build a single programme which reflects the diversity of interests and identities that exists within society ensures that different interests will seek many other forms of expression and influence other than through vote-seeking parties.

In recent years many so-called 'new social movements' of feminism, gay rights, environmentalism, and animal rights, have established their claims on society through activities largely outside the formal political structure, though they have at times impacted on it in influential ways (as with the formation of 'Green' parties, and with the inflection of all-party programmes in an environmentalist direction). These activities include direct recruitment of members, achieving issue visibility through the mass media, the creation of new subcultures, lobbying, and direct action – as seen in the recent protests against live animal exports or road building. It is highly rational for citizens to decide that if they care about the provision of hospices, or aid to underdeveloped countries, or preventing environmental damage, there are more effective ways to use their resources than to involve themselves with political parties.

A more influential and long-established channel of influence and virtual representation lies in the mechanisms of lobbying and pressure groups.

Institutions of every kind, from private capitalist corporations, to trade union and professional organisations, to voluntary associations, hire armies of professional publicists and brokers, whose purpose is to ensure that their employers' interests are considered in the making and implementing of decisions by legislators and their administrative servants. And since all public and many private decisions take place in a field of discourse shaped by mass communication, another form of 'virtual representation' lies in those who construct mass media outputs, and who seek to influence their agenda and content. The periodic contests which take place by election are therefore only one of many means by which 'representation' is effected and influence exercised, even within the sphere which can be defined as 'public'. This is to leave aside all those areas of decision making which properly or improperly lie outside the public sphere.

The concept of representation is a complex one, as social critics such as Iris Marion Young have pointed out. The construction even of such apparently elemental entities as 'nations', 'peoples' and 'classes' is an act of intention and will, not the 'representation' of an intrinsic social reality. What is 'represented' comes to exist in part as consequence, not merely as cause, of the processes of 'representation'. Political entities are called into being by their advocates, and do not unproblematically exist as latent realities lacking only their self-expression. Representation is thus intrinsically ideological and exclusionary in its nature, and we have every reason to be sceptical of the claims of any institution to 'represent' the social totality.

The manipulation of the modern political process through the mass media has made politics a peculiarly empty form, a means of systematic misrepresentation rather than representation of social reality. Some of the lessening of public confidence in the formal political process which many analysts have noted may be to do with the accurate public perception of politics as one self-interested trade among many, not as the collective embodiment of alternative conceptions of a larger social good. Important as it is to democratise the still largely oligarchic and authoritarian system of political representation itself, the new spheres of democratic representation are, as Ulrich Beck has argued,[3] the courts, the mass media, and science and technology (which shapes the future conditions of life). Beck is nevertheless wrongly and inconsistently silent on that other area of 'incomplete modernity', the sphere of capital.

The Retreat of the Public Sphere

The discrediting of public sector provision in the past two decades has gained some of its strength through the recognition of the inadequacies of the concept of democracy advanced by radicals, and its sometimes self-serving nature. The intellectual initiative which for fifty years centred on critiques of the market and arguments for the superiority of planning, shifted during the 1970s and 1980s. An academic literature – among whose components were the theory of non-market failures, the 'impossibility' of planning, public choice theory, and the idea of government 'overload' – gained influence. The Conservative programme in Britain always had its own redistributive purposes. Its narrow interest base and tendency to degenerate into sleaze has become more evident as its political position has weakened. But there was also an ideological conviction among radical reformers of the right, many of them the socially mobile products of modest backgrounds, that the 'enterprise culture' really did provide wider opportunities than the culture of state provision. They perceived the professionals, managers and unionised employees of the 'welfare state' as a merely sectional interest, gaining security, privilege and power from their self-proclaimed mission of emancipation and social care. The right to purchase, it was argued, conferred more meaningful rights and powers on citizens than the right to vote for this or that public service, the main beneficiary of which was usually its producers, not its consumers. Attacks on 'loony left' councils were intended to dramatise these abuses of elective power by identifying its allegedly extreme cases.

New Labour's caution about restoring trade union powers, renationalising privatised industries, or returning the lost powers of local government, indicates how far they think these critiques have struck home with the public. Some of the reforms of the public sector initiated by the Conservatives in the past seventeen years have given expression to critiques of this kind. Much of the effect of this has in fact been negative in democratic terms. Power has mostly been transferred from imperfectly democratic public bodies, to considerably *less* representative private ones – of which the privatisation of the public utilities is one notorious example. Another mainly negative development has been the politicisation of institutions hitherto occupying a non-political or 'neutral' public space, by imposing tighter political control over them (large swathes of the civil service), or by packing them with Tory Party members or sympathisers (Health Trusts, for example). In some cases where institutions have been removed from the elected control of local government (for example, the ex-polytechnics, which became higher education corporations), the principle of representation imposed on them has been heavily biased in favour of one particular interest, that of private business. The 'independent governors', who were given control of the governance of these new universities by arcane rules which gave some categories of 'governor' more powers than others, had by definition to be private businessmen. Meanwhile the elected local authorities who had previously had statutory control over these institutions were denied even a right of representation on the governing bodies.

But other aspects of this programme have in fact been more positive. There are prospective benefits in the contracting-out of some local authority services, for example to voluntary organisations, in so far as this creates a more diverse and locally managed system of service provision. The devolution of budgetary and management powers in the school system to schools themselves and away from the bureaucracies of the local education authorities, in effect transfers power from political representatives who are necessarily remote from neighbourhood communities to parents and staff in a school who can be expected to be closely in touch with them. Many have had the opportunity to compare the liveliness and energy of parent teacher associations with the activities of the ward party in the same territory, to the advantage of the former. Those who have responsibilities for managing the new-style 'trusts' operating in higher education and health will recognise the opportunities for autonomy and innovation which these have conferred. In the field of urban and regional regeneration, the development of new agencies such as development corporations and city partnerships side-by-side with elected authorities, has brought new initiatives and energies. Although the imposition of the London Docklands Development Corporation on East London and the temporary suspension of local government planning powers within its territory is not a model one would wish to see repeated, there can be no doubt that it has led to a scale of development which the divided local authorities in the region, with or without the Greater London Council, are unlikely to have achieved.

STAKEHOLDING IN THE PUBLIC SECTOR: DIVERSITY AND ACCOUNTABILITY

What is positive in these various developments is the idea that there are various forms of legitimate representation in a community. Neither the market (and the owners of capital and property whom markets disproportionately empower), nor the elected representatives of the national or local state, should hold monopolies of power. The idea of 'stakeholding' enables us to recognise a diversity of legitimate entitlements to representation within the public as well as the private sphere. Parents are legitimate stakeholders in the management of schools, as are patients and their representatives in the management of hospitals and medical practices. Employees are legitimate stakeholders in all institutions, both public and private, in which there is employment, and should always be represented in their governance. I have also argued elsewhere for the potential role of 'juries' of local citizens (together with 'professional' assessors and experts) in a system of 'quality assurance' or 'inspection' of local public services, providing a new form of accountability of public institutions.

There is an important issue of principle at stake in all this for political parties traditionally attached to the ideology of the democratic state, as well as for parties now ideologically committed largely to the market. This is the pluralist idea that there is no single legitimate system of exclusive representation, whether elective or consumer driven. Power in a democracy needs to be shared and its exercise negotiated. Such sharing can be accomplished through more representative electoral systems, mandating coalition government as a common pattern, and through regional and local devolution, and it should be. But it can also be achieved through a system of representation of stakeholders in the governance and regulation of the various dispersed institutions of the democratic state.

Such a system would require a self-denying ordinance by Labour if it again became a majority party. Implementing this new style of governance would require an acceptance of the view that winning a parliamentary majority would no longer entitle a party to insist on a nominated majority on all public bodies. Diversity of representation on all public bodies would become a guiding principle. There would need to be more public and accountable methods by which such representation is achieved, some by election from appropriate constituencies, some by selection through an open competitive process akin to that of an appointments procedure.

In a democracy, a majority political party will of course expect to exercise the largest influence over public policy and administration. But more will be gained in establishing a wider basis of representation, even if representatives are not beholden to the party itself, than will be lost in direct control. A concept of 'stakeholding' will allow the emergence of more durable compromises between different social interests, more effective alliances in particular areas and regions, and above all a more democratic sensibility. The development of a more diffused and accountable democratic practice in the public sector will give a legitimacy to democratic stakeholding within the private sector that it will not otherwise obtain. For as long as democracy in the public sector is a hollow shell, it will be difficult to convince anyone that democratic accountability is feasible and necessary within the private sector.

NOTES

1. M. Walzer, *Spheres of Justice* (Oxford: Blackwell, 1983).
2. This idea was embodied in the constitution of the 'old' Labour Party after all.
3. Ulrich Beck, *Risk Society* (London: Sage, 1992).

9 Towards a Stakeholder Democracy

Anthony Barnett

'Voice is an art constantly evolving in new directions.'
Albert Hirschman[1]

When used to describe democracy, stakeholding is a *metaphor*. The danger of metaphors in political language is dullness or evasion, both of which trade on predictability. For example, when politicians use sporting metaphors it is a warning to be on the alert for sleight of hand or looseness of brain. Or when state, government or society are compared to an organic community or individual it usually signals the rhetoric of knee-jerk reactions. Even worse is the common use of the economic metaphor that compares countries to companies. Almost everything that is important about a country is lost in the analogy with a commercial enterprise based on contract and rates of return. They are not communities of life or fate in the way that a country is. It is not just that Britain is not a PLC; comparing it to one diminishes the imagination and lessens understanding.

Why, then, give any time to the economic metaphor of a stakeholder democracy? The answer is because it need not be a dull trope of intellectual fashion. Metaphors can be stimulating as well as deadening. Just as stale ones reinforce mental routines, so fresh analogies may illuminate, and stakeholding is a new term that could help us gain a fresh angle on democracy, that is to say on the way power can be distributed and exercised.

Stakeholding proposes a key principle of economic organisation. That good long-term decision making over investment and disinvestment must try to identify with all the interests and individuals affected by the decisions. As a form of economic organisation, stakeholding covers various possible ways in which the interests of different parties can be incorporated. These range from an obligation on the decision takers that is merely hortatory (a kind of government advertising campaign), to a genuine change of culture, or a set of more or less extensive legal obligations on managers. A set of questions follows on from this broad meaning of the word. For example, how are varied interests to be balanced and which obligations should be primary? These lead on to the dynamic consequences of stakeholding, its ability to deliver better results, more responsive policies and higher quality outcomes for firms, sectors, and the economy.

Naturally, an argument then develops over the possibilities of a stakeholder economy as a whole – in which competition and mutual interest would have stakeholding woven through it. This society-wide use of the term is not metaphorical. Although extended, its focus remains the organisation of the economy. If we are going to consider the necessarily more aspirational possibilities of the metaphor as applied to democracy, it is best to start with as anchored as possible an understanding of what the broad economic concept of a stakeholder society might mean.

Summing up his speeches in Japan and Singapore, when he made stakeholding a central theme of Labour's approach, Tony Blair provided a working definition: 'Our task ... is to equip our people and business for massive economic and technological change and to do so on the basis of a stakeholder economy, in which economic opportunity is widely disbursed and in which no group or class is excluded.'

Sceptics, like William Keegan writing in the *Observer* immediately after Blair's pronouncements, found them wanting: 'As I see it, the stakeholder economy is not so much meaningless as a concept capable of having far too many meanings attached to it. The atmosphere was noisy last week with the sound of people climbing on the stakeholder bandwagon or claiming to have invented it.' For Keegan, the best way to ensure better economic change remains Keynesian macroeconomic demand management.

In any policy debate, however, it is important not to take concepts too literally or academically. Meanings in politics are dynamic and the defining sense of stakeholding is that it draws a line in the sand against the pure free market and argues instead for capitalism to be organised so as to restrict short-term maximisation in favour of longer-term wealth creation. The approach is not incompatible with Keynesianism, but insists that no policy run centrally 'from above' will ensure constructive investment unless financial structures which facilitate stakeholder companies are in place.

Stakeholding is not a socialist argument. It is a capitalist argument that observes a chronic inadequacy and danger in leaving all wealth creation to the hidden hand of the free market. It argues for a better form of maximisation – that includes as part of its calculation the wealth and well-being of the population as a whole.

Two basic assumptions are implicit in stakeholding. First, that policy making can be a positive good. The role of government should not be limited to minimising the influence of the state. Instead, good government can contribute positively to capitalist wealth creation, and taxation need not be pure loss to the wealth of nation and citizens. Second, that the true calculation of a society's wealth has to be more comprehensive than its stock market value. From the quality of the environment to the misery of the poorest families, a stakeholding definition of economic growth is inclusive and shared.

These two assumptions are anathema to the approach known in Britain as Thatcherism. This holds that the less the state does and the more the market decides, the better the economy will compete and the greater the wealth it will generate; which in time will lead to the benefit of all.

This is the crude but still dominant philosophy of Britain's governing class. Those who argue *for* stakeholding are arguing *against* this philosophy. When Blair made his speeches in the Far East calling for a 'one nation' stakeholding approach, Thatcher responded with an anti-European tirade in which she declared that those who called for one nation wanted 'no nation'.

Why, it might be asked, should there be anything surprising in a Labour leader advocating an approach that opposes Thatcherism? The answer is that compared to traditional Labourism, stakeholding accepts much of the legacy of Thatcherism and one of Blair's distinctive contributions has been to force his party to accept that it cannot advocate a return to the period before Thatcher. As many have observed, she was a radical and Blair has insisted that much of her radicalism was necessary.

Part of Blair's argument is clearly developed in the introduction to Labour's draft manifesto, which states that much of the opposition to Thatcherism is a doomed form of conservatism. That far from being principled or progressive, traditional Labourist resistance is a pointless wailing that advocates no credible alternative, even if it could win electorally. This critical assault on Old Labour for its conservatism is convincing. The danger is that the terms which follow will be set entirely by the success of the free market ideology in Britain – success, that is, in terms of the influence its ideas now have in the City and civil service. What was welcome about the advocacy of stakeholding in January 1996 (and is disappointing about the apparent backing away from the approach in the draft Labour manifesto) is that it provides a cogent answer to Labour's two-fold problem: first, how to embrace the emancipatory aspects of Thatcherism's radical assault on deference and corporatism; second, how best to combat Thatcherism's reprehensible short-termism and socially reactionary divisiveness.

Three themes may help sketch how stakeholder democracy could achieve these two objectives, and illustrate its potential as a non-Labourist alternative to Thatcherism: change, inclusion and sovereignty.

CHANGE

Umberto Eco once commented that an Italian finds it strange the way the English regard a crisis as entirely negative. In Italy a crisis has positive connotations, as a moment that can lead to resolution of a problem, which you come through strengthened and improved. But in England, a crisis is usually spoken of as something that cannot lead to a better future whatever the outcome, it is a pain whose outcome can at best lead to no further aggravation. You cannot have growth without crises, and in English politics growth and change are perceived as inherently leading to loss rather than gain.

As a description of London finance capital, or of British society and personal attitudes, Eco's comment would be inadequate. But as a description of the formal political system, ever conscious that it has seen its finest hour, the observation is astute. We can see it today in the debates over Europe, Scotland and the Lords. Some reforms may be necessary. But they are undertaken with a sigh. To be modern is to be worse.

But change is essential, its pace will accelerate, its breadth and consequences will increase, and for a political culture to survive it needs to internalise change – to live, breathe and welcome it. Blair's description quoted above is striking in its emphasis on the need for British society to embrace change and make it its own. It also gives stakeholding a dynamic meaning. It is about how to invest, not who already has vested interests. It is about how to negotiate and implement change, not how to resist it. It is a progressive not a conservative concept.

The idea of stakeholder democracy is more radical in the British context because the British state is founded not on democracy, in which citizens are sovereign, but on consent orchestrated from above to protect the parliamentary rule of the elite. Here the people are not the rulers. *The great change* threatened by stakeholding in the UK, it could be argued, is the advent of modern democracy itself. A possibility that is best illustrated by comparing the stakeholder approach to its two postwar predecessors of consensus and conviction politics.

	Consensus Politics	Conviction Politics	Stakeholder Democracy
Change	NO	YES	YES
Inclusion	YES	NO	YES
Shared power	YES	NO	YES
Openness	NO	YES	YES

The starting point for any discussion of contemporary British politics remains the wartime and postwar settlement, that goes by the term consensus politics. It was constructed after 1940, with the wartime coalition under

Churchill, and lasted in its formative phase until the devaluation crisis (that word) of 1947. Consensus politics was an all-party affair. Its political axis joined Labour with Conservatives, its intellectual axis was forged by two liberals, Keynes and Beveridge. It was a very particular mixture that preserved the institutions and character of the British state while incorporating the labour movement, once seen as its historic enemy, into it. So far as change was concerned, the later stages of consensus politics did its best to resist any fundamental changes to the institutions of high politics. At the beginning of the sixties, Prime Minister Harold Macmillan advocated embracing 'the wind of change', by which he meant bending with the wind to protect the roots, while his eventual successor Harold Wilson provided an equivalent verbal gloss of modernisation as he sought to defuse crisis after crisis. Both looked backwards and saw their role as to preserve as much as possible of Britain's world role.

While opposing change, consensus politics accepted public responsibility for the unemployed, the ill and the old, not simply as a matter of charity, but as part of the public good. This inclusive approach to those outside the political and influential classes was accompanied by a culture of political understanding that ensured government remained a bipartisan affair. This constrained the exercise of power. But it did so within terms set by what was described as 'The Establishment'. Parliament was the chief club among other clubs that exercised a common influence and decided, for the good of the whole nation, naturally, who was sufficiently a chap to become part of the club, and who was not. At the height of its tragic attempt to deploy consensus politics for progressive ends in the 1960s, the Labour government was overwhelmingly an Oxbridge affair. The paternalism of consensus politics sought to ensure that all classes were looked after. Furthermore, *within* its restrictive composition it did attempt to ensure that all reasonable views were taken account of. But consensus politics was, like all paternalisms, a closed system. It resisted an open society even if it did believe in a comparatively fair and inclusive one.

Margaret Thatcher's conviction politics burst apart the old consensus and still traumatises Westminster. Her achievements have been much overestimated. She was far more the agent of OPECisation, even if the UK was a beneficiary rather than a member of the oil cartel, than the creator of a new political philosophy. She turned against her own party's role in consensus politics, branding it as a socialist trap. In effect she reversed the terms of the postwar settlement, thus showing herself to be its rebel child rather than the architect of its replacement. It resisted change, she advocated it. It was socially closed, she opened up politics, recruiting outsiders rallying them against the restrictive practices of the old paternalism. It accepted the rightful influence of those outside the Cabinet, she assaulted every impediment to central power she could identify. It stood for inclusion, she celebrated the extension of division, even supporting the poll tax in part because it would drive the poor from the electoral register.

Conviction politics was radical in the way it opened up the old regime to the modern world. But it exploited rather than transformed the powers of the British state. By concentrating executive power and dismantling the often informal networks of local and traditional influence over its application, conviction politics shattered the political culture of enchantment and deference that oiled the Victorian machinery of consensus. Populist rather than democratic, conviction politics was reactionary in its narrowing of the definition of the interests of the state and in its opposition to democracy. Its hostility towards sharing power externally within Europe and internally within the UK followed from its opposition to constitutional diversity, and showed it to be a false modernisation as well as a wasted opportunity. Just as the much vaunted conservative revival of Reagan was built upon a vast budget deficit fuelled by military spending that must have made Keynes spin in his grave, so the triumph of Thatcher's conviction politics depended upon the squandering of North Sea largesse.

A Labour government that seeks office today must accept Thatcher's destruction of consensus politics. This means it has to govern differently from previous Labour administrations. Yet this makes it all the more important that, should it form the next government, it does not confuse the necessary negative radicalism of Thatcher's destruction of consensus with the supposed positive radicalism of monetarism and free market hostility to the state. Stakeholder democracy points towards a politics that meets this dual requirement and for the first time could provide a Labour government with an approach that does not subordinate it to elite rule.

Stakeholder democracy should retain Thatcherism's formal commitment to openness and change. At the same time, by returning to an inclusive approach towards all citizens and a pluralist acceptance of the legitimacy of other political interests, stakeholding would provide a framework of reciprocal rights and interests that would make explicit the implicit toleration that once marked British politics. To put it another way, stakeholding would ensure that a positive approach to change and to openness was applied to the heart of government itself where it is now needed most of all.

A positive attitude towards the process of European Union is the most obvious example of a reform that would embrace modern change. Domestically, the most telling example is decentralisation based upon consent, a process that would introduce a dynamic element into the reform of British government that would be outside the control of the centre. The more that people can undertake government on their own initiative, the more chance there is of widespread change succeeding. The argument, now most vigorously pursued by Simon Jenkins, of the need to relinquish all capping powers over local government expenditure in order to reinvigorate local democracy by making local people genuinely responsible for its expenditures, is a commanding example of the stakeholding approach. Central government must allow others to make mistakes – instead of seeking to monopolise error for itself. Trust is one of the themes Labour has made much of in its stakeholding approach. Trust only exists, however, when it is reciprocated, when it is two-way. It takes two to trust. This should be the motto of the renewal of the relationship between government and the governed. But who currently distrusts whom the more? Much has been made, including by this writer, of the disenchantment of people with contemporary government. Perhaps the disenchantment of leaders with the people who elect them is the greater. And it shouldn't be.

At any rate, one determining piece of constitutional legislation will test a new Labour government's commitment to changing the administration of the British state. Labour is committed to delivering a Scottish Parliament based upon the wishes of the Scottish people as expressed in a referendum. But if, as it is assumed they will, the Scots support a Parliament with tax varying powers, what form will the legislation take? Once Scotland has staked its claim, a government interested in ensuring that change follows smartly will reject the traditional civil service advice that the legislation must spell out exactly what powers Scotland shall then exercise. The British mandarinate should not be encouraged to play God and draft pages of detailed legislation that spells out what the people of a nation within the UK that has demanded the right of self-government may or may not do. A short, enabling bill, that states what area of competence will be exercised by the British Parliament and what by the Scottish, should be sufficient along with the appointment of a commission acceptable to both Parliaments empowered to resolve future difficulties within the framework of the principles laid down. Scotland should then elect its Parliament and get on with the job of self-government. My attempts to advocate this approach have been met with horror and alarm. It would mean letting go! It would store up problems for the future (as if these won't happen anyway). Such reactions betray the old consciousness. Scottish home rule will be a process not a piece of legislation: the *Scots* must undertake it. Only by investing a Scottish Parliament with this trust will it be reciprocated. The more it is invested with distrust and tied down by controls and checks created by Westminster in advance, the more likely it is that future Parliaments in Edinburgh will reciprocate in kind. This will generate a predictable tragedy of exactly the kind that, in its hubris, Whitehall believes it can prevent.

INCLUSION

The most morally compelling aspect of one-nation stakeholding is that no one should be excluded from society and that the creation of a permanent underclass of 'have nots' must be prevented. Pragmatically, so the economic argument goes, the full social costs of such exclusion – starting with crime prevention and security measures – will be of a similar order of magnitude to the costs of ensuring a productive role for all. Such practical justifications of an ethical principle rarely convince. Either you can accept the development of a high-tech, information-based apartheid society in which the outcasts are defined less by skin colour than by a vicious cycle of unemployment, immiseration, lack of education, family breakdown and criminalisation; or you cannot. If you do not, then it is not hard to be persuaded that the wealth generated by the intense productivity of modern societies is adequate to cover the investment needed to ensure the inclusion of those who might otherwise form such an underclass. There are important questions over how such inclusion can be achieved, from motivation and welfare dependency to the geography of poverty. But convincing people that it should be done will not come through cost–benefit analysis. Privately, many of the rich appreciate that large-scale unemployment keeps down wage costs and protects their fortunes from inflation. The existence of the outcasts of the earth makes them feel good not bad. The less it costs to keep them that way, the better. In our formally democratic times, such arguments are not usually made in public. But they are what stakeholding is up against.

The political equivalent of preventing an economic underclass is universal voting; not just the opportunity offered by the franchise but the actual use of the vote by everyone. But while the base lines for inclusive citizenship are working and voting, this is too defensive and limited a description of what a stakeholder economy and stakeholder democracy are about. The concern is not simply with the involvement of the poor and marginalised, perhaps extended to include women, blacks and minorities, into the existing order of things. It concerns the way everyone might make a difference and may help to make change better and more effective. An analogy can be drawn with rights. In the first instance, formal rights are needed to protect minorities – if necessary *from* the majority. But rights are also for everyone, and a Bill of Rights will enhance decision making and improve everyone's sense of who they are and their respect for others.

Albert Hirschman's *Exit, Voice and Loyalty* is an illuminating and entertaining meditation on the larger issues of involvement, and he draws upon economic theory to extend the understanding of politics. The classical notion of economic behaviour is based on exit. If buyers cease to favour a product because of its price or quality, they leave it for another. But if there is customer loyalty or producer monopoly the consumer may attempt to change the product by persuasion, what Hirschman calls voice, rather than exit. Can voice be a substitute for exit, if so under what conditions, and what is the nature and consequences of the loyalty that encourages voice? Hirschman pursues these questions in a fine, understated discussion of how people may respond to change. He argues:

> In the choice between voice and exit, voice will often lose out, not necessarily because it would be less effective than exit, but because its effectiveness depends upon the *discovery* of *new* ways of exerting influence and pressure towards recovery. However 'easy' such a discovery might look in retrospect ... creativity always comes as a surprise. Loyalty then helps to redress the balance by raising the cost of exit. It thereby pushes men into alternative, creativity-requiring courses of action from which they would normally recoil ... .[2] (emphases in the original)

Stakeholding is about both inventing new forms for the expression of voice and making exit harder, including for those who already enjoy influence. Inclusion is not just about preventing exclusion, it is also about generating the framework of loyalty for a process of mutual influence between partners with different stakes.

Just as there is a mental presumption in Britain that stakeholding is another form of static, corporatist arrangement of existing interests, rather than a means of enabling and encouraging changing interests, so there remains a paternalist presumption about inclusion – that it can be done from above, that it involves people trusting a suitably thoughtful authority, rather than authority trusting the people.

An illustration of the complexity and sophistication of contemporary voice is the Citizens' Charters. These were invented to give people a capacity to complain more effectively. But, as Francis Maude, who helped to develop them when he was an MP commented, they provide 'remedies not rights'. The voice to which Citizens' Charters help give expression is the voice of the customer, not the voice of authority.

Yet, as Hirschman points out, in politics citizens can be the producers of their society as well as consumers of it. Stakeholder democracy would hold citizens to be producers of government, its shareholding owners and its customers. Different voices are used in each respect, and voice is a better concept than trust in illuminating the potential of stakeholding because it is less passive and more intelligent. Voice must be two-way, for what influence can there be in speaking if in response there comes only silence?

What kind of laws and government best illustrate stakeholder democracy with respect to inclusion and voice? Labour's commitment to ensure work for 250000 unemployed youths is a good example. True, it combines principle with self-interest – for how can Labour hope to govern for a generation if it allows the younger generation to rot and thus certain to riot at some point within the next decade? But this gives one hope that the commitment will be carried through even though it is bound to cost more than the revenues raised by a windfall tax on the privatised utilities. The wider process of inclusion is more complex. It could start with an obligation to vote, as legislated in Australia, provided this allows voters to spoil their ballot paper if they wish to reject the choice on offer.

Perhaps the best example of inclusive legislation is a Freedom of Information act, because even a weak or restrictive act would nonetheless establish the principle that information generated by the authorities at the public expense belongs to the public. The public has a right to know unless the authorities can show good reason why information should be withheld, for example because of national security or individual privacy. In Britain the authorities presently regard information as belonging to them, and they will only allow the public to know what it is good for them to know – an attitude that regards the public as natives to be ruled rather than citizens to be respected. From the point of view of the public, a Freedom of Information Act opens up new ways in which people can establish their voice and ensure their inclusion in decision making, whether this affects them personally or in terms of policies they care about. A better form of relationship will be established, more open, more mutual, between government and the governed. And this will lead to improved decision making, placing authorities on their guard against arbitrary, slovenly, or inadequate decisions.

Will a New Labour administration legislate a Freedom of Information Act as it has promised in its draft manifesto, and if so, when? The introduction of stakeholder democracy involves constitutional reforms. Often these are tricky, controversial and time consuming. Abolishing hereditary peers is popular but replacing the Lords difficult. A Scottish Parliament is essential if the Scots vote for one, but it raises all sorts of English questions. Incorporating the European Convention of Human Rights is a good first step to a Bill of Rights, but the move will bring parliamentary sovereignty into question and this could frighten swing voters. Those who advocate constitutional reform should be the last to underestimate the difficulties and the strength, however misbegotten, of opposition to such change. None of this applies to a Freedom of Information Act. The idea is immensely popular, not least with Conservative voters. The legislation exists in draft and has been tried and tested in other parliamentary systems. It embraces everyone, unifies rather than divides, is easy to pass, is almost impossible to oppose publicly, builds on the Tory commitment to 'open government', and is supported by the tabloid press. Here, then, is an opportunity crying out to be seized. By passing a Freedom of Information Act as soon as they come to power, a Labour government could establish the credibility and achievability of constitutional reform. There is no better symbol of a stakeholding approach to democracy.

SOVEREIGNTY

Stakeholding implies sharing power. Well worn terms trip from the word processor: pluralism, decentralisation, participation. They often sound worn and devoid of meaning in Britain because we have little experience of what they might mean. They also frighten decision makers who fear that the alternative to centralised sovereignty is no sovereignty at all. Perhaps, therefore, we should start with an imaginary example from a stakeholder company to locate what principles there might be to stakeholding decision making.

Suppose that two factories in a large company start to become uncompetitive due to innovation in methods of production, and that it is obvious that unless production is concentrated in one, both will become loss-making. Presented with the analysis of the trends, the directors have to take a decision. In a stakeholder company, the factory workers as well as management will be informed and will have *the right* to present alternative courses of action to closure and to have their viability assessed. A decision will still have to be made as to which factory is to lose its production and which is to gain. This has to be taken by directors who assess the larger picture. Increasing the productivity of one factory while shutting down production in another involves a mix of positive and negative decisions. But the way these decisions are taken will have been shared, and the productive resources in the closing factory might well be transferred to new opportunities that could only be perceived locally. Even if this is not possible, the way the change takes place will be improved. Part of the improvement will be that those whose lives are negatively affected will feel that they understand the reasons, that they have had a say, and their self-pride and capacity will be less damaged.

Painful decisions are still taken, but they are taken differently from a company that believes only the directors know best.

Embedded in this example are some of the principles of stakeholder democracy. First, there should be no centre of absolute power. Here in the UK we are told that we enjoy 'the absolute sovereignty of parliament' as one of the glories of our traditional constitution. It is doubtful that this description can be sustained as an interpretation of the past. It certainly no longer applies. Since the Magna Carta of 1215, Britain has witnessed distinctive and successful resistance to attempts to claim absolute power. The divine right of kings was brought to an end at Naseby. Today, the attempt to assert the absolute power of the executive as expressed in the divine right of Parliament will not last for long. Power is being shared. This is a European process. It is perhaps above all a regional and local process. It does not follow that there will not be ultimate decision takers, just that there will no longer be only one of them – Whitehall. To replace absolute sovereignty with democratic sovereignty is not to replace sovereignty but to alter the process of legitimate decision making – it puts an end only to absolutism.

The sharing of power makes democracy a continuous process. Instead of being defined by a quinquennial plebiscite over who should take decisions, citizens are succeeding in expressing their interests and influencing government in new and more continuous ways. However much those who believe they 'run' the country may regret it, this process is unstoppable, hence the opportunity that awaits a government which decides to put itself at the head of the process rather than resist it.

An outstanding example of the way influence over decision taking is being expanded to take in new voices is the evolution of public interest law. The courts have begun to accept that public interest groups have the right to insist upon judicial review of decisions even when such groups fall outside the older definition of interested parties, namely individuals personally affected by a decision. Thus Greenpeace was accepted by the courts as a bona fide applicant having the right to object to the commissioning of THORP, the nuclear reprocessing plant constructed at Sellafield. Across a whole range of decisions (especially on the environment, but this will doubtless expand into other areas) official decision makers must now take into account the fact that their policies may be challenged in the courts by knowledgeable experts who in the past would not have been accepted by the courts as having the standing to make such objections.

We can call this stakeholder sovereignty because these self-organised public interest parties are winning the right to influence policy. Of course, this example will make the opponents of stakeholding say 'I told you so'. The power to resist decisions in court is antagonistic, delaying, costly and negative. But once this power exists, the obvious way to prevent its negative deployment is to listen constructively and in advance to the interest groups concerned. Now that they have a stake they should have a share in the decision taking.

Why can we be confident that this process is unstoppable? First, because government decisions are becoming much more knowledge based and risk incurring; second, because they therefore call out for better and more continuous scrutiny; and third, because the population is becoming far better educated and articulate. The kinds of decision now taken by government need to be scrutinised more thoroughly and the public is increasingly capable of doing so, both individually and through dedicated organisations.

CONCLUSION

A stakeholder democracy would be one that develops new institutions that encourage all citizens to influence decisions, local and national, on the basis of shared power, and to do so freely not bureaucratically, with the aim of embracing and handling change. Once these aims might have sounded nice but costly aspirations that a competitive society could not afford. Today, because the very basis of our risk society, to use Ulrich Beck's term, is changing so fast, stakeholding is likely to prove a competitive necessity. A knowledge based society must broaden the basis of knowledge, so that it is actively applied throughout society. It will need to utilise different forms of shared power to do so, if it is not to break apart.

Two linked aspects of this modernisation of democracy sum up its objectives: the demand for self-determination, and quality. Representative democracy as it has developed since the nineteenth century is a largely fatalistic form of politics that encourages a defensive expression of interests rather than self-determination. For ill as well as good, contemporary society is lessening the degree to which people regard their situation as a consequence of fate. Thatcherism exalted competitive opportunity as the means to overcome it, but by the same token legitimised the price of losing in the great game of competition, as almost everyone does. Stakeholding opposes this philosophy and implies that through mutual action the hand of fate can be lessened and opportunity enhanced and made good without stifling competitive creativity.

Stakeholder democracy is about making change and the change people want above all is for the standard of their lives to improve. Today this means the quality of life, not as a matter of luxury but as felt necessity: the quality of cities and communications, our public and private space, the quality of what one eats, sees and learns. Quality is a continuous process and much of the appeal of a stakeholding approach, as opposed to one that advocates economic growth on the basis of low costs and cheap labour, is that it points towards the long-term benefits of a high-quality existence for all.

Which brings us back to change, where we began. British Conservatives are now arguing that in order to handle economic change the country needs to preserve its institutions: that, in the words of David Willetts (slightly misquoting T.S. Eliot), Westminster and Whitehall should be the 'still centre of a changing world'. This vision may be attractive to those who inhabit the still centre. Looking out from it they may fail to comprehend that the world is changing not by going around them, as if they were its centre, but by leaving them behind.

Britain cannot embrace technological and economic change unless its leaders also embrace a profound transformation of their own system of power. We must modernise our government to modernise our democracy. For the United Kingdom, this calls for nothing less than a Copernican revolution that recognises it is no longer the centre of power around which everything revolves. Once it was – at the height of Empire, when the institutions we know today were forged, and very able it was too. Now, it must embrace the change it insists the rest of society must undertake. It sounds paradoxical, but the British government must let go of power if it is to lead successfully. This is a fact not a metaphor.

NOTES

1. A. Hirschman, *Exit, Voice, and Loyalty* (Cambridge, MA.: Harvard University Press, 1970), p. 43.
2. *Ibid.*, p. 80.

Part III

Social Justice and the Stakeholder Society

10 Social Inclusion and Exclusion
Ruth Lister

A useful starting point for a discussion of social inclusion/exclusion in the context of 'stakeholding' is the language used to frame current debates, for language is important in shaping perceptions of social phenomena and their causes. The language of social inclusion/exclusion (SIE) permeates a number of recent key texts including, in particular, Will Hutton's *The State We're In*[1] and the Dahrendorf *Report on Wealth Creation and Social Cohesion*. The latter states:

> Exclusion is the greatest risk accompanying the opportunities of the new economic era. Significant numbers of people lose their hold first on the labour market, then on the social and political participation in their community.[2]

The Report links social to civic exclusion – insecurity giving rise to hostility to 'unwelcome others' and 'in this condition, minorities are particularly vulnerable; the risk of xenophobia, racial hatred and religious intolerance is ever-present'.[3] Conversely, the Report notes: 'the best concept which we have found to describe an economy and a society based on social cohesion is that of *inclusion*' which it equates with citizenship.[4] It also argues that 'a stakeholder society is an inclusive society'. For me, the language of citizenship and social inclusion has greater resonance than that of stakeholding when talking about a society rather than an economy. Stakeholding smacks too much of 'management-speak' and, I would argue, lacks the political and more dynamic edge of citizenship and social inclusion. Indeed, it is interesting that explanations of the meaning of a stakeholder society tend to have recourse to the language of citizenship and social inclusion to the extent that it is not clear what the notion of stakeholding itself adds.

The concept of social exclusion has also been promoted by the European Commission which runs an Observatory on National Policies to Combat Social Exclusion. In its third report, the Observatory notes the increased use of the term in a number of member countries.[5] The Observatory's own working definition of exclusion, which emphasises its multi-dimensional character, is framed in terms of 'the absence or denial of social rights', again drawing on the vocabulary of citizenship. The European Commission itself has tended to use the term social exclusion in place of poverty, even though it goes wider. Although there are dangers in this, it does represent a more dynamic language which encourages a focus on the processes and institutions which create and maintain disadvantage rather than a preoccupation with individual behaviour and experience – a point also well made in a recent Northern Ireland Democratic Dialogue Report, *Social Exclusion, Social Inclusion*.[6]

At the same time, a focus on process and not just outcome underlines the importance of the voice and agency of 'the excluded' in any politics of inclusion. I am deliberately not referring to the excluded as an 'underclass' – a label which is in itself excluding and not conducive to a politics of inclusion and which is used much too uncritically by many on the left despite the lack of evidence for its existence, whatever 'it' might be, given the lack of agreement on what is meant by the term.

The notion of an 'underclass' also lumps together a number of different groups, but the excluded are not a homogeneous group. Moreover, the processes of exclusion operate both *within* and *at the frontiers of* nation states, which links to the Dahrendorf Report's point about civic exclusion. Thus, within the nation SIE is not just about poverty and class differences but also the social divisions, such as gender, 'race' and disability which interact with them, while SIE at the frontiers raises questions about, for example, immigration laws and policies towards asylum seekers, which are not dealt with here but which are of fundamental importance to the way in which an inclusive society positions itself internationally. As both the UK and the wider EU pursue ever more restrictive policies in this area, they are signalling an increasingly exclusive stance towards membership of their respective communities. This also raises broader questions of the potential for global citizenship.

THE ECONOMIC DIMENSION OF INCLUSION AND EXCLUSION

Strategies for social inclusion within the nation state need to be considered at three different but interrelated levels: the economic, the social and the political.

Clearly the economic level is of fundamental importance given the extent to which social exclusion is being driven by economic policies and labour market trends. That is not to say, though, that exclusion only concerns the labour market, an approach that has been criticised by Ruth Levitas, who also poses the important question, exclusion from what?[7] In other words, if we concentrate only on exclusion, there is a danger that we lose sight of the inequalities that exist in the wider society. This had led some to suggest that the concept of social exclusion needs to be complemented by that of social polarisation.[8]

Although not the main focus of this chapter, I will make just two points about the economic dimension of exclusion. First, it is important to underline the dangers of abdicating responsibility for inclusionary economic/social policies in the face of global economic forces. Whilst it may be true that these forces limit the power of nation states to set their own economic and social agendas (though some would query even this), this should not become an alibi for inaction, a point underlined by Paul Hirst and Grahame Thompson in their recent critical study of globalisation.[9] As the Joseph Rowntree Inquiry into Income and Wealth argued, although 'policy-makers have to operate under constraints set by global forces, which may well be tighter than in the past, we do not believe that they have lost all freedom of manoeuvre'.[10]

Second, I would point to the need for the kinds of policies advocated by the Commission on Social Justice (CSJ) to create a more inclusionary labour market by breaking down the main barriers which exclude disadvantaged groups from the labour market or marginalise them within it. These policies include: a jobs, education and training (JET) programme directed primarily towards the long-term unemployed and lone parents but as part of a broader priority given to investment in lifelong learning and training; the expansion of high-quality and affordable child care facilities together with the development of family-friendly employment policies; the strengthening of anti-discrimination measures; and finally, the guarantee of adequate rewards from employment through a statutory minimum wage and strengthened employment rights, including the outlawing of zero-hours contracts.

THE SOCIAL DIMENSION OF INCLUSION AND EXCLUSION

For the Commission on Social Justice, paid work represents the most effective route out of poverty and social exclusion. Its proposals on the employment side are thus underpinned on the social side with what is now widely known as a 'welfare-to-work' strategy, also central to the Rowntree and Dahrendorf reports. The Rowntree Report, for instance, directs many of its recommendations towards 'encouraging and helping people back into work [as] a crucial step in any policy to combat poverty, at the same time giving them a sense of usefulness and a stake in the country's economy'.[11]

The policies on the social security side of the welfare-to-work strategy are aimed both at improving the incentive to work by raising in-work incomes, and at easing the transition from benefit to both full-time and part-time work. The importance of the latter in particular has come to be recognised recently, as research has shown how the benefits system itself creates barriers against those who want to move from income support to paid work and how the insecurities and uncertainties associated with the transition are an important factor here.

More broadly, inclusionary social policies need to be informed by principles of social citizenship – again a theme which runs through both *The State We're In* and the CSJ and Dahrendorf reports. The first step is to reaffirm the importance of the welfare state as a force (or at least a potential force) for inclusion in the face of exclusionary economic trends. As the CSJ argues, 'far from making the welfare state redundant, social and economic change creates a new and even more vital need for the security which the welfare state was designed to provide'.[12] Similarly, Hutton emphasises that 'the vitality of the welfare state is a badge of the healthy society; it is a symbol of our capacity to act together morally, to share and to recognise the mutuality of rights and obligations that underpins all human association. It is an expression of social citizenship.'[13]

What this might mean in relation to incomes can be explored in relation to three main choices underlying much current debate on social security reform: universalism versus targeting, public versus private provision, and unconditional versus conditional benefits. However, having presented each as either-or choices, in fact it is more a question in each case of different positions on a continuum.

Universalism versus targeting.   When the CSJ was set up, the media and many on the left as well as the right saw its main task as getting Labour off the hook of its traditional commitment to universalism in the name of modernisation. Instead, the Commission aimed to demonstrate that it is means testing and not universalism which is anachronistic, for the former is ill-suited to modern conditions of rapid change, fluctuating incomes and insecurity. Moreover, because it is based on the joint incomes of couples, it threatens to undermine women's financial independence and means that one partner's economic activity affects the other's benefit entitlement. Interestingly, even Peter Lilley, the Social Security Secretary, now recognises some of means-testing's disadvantages, though his concern is more with its damaging impact on incentives to earn and save, a theme which has been pressed forcefully by the Social Security Select Committee.

Furthermore, the experience of the US suggests that a residual means-tested safety net as the centrepiece of a country's income maintenance strategy, which is the direction in which current government policy is taking us, will not necessarily, as claimed, target more resources on those in poverty. Instead it is likely to marginalise the poor and their interests even further as the rest of society no longer has any stake in the welfare system. Means tests thus represent a force for social exclusion rather than inclusion.

Public versus private provision. The issue of the balance between public and private welfare provision is becoming increasingly critical. On the far right there are various proposals to phase out social insurance in favour of private insurance, backed up by a residual state assistance scheme. The government itself has been pursuing policies aimed at encouraging more people to take out private insurance, especially in the areas of pensions and mortgage protection. Now people like Frank Field are arguing for compulsory private insurance as the best way of promoting 'stakeholding' in welfare. It might well do so for those who can afford the premiums, but for the significant minority who will not be able to buy their stakes and whose premiums will have to be paid for out of taxation, arguably it could drive a wedge between them and 'the taxpayer' rather than promote solidarity.

Whilst endorsing a mixed economy of welfare and recognising a role for private provision, the CSJ makes clear that it is not a substitute for a comprehensive, modernised social insurance system, on the grounds that social insurance protects people more cheaply, efficiently and fairly than private insurance; plays a key role in helping people redistribute income over their increasingly varied lifecycle (though compulsory private insurance could also do this); represents an expression of social citizenship in its balance of rights and responsibilities through an ethic of mutuality; and exemplifies the approach prioritised by most of our EU partners.

Thus, the centrepiece of its proposals for welfare reform is a modernised, inclusive social insurance system better attuned to contemporary employment and family patterns and especially the position of women. Part-time workers, in particular, would enjoy new rights and in the longer term, it is suggested, social insurance could cover new contingencies such as parental leave and learning sabbaticals. The Commission has also floated the idea of enabling those who want to, to pay in extra to the scheme so that they can draw out more when they need it.

Conditional versus unconditional. The issue of conditionality goes to the heart of the question of the relationship between citizenship rights and obligations, and in particular work obligations. In a number of societies, European as well as American, there is increasing emphasis on work obligations as a badge of social inclusion and citizenship.

Workfare represents its most extreme form, and government policy is moving increasingly in that direction, especially with the new Job Seeker's Allowance and the recent announcement of pilot workfare-type schemes. The CSJ rejects workfare, primarily on the grounds that its emphasis on compulsion could be counterproductive. Rejection of workfare does not, however, necessarily mean rejection of all notions of responsibility amongst unemployed benefit recipients to take available suitable work or engage in training. We need to distinguish beween this principle and the present government's increasingly punitive interpretation of it.

Where the CSJ goes, controversially, further than the present government is in its recommendation that parents of older children should be required to be available for part-time work, provided adequate child care facilities were available and subject to various other safeguards. The proposal would only be activated in the context of the successful introduction of the JET package mentioned above. This has been interpreted in some quarters as an attack on the rights of lone mothers. However, the UK is very unusual in allowing lone parents to remain on social assistance until their youngest child is aged sixteen and it is debatable whether such a liberal rule is actually in their own interests. The evidence of the long-term damage done to the economic interests of women absent from the labour market for long stretches means we have to question whether we are doing lone mothers any favours by assuming that they can continue to remain outside the labour market for so long.

At a time when actual policy is moving towards greater conditionality in a number of countries, there is growing support for a policy which stands at the other end of the continuum: citizens income (CI), which would be paid to each individual without any conditions attached. For many of its advocates it represents the ultimate expression of citizenship and social inclusion. Also, it is well suited to part-time work and ensures an independent income for women. However, there are also problems, including its political acceptability and economic feasibility, and arguably it upsets the reciprocal balance between rights and obligations. Although the CSJ does not endorse it as an immediate strategy, it does advise against ruling out a move towards CI in the longer term and in the meantime gives support to the idea of a 'participation income' which goes some way towards CI. Where appropriate, the income would be conditional on some form of active social contribution, defined more broadly than paid employment to cover care and, in some versions, voluntary work.

The idea of a participation income goes some way towards addressing one of the tensions with which the CSJ had to grapple: how to balance the imperatives of a strategy predicated on the central importance of paid work to tackling social exclusion with recognition of the value of unpaid caring work. Linked to this is the question of how best to ensure an independent income for those providing care (still mainly women) through the benefits system, without at the same time reinforcing the gendered division of labour, thereby locking women further into caring responsibilities in the 'private' sphere and out of full participation in the 'public' sphere and potential economic and political autonomy. Part of the answer has to lie in policies which address men's absenteeism from the responsibilities of care, such as have been attempted by some Scandinavian countries.

The other main danger with the current conventional wisdom around the centrality of welfare-to-work is that the immediate needs of those unable to cross the bridge from welfare to work will be forgotten. Tony Blair has made clear that his welfare agenda is not about 'better benefits' which a number of Labour spokespersons now seem to associate with a 'dependency culture' that research has yet to show exists. Clearly the success of any welfare-to-work strategy is dependent on the work becoming available, and that will take time. So, deeply unfashionable as it is, we need to remember that lack of money is, in itself, a source of social exclusion. According to a special report from the Joseph Rowntree Foundation, an additional £15 a week would greatly improve the ability of people on very low incomes to cope.[14]

Of course, any increase in benefit levels has to be paid for and this implies another deeply unfashionable notion that we might once again use the tax system as an instrument of redistribution towards the excluded and as a mechanism for social inclusion and an expression of citizenship. The CSJ Report may not have gone as far as some would have liked in its recommendations for a fairer tax system but it does reiterate 'an old principle: taxes are the contribution that we all make towards building a better society. Taxation in a democratic society is based upon consent; it is a desirable good, not a necessary evil ... fair taxes, wisely and efficiently used, are a responsibility we should share and accept.'[15] Unfortunately, in trying to compete with the Tories as the party of low taxation, Labour is in danger of losing sight of this principle and of reinforcing the increasingly dominant view of taxation as inherently undesirable. Taxation is a central political issue and yet, as the Dahrendorf Report notes, the issue of taxation has become practically taboo in public debate.

THE POLITICAL DIMENSION OF INCLUSION AND EXCLUSION

Moving finally to the political dimension, I will focus on inclusion as a political process which needs to involve the excluded themselves. This also means understanding citizenship not just as a question of rights but as an active process of political participation (broadly defined) – a rather different understanding of active citizenship than that promoted by the Tories. In its outreach visits, the CSJ took inspiration from the many examples of such active citizenship that it witnessed in some of the most deprived communities, often spearheaded by women. In order to enhance this culture of active citizenship the Commission puts forward various proposals to promote bottom-up community regeneration, including the establishment of community development trusts. Support for such trusts has also come from the Northern Ireland Opsahl Commission.[16] They were defined by one Northern Ireland community group as 'an independent, not for profit organisation which takes action to renew an area physically, socially and in spirit. It brings together the public, private and voluntary sectors ... [and] it encourages substantial involvement by local people.'

Also from Northern Ireland, the Democratic Dialogue Report on social exclusion and social inclusion emphasises the importance of a vibrant civil society as a public forum for excluded groups and suggests that resources and leadership training should be made available to them.[17] This sometimes needs to be more basic – at the level of assertiveness training and confidence-building, for example.

Similarly, there is growing recognition in some quarters of the importance of user involvement in welfare services as an expression of active rather than more passive forms of social citizenship. Such initiatives are about giving voice to groups who are normally treated simply as the objects of welfare policies and whose voice is largely excluded from political debates.

We are seeing an intensification of processes of political exclusion alongside social and economic exclusion. Galbraith has observed how the contented majority (though perhaps they too are increasingly less contented in the face of growing economic insecurity) 'rule under the rich cloak of democracy, a democracy in which the less fortunate do not participate'.[18] He was speaking of the exclusion of the poor, but the rich cloak of democracy also hides the extent to which social divisions of gender, 'race' and disability translate into political exclusions behind it. This points to the need to open up political space to 'the excluded', both by making formal politics more open to informal, community-based forms of politics, and by opening formal politics up to groups and individuals currently marginalised. In this way, deprived individuals and communities can also become political stakeholders.

To conclude, I would echo Will Hutton's emphasis on the interrelation-ships between the economic, social and political aspects of social inclusion/exclusion and between different components of citizenship. In his review of the CSJ Report he wrote of 'the point/counterpoint between the economic, social and political that must be at the heart of any reform programme'.[19] In similar fashion his book ends by stressing the urgency of the need for such a programme. At a time when a quarter of the population and a third of children are living with below half average income, the nearest we have to a poverty line, and when the gap between the poor and the wider society is growing into a chasm, policies to reverse the processes of social exclusion through a positive spiral of economic, social and political inclusion must be number one priority for an incoming Labour government.

NOTES

1. Will Hutton, *The State We're In* (London: Jonathan Cape, 1995).
2. R. Dahrendorf *et al.*, *Report on Wealth Creation and Social Cohesion in a Free Society* (London: The Commission on Wealth Creation & Social Cohesion, 1995), p. 15.
3. *Ibid.*, pp. 15–16.
4. Dahrendorf *et al.*, *Report on Wealth Creation*, p. 34.
5. D. Robbins (ed.), *Observatory on National Policies to Combat Social Exclusion* (Lille: EEIG 'Animation and Research', 1994).
6. R. Wilson (ed.), *Social Exclusion, Social Inclusion* (Belfast: Democratic Dialogue, 1995).
7. R. Levitas, 'The Concept of Social Exclusion and the New Durkheimian Hegemony', *Critical Social Policy*, Vol. 16, No. 1, 1996.
8. F. Williams with J. Pillinger, 'New Thinking on Social Policy Research into Inequality, Social Exclusion and Poverty', in J. Millar and J. Bradshshaw (eds), *Social Welfare Systems: Towards a Research Agenda* (Bath: University of Bath/ESRC, 1996).
9. P. Hirst and G. Thompson, *Globalization in Question* (Cambridge: Polity, 1996).
10. Joseph Rowntree Foundation Income and Wealth Inquiry Group, *Income and Wealth* (York: Joseph Rowntree Foundation, 1995), p. 38.
11. *Ibid.*, p. 43.
12. Commission on Social Justice, *Social Justice, Strategies for National Renewal* (London, Vintage, 1994), p. 222.
13. Hutton, *The State We're In*, p. 306.
14. E. Kempson, *Life on a Low Income* (York: Joseph Rowntree Foundation, 1996).
15. Commission on Social Justice, *Social Justice*, p. 376.
16. A. Pollack (ed.), *A Citizens' Inquiry, The Opsahl Report on Northern Ireland* (Dublin: Lilliput Press, 1993).
17. Wilson, *Social Exclusion*.
18. J.K. Galbraith, *The Culture of Contentment* (London: Sinclair-Stevenson, 1992).
19. W. Hutton, 'One Step Nearer to Genuine Citizenship', *Guardian*, 24 October 1994.

11 Mapping the Stakeholder Society

James McCormick

We will only really know how successful the ideas and policies coalescing around the notion of a Stakeholder Society are when the first Conservative government wins power *after* the next Labour government. The left must be no less ambitious than to help build a new consensus able to survive a change of government largely intact, because its reforms have been sufficiently rooted in the interests of most people. The capacity of Conservatives to dismantle significant elements of the settlement they inherited in 1979 tells us something about centralisation and the power to secure huge parliamentary majorities on a clear minority of public support, and something about the deployment of 'the strong state' in the task of rolling back its influence. But it also tells us something about the settlement itself. Even if Thatcherism had never happened, Britain would not find itself absolved of the need to modernise the welfare state or revisit the relationship between the state and individuals.

We begin from where we are, not from where we would choose to be. The left needs a vision of what it has traditionally called the Inclusive or Good Society – and now the Stakeholder Society. It requires a map of the principles and the practical policies which will lead us in that direction. The journey should persuade enough people that it is preferable to the alternatives. The political terrain which the Stakeholder Society will lay claim to must have clearly defined boundaries. This chapter sets out some of these guiding principles and policy reforms.

A MAP OF PRINCIPLES

The broad objectives of a Stakeholder Society might be to tackle market failures, to address distributive injustice and to enhance incentives for participation. Some central principles should be threaded through these.

'The Social' and 'The Economic'

The left has for too long conceded economic production and efficiency to the right, leaving itself with the task of after-the-fact distribution of income and wealth through the tax and benefits system. The rise in income inequality is not only a British phenomenon (although it is particularly marked in this country) and it is indeed driven in part by beneficial tax changes for those on high incomes and the failure of benefits and pensions to keep pace with earnings for those on low incomes. But it is the *earnings* element of income which shows a more marked dispersal. Access to earnings must be central to a stakeholding strategy. Put simply, welfare is too important to be left only to the welfare state.

Redistribution of income is an insufficient policy instrument given the ambitious nature of the task. The tax and benefit systems must be reformed, but more money for those at the bottom is a holding option. It does not, on its own, assist people to be mobile, to equip themselves to cope with change. It does not endow them in an actively egalitarian way. We cannot ignore the primary distribution of resources – skills, talents, knowledge and earnings – in preference to a focus on secondary outcomes.

Stakeholding has generated disagreement as a model for intra-company relations and corporate governance. Leaving aside those who dismiss the concept as a backdoor route to re-regulation, other critics have argued that the capitalist firm cannot be made more responsible and should simply be left to do what they do best (create wealth), while the state's task should be to protect consumers, employees and the environment separately – the politics of secondary distribution rather than primary allocation of resources and opportunities. Whatever the obstacles to building economic citizenship through stakeholding, the left cannot afford to accept that the role of public policy only begins beyond the market. The emerging consensus on the economy is compelling – markets are not 'given' objects with an inbuilt capacity to reach a virtuous equilibrium between levels of investment and employment. They exaggerate success and failure. They are the product of negotiation and future calculations which government should seek to influence in a productive way. In order to persuade employers of the value of stakeholding, the links between information, motivation and productivity must be demonstrated.

New Labour orthodoxy holds that extending social justice is a requirement for economic efficiency. Social justice is defined in terms of 'investment'. The 'Intelligent Welfare State' proposed by the Commission on Social Justice is rooted in improving opportunities to earn.[1] Thus reforming means-tested benefits and strengthening the insurance basis of benefits should reduce the barriers facing unemployed people getting back into work and reduce the duration of having to claim benefits. Social justice is not just about cash transfers, however. Wider access to affordable child care services should also help low-income parents back into jobs and assist others to remain in employment.

Yet, getting people off welfare (or off benefits) and into work is problematic for at least two reasons. It pushes the definition of welfare towards the narrower American term – means-tested cash support for those outside paid work – rather than the more helpful definition which includes universal services and draws wider political support. The notion of leaving benefit behind is misleading because the low-paid work which many will take requires in-work benefit top-ups for families or housing costs, for example, even with a minimum wage. The transition is not off benefit into work, but more accurately from out-of-work benefits to earnings plus in-work benefits. There is a further problem with the harmonious marriage between social justice and economic efficiency which has been highlighted by Stuart White and others.[2] Social justice requires investment which will make no obvious contribution to economic productivity. Higher investment in care services and benefits for people of working age with severe disabilities is a matter purely of cash transfers. New Labour may be offering 'New Life' for Britain but it cannot enable the severely disabled to take jobs or cure those with long-term illnesses. This is more than angels dancing on the head of semantic pins. Helping more people into jobs is essential to social justice but cannot be the whole strategy.

Security must be Reclaimed

The Left has undoubtedly struck a nerve with its critique of a labour market rife with insecurity. But the trouble with security is that it can sound like a luxury we can no longer afford if we are to be competitive. Conservatives will accuse those in favour of security of wanting to cling to the past and hide from change. It will appeal to people's hard experiences of the labour market, where change is uncomfortable but everyone knows it to be inevitable. It is not hard to imagine opponents trying to portray New Labour as New Luddites. Stakeholding has to tackle insecurity without confusing it with *uncertainty*. The future has always been uncertain. The real task is to endow people with the skills to negotiate the quickening pace of change rather than be defeated by it. That is only possible if there is a reliable baseline level of security.

A 'Something for Something' Society

I am also struck by Stuart White's argument that the centre-left should not give up on the notion of reciprocity simply because Conservatives have colonised the territory practically unchallenged. A stakeholder society should be built on the strength of the contributions made by every citizen *who is able to contribute* and the entitlements drawn upon across the lifecycle. Some on the left are clearly uncomfortable with the new Clause IV rhetoric of 'the rights we have reflect the duties we owe'. However, the policy implications of genuine reciprocity may turn out to be more radical than we expect. We cannot seriously expect all those who are low-skilled and long-term unemployed, living in local labour markets with very low rates of job creation, to find work (or at least work classed by the Benefits Agency as 'legitimate'). The responsibility to take jobs must ultimately turn on the joint responsibility of employers and government to create jobs. This raises questions about whether the state can or should guarantee employment of last right – whether there should be a right to a job for those who seek one.

Conservative ministers have criticised a 'something for nothing' society when attacking long-term benefit dependence, but ignored the effect of the Job Seeker's Allowance (which provides the claimant with something, but rather less than the entitlement they had expected). In a different way, they have helped to *encourage* a 'something for nothing' approach by holding out the promise of cost-free tax cuts and giving the impression that welfare costs can be lowered by moving to private insurance. The left should turn this back on advocates of this position by restating the first principle of welfare: however it is organised it still has to be paid for. Tax cuts in the public sphere will have to be matched by rising insurance premiums in the private sphere for cover which is less than comprehensive.

If 'rights and responsibilities' are to provide us with any guidance they have to be applied universally. In other words, rights must go all the way down (including the economic sphere) and responsibilities must go all the way up. If benefit fraud should be tackled, so must tax evasion. Both erode the foundations of a Stakeholder Society.

A LONG-TERM STRATEGY

We can only gain a limited sense of how societies are shaped from a snap-shot glimpse. Stakeholding is only in part about the resources and opportunities held at one point in time. Stakeholding must be a dynamic process rather than an event. At one level, it is about holding common resources in stewardship for the future: social justice between generations. A reshaped economic model should be committed to high levels of productivity and wealth creation, but in a sustainable manner. Examples of using the tax system towards this end should be considered. When the Dutch government introduced preferential tax treatment for pension and insurance funds screened for environmental impact, the result was a large movement of funds away from investors unable to meet ethical targets.

The debate about taxes is restricted to tax rates rather than considering the question of how we raise taxes in the first place. Increasing income tax for high-income earners is progressive, but there are limits to how far tax can be raised on labour. Arguments in favour of environmental tax reform, raising a higher proportion of revenues from waste, pollution payments and energy consumption and a lower share from labour should be fully considered. Evidence on the scale of employment gain is mixed, but the prospect of more jobs and a more sustainable environment without a significant increase in public spending is worth exploring.

At another level, stakeholding should be a lifetime strategy for individuals. In some ways this is no more than a modern expression of the social insurance principle. Contributions should be paid during times of economic activity and entitlements should be drawn when earnings are interrupted or in retirement. The British model has emphasised reciprocity rather than insurance in the actuarial sense. The Singapore model of compulsory savings funds is closer to an individual bank account with limited overdraft facilities. The first is more redistributive than the second. However we choose to insure against lifecycle risks, we should be clear that the level of investment for the future has to rise relative to the level of current consumption. Inclusion in paid work currently offers no guarantee of becoming a stakeholder in retirement (particularly for women in part-time jobs which pay below the National Insurance threshold).

SOME LIMITS

Boundaries offer clarity and room to explore the possibilities for reform. But they also imply limits. Stakeholding will not get us very far if it results in policy wish-lists. So it is as well to discuss what we do *not* expect. A Stakeholder Society will not be one without risk, uncertainty, unemployment, low pay or inequality. This is not to say that all of these cannot be reduced. They can be and it is essential that they are. But the urgent task should be to seek a just distribution of however much disadvantage remains through a more just distribution of life-chances. One of the priorities must therefore be to lower the duration of experiencing disadvantage. If exclusion is semipermanent for some families and communities they cannot be said to hold any meaningful stake in society.

On any credible definition of poverty in the UK more than one in four children are in poor families. It is one thing to be born poor but quite another to grow up poor. The growth of low-paid jobs is only a disaster if employees face 'no exit' signs rather than doors open to better jobs. A falling rate of registered unemployment only tells us part of the labour market story. If the headline figure conceals a core of very long-term unemployed people whose chances of finding a job diminish the longer they are out of work (as it does in the UK), we are facing a significant market failure. The number of people in employment is at a postwar high, yet the number of working-age households with no earnings has reached one in five.[3] The risks of ill health, low-quality housing and a poor environment have become concentrated in communities which already face disconnection from opportunities to earn. The American philosopher Michael Walzer presents a model of complex equality in his book *Spheres of Justice*, where disadvantage in one 'sphere' (health or education) should not spill over into other spheres (housing, for example).[4] The UK shows strong signs of a simple, cumulative type of inequality where one sphere reinforces the other.

A MAP OF POLICIES

A just distribution of risk and opportunity requires powerful policy instruments. If stakeholding is about a different form of capitalism, perhaps we should begin by seeking a broader understanding of capital than the simple monetary definition. Successful economies require more than money in the same way that effective welfare states deliver more than cash benefits.

Citizens' Capital

Following the Social Justice Commission's four-tier model of social justice, every citizen must be able to hold a minimum stake or be able to meet their basic needs and maintain a decent level of civic participation. This is the 'baseline' model of egalitarianism. The assumption is that the state should *enable* everyone to meet their basic needs rather than automatically *provide* the resources. Access to primary and secondary education is a right. But there is no universal entitlement to an income (although Child Benefit might be seen as a citizens' income for the parent). For those seeking work but unable to find it there is an entitlement to means-tested income support, but there is no housing guarantee for those who wish to rent (or have no other choice). Instead there is rationing of however much socially-rented housing is available. The waiting list principle is also applied to ration access to health care.

That rationing is inevitable does not mean the level of resources to be rationed is fixed or that the current pattern of priorities is the most just. We might support more affordable housing for rent and the creation of more jobs for lower-skilled workers, for example. We might question why the state offers tax relief for being married, for having a mortgage and for running a company car instead of investing some of the resources in the life-chances of children (regardless of the marital status of their parents), in easing housing costs regardless of housing tenure, and in commuting by public transport.

We might term a package of basic entitlements 'Citizens' Goods' or 'Citizens' Capital' – resources which offer a baseline level of security and the minimum stake every citizen should hold. As well as improving on existing goods, citizens' capital could be extended in at least three ways:

1. For families with children, access to nursery education could become a new entitlement. The 'marriage dowry' proposed by Peter Mandelson and Roger Liddle has been criticised because it continues the state's preference for one form of relationship (as reflected in the Married Couple's Allowance), when the priority ought to be support for parents and children. A 'first born' dowry is suggested instead by Patricia Hewitt,[5] although it is not self-evident that a universal cash sum is a higher priority (or more just) than universal nursery education.

2. For adults, a second chance of education could eventually become an entitlement. This could take the form of access to three years' post-compulsory learning in any sector, funded by a learning loan to be repaid only if future earnings are high enough. State and employer contributions would be required to match individual contributions, and initially support would have to be targeted on those with fewest qualifications.

3. For those already retired and on low incomes a minimum pension guarantee could be established by integrating taxes and benefits. This would introduce a citizens' pension threshold set above the current benefit cut-off, below which no one would fall.

Income to boost the total stock of citizens' capital can come from two sources: taxes or a capital-funded revenue stream. Gerald Holtham proposes such a Community Fund, resourced by the market return on the small stake government could take in publicly quoted companies.[6] This might be one way of giving meaningful economic expression to the revised Clause IV. In the same way that a combination of state and second pensions pools the political risk (of government raiding the National Insurance funds) and the financial risk (of capital market volatility), a Community Fund would help to ease any risk of voter resistance to higher taxes. Holtham suggests that the government's initial stake could be raised by increasing the yield from inheritance tax. (Inheritance is another powerful driver of wealth inequality, where rewards are allocated by the principle of brute luck rather than effort or merit.)[7] In the same way the National Lottery has created a £5 billion industry in the space of a year, handing the Treasury a mini-windfall tax (worth £600 million). As a new tax, it could be added to the government's Community Fund downpayment. The Fund would take time to mature but would offer a faster-growing yield than that obtained from tracking GDP. Revenues could be ear-marked for public education and the NHS.

There may, however, be a strong case for investing these resources in new areas. Citizens' capital should be about more than the here and now. It should, where possible, offer a way of redistributing other resources across people's own lives. If I take ten years out of the labour market to care for a relative with Alzheimer's disease, it is surely unjust to find myself with nothing to show for that investment of time (which may not have been undertaken by anyone else). Such forms of unpaid work should be valued more highly than at present, perhaps through credits towards a second pension in retirement. By crediting-in those who are on parental leave, volunteering, studying or seeking work, a participation income would be developed (as distinct from a citizens' income paid without any contribution conditions).[8] It would introduce a new model of redistribution, allowing periods of time to be taken out of employment in mid-career, for example, perhaps with the option of a later retirement age, and implying a redistribution of resources towards women and families with children. Contributions from the Community Fund might offer one way of valuing unpaid work.

Beyond meeting basic needs, a just society seeks the widest possible distribution of life-chances and opportunities. I focus in the rest of this chapter on access to economic capital (particularly the improved earning prospects which access to training ought to provide) and social capital (including the resources of information and social trust traditionally viewed as 'soft' but increasingly understood as important tools in the distribution of opportunities). A number of specific examples are used to highlight key themes.

In addition to baseline egalitarianism this approach assumes the objective of *endowment egalitarianism*. The correction of market-generated income inequality through cash transfers is one type of 'downstream' redistribution. Intervening earlier, by building capacity to acquire income in the first place is also essential, with one proviso (addressed below): it does not answer the hard question of how to treat earned income from sources which may be classed as 'illegitimate'.

Economic Capital

If companies are to become better stakeholders, institutional changes are required. The Social Chapter offers the prospect of Works Councils and an opening up of information about the company for employees. Various share ownership schemes offer employees a financial stake in company profits. The Australian economic settlement was built over a decade by remaking relations between the state, employers and trade unions. If the task is to infuse intermediate institutions lying between the individual and the state with the practices of stakeholding, it would be odd to exclude trade unions. Here is one area where new thinking is certainly required.

There are other examples of employers committed to adding value in the workplace. Ford's EDAP initiative (Employee Development and Assistance Programme) provides all employees with credits towards a range of learning opportunities from learning a foreign language to a new sport. It is underpinned by the belief that any form of learning is to be valued. The take-up rate is high and rising and Ford's management insists that clear economic benefits result from such an investment strategy. Although Ford is in some ways a model stakeholding company, most people work in much smaller firms which are unable to deliver the scale economies involved in schemes like EDAP. Moreover, some of those firms will fail to provide even the specific work-related training which employees require. We should not lose sight of the urgent question of access to basic economic capital in the form of training entitlements when considering how to improve on existing provision.

Recent evidence suggests that the real British training crisis is one of distribution rather than volume. Those who most need in-work training are least likely to get it.[9] If wider access to learning is one of the key forces behind the distribution of opportunities (and therefore a primary element of any 'endowment egalitarianism' strategy), the training infrastructure must be reformed. The creation of low-paid work is likely to continue and it is likely to be the first rung on the ladder for most of the long-term unemployed. A national minimum wage is a valuable instrument of inclusion, providing a floor under low pay and some help to spring the benefits trap. However, it will not reduce the risk of low pay on its own, since *some* of the problem reflects the low level of skills at this end of the labour market. (This is not to argue that rates of pay neatly reflect skill levels. There is strong evidence that pay rates in the care sector for example are set significantly lower than the value added by care workers.)

A minimum wage will help those with fewer skills gain access to jobs but it will not help them gain access to *better* jobs in the future. Low-paid employment in itself is not unjust, as long as employees are offered chances to move up the earnings ladder. Ultimately, access to effective training is the more powerful instrument, since it offers the chance of greater mobility in the labour market. In theory at least, those employers who are not committed to training as part of a stakeholding model should find themselves 'crowded out' by those who are.

There is one particular problem of inclusion which could be addressed quickly. A sense of reward and progression through work is essential, and particularly so for young adults entering the world of training and work for the first time. Early experiences will colour future expectations. If those on the first rung of the ladder find themselves no better off in Youth Training than from claiming a means-tested benefit like Severe Hardship Allowance, and no better off than their counterparts a decade ago, then we can hardly expect them to show a great deal of motivation. Trainees aged under eighteen will generally have lower levels of productivity than older employees, justifying a lower rate of minimum wage, but there is no economic theory in existence which points to no improvement in productivity in the last ten years – yet training allowances have been frozen for that period. Stakeholding is not only about money but Labour is right to propose job and training guarantees paid at a higher rate for long-term unemployed young adults. For older adults (including the 'hidden' unemployed – lone parents and disabled people who could work with more assistance), various proposals for a British JET (Jobs, Education and Training) programme have been made, mostly offering supply-side assistance. Strategies for creating part-time jobs in the non-tradable sector or alternative demand-side interventions focused on the long-term unemployed are also being proposed.[10]

There is a further distributional factor which influences the pattern of access to new jobs (as well as how unpaid work is distributed): gender. The Equal Opportunities Commission has reported that more than half the complaints it received last year came from men, largely because of failure to get part-time jobs in sectors which have traditionally been viewed as 'female'. We should avoid pinning too much emphasis on this example of unequal access. Nevertheless, it provides us with a glimpse of how opportunities to earn low wages are being distributed in places which traditionally relied on jobs of the full-time, lifetime, male variety. Although the reluctance of former miners and car workers to retrain as care workers or sales assistants is unsurprising, it is more a matter for concern if their sons are waiting for the old jobs to return (or the new jobs in electronics to arrive in sufficient numbers). There is some evidence of a double gender lock, firstly in the minds of young, working-class men reluctant to apply for non-traditional work, and secondly in the minds of employers who associate low-paid, part-time work in the service sector with women (and are therefore less likely to consider men anyway). Reforms to the benefit system to allow part-time benefits to top up part-time earnings may hold part of the answer. But a longer-term readjustment of expectations is required if there is to be genuine competition between the sexes. A stakeholder society cannot sustain old notions of 'men's jobs' and 'women's work'.

Social Capital

That the importance of social capital has gained the attention of centre-left academics and politicians in the UK is largely due to the work of Robert Puttnam.[11] As an organising principle for economies, Francis Fukuyama's recent work on trust has stimulated the debate still further.[12] The result is that the intangible web of resources built through networks of all kinds – information, trust, cooperation, relationships – ends up shaping life-chances in more forceful ways than policy makers have allowed for. Societies, communities and companies which 'think civic' in the broadest sense appear to be better able to cope with change (and sometimes to shape it). Because social capital is imbedded in *inclusive* networks and practices, it is a resource for stakeholding. In this section the focus is on how social capital helps to build capacity for those who currently have the least stake in society.

Evidence from the Social Justice Commission's outreach visits has shown the concentrated disadvantage of many low-income communities. If the macroeconomy does reach a higher and sustainable level of job creation, there are places which will simply fail to share the benefits. They are effectively 'no-go' areas for the labour market, the housing market, and financial services. There is evidence of a market failure in the sense that labour demand and supply are structurally out of step in the long term. But there are other associated failures.

In one community in Manchester local economic decline was so marked that even the Job Centre relocated out of the area. Given the strong probability that friends and neighbours of long-term unemployed residents are also out of work, the failure of information networks is equally damaging. Informal job search methods – by word of mouth – result in up to half of all job changes. Communities which are largely disconnected from *knowledge* about job opportunities are doubly disadvantaged. In the Manchester example a Community Development Trust was established by residents with the support of churches, voluntary sector groups and the city council. It has managed to create a number of community businesses and local jobs, but its most important achievement is its Job Search facility. The Trust understood what the Employment Service and Benefits Agency too rarely recognise – that many people who are long-term unemployed are simply not in a position to hold down a job or training place without additional support.

Long-term unemployment erodes self-confidence and a sense of what employers are looking for. The Trust developed individually-tailored training designed to bring people back to the starting line, whether that required intensive support with literacy and numeracy or more general confidence-building. It has created an on-line catalogue of employers in the Greater Manchester area, eroding the informational barriers facing residents. But perhaps most importantly it has succeeded in persuading employers that the people who have trained with the Trust are equipped for the labour market. The Trust has established the reputational capital which Job Centres lack. Other microeconomic initiatives, including the best-known example of the Wise Group in Glasgow and London, are also committed to the notion of intermediate investments to boost the 'soft' as well as the 'hard' skills required to find jobs and keep them.

An approach dedicated to the goal of reshaping networks of skill and self-confidence has been received with enthusiasm by Labour's Social Security team. One way of giving expression to local social capital could be to enable more community and voluntary sector groups to deliver job search opportunities, as in Australia. The obvious criticism is about churning: if more of the long-term unemployed are getting jobs, more of those they are competing with – the insecurely employed – may lose out. It demonstrates why demand for lower-skilled labour must be boosted if supply-side innovations are to truly add value. Nevertheless, we are left with a hard choice. Unless and until this condition is fulfilled a lower rate of long-term unemployment may result in a higher rate of short-term unemployment. If a just distribution is a priority, that may be a necessary trade-off.

Social capital is not just a means of accessing economic capital. It is primarily a means of connecting people into mainstream opportunities. One of the most impressive examples in the area of learning is Liverpool's Parent–School Partnership programme. The insight of education policy makers was that parents who feel no stake in their own education are in a weak position to support their own children's learning. The city established parent support centres in thirty primary schools, offering creche facilities and various ways to become involved in their children's and their own education. Parent and child literacy programmes have been proven to boost reading skills significantly. Parents speak about their growing self-confidence and status as role models for their children; lone mothers in particular speak about overcoming their sense of isolation and low self-esteem. The distinctive feature is not that adults are returning to education but that parents are seeing themselves as *educators* as well as learners. If Labour wishes to breathe life back into urban policy and boost social capital in a sustainable manner, such initiatives could provide a model for learning-led regeneration. Combined with information technology training, it is one element in the wider task of ensuring that the economic 'have nots' do not become the *information* 'have nots'.

There is growing interest on the left in reviving networks of mutual association and self-help, partly to deliver pensions and insurance cover but also as a community development resource. Social capital may be boosted by such forms of relationship welfare more effectively than traditional forms. But how do we respond to forms of self-help which are not encouraged by government? What counts as 'legitimate' self-help?

On most estates with a high rate of unemployment and poverty it is not difficult to uncover thriving networks of self-help. They are often cash in hand and, for most people on benefit, classed as illicit. Much of the activity that occurs appears to meet the service demands of low-income consumers which the formal market does not, and to boost incomes. There is clearly a dark side to the 'shadow economy' related to drug dealing and violence. But there is also economic activity which enables people to hold a stake in their own communities. This may be the uncomfortable side of stakeholding but we can no longer ignore it. We do not know if there are ways of bringing some of this activity out of the shadows and developing a low-taxed small business sector, but it is surely worth finding out.

Suspicion is the enemy of trust. It is the debilitating result of Britain's long-run growth in inequality. Employers are suspicious of those with a two- or three-year gap in their work record. Taxpayers are encouraged to be suspicious of benefit claimants. Suspicion in low-income communities is common, particularly towards the police and the council. A Stakeholder Society must be a high-trust society. Efforts to tackle distributive injustice must be matched by efforts to share knowledge and enhance participation, whether that is for employees within companies or for citizens who require information on major issues of public policy (financing long-term care and rationing of health services, for example).

CONCLUSION

Stakeholding does not provide us with precise answers to policy questions. It does not tell us how much of the power held by shareholders should be retained, just as the principles of social justice do not tell us whether the top rate of income tax should be 50 per cent, or the bottom rate 10 per cent. But both provide us with a guide to policy. There is in addition a more general question about *how* policy reforms are to be carried out. A new government led by a party which has been out of power for almost two decades will need to draw widely on sources of policy innovation. It will wish to learn from the successes (and mistakes) of other countries, but it should not overlook the local initiatives which have in a small way started to improve life-chances in this country *despite*, not because of, the public policy climate they have worked in. It should also conduct local pilots when the impact of proposals is genuinely unclear.

One of the baseline principles of stakeholding is to think long term. That should encourage the left to think ambitiously. Critics insist that stakeholding is 'not British' because it draws on ideas from Germany and Scandinavia, the Far East and Australia. One measure of how successful a synthesis is achieved will be whether Stakeholding-UK becomes an export commodity.

NOTES

1. Commission on Social Justice, *Social Justice: Strategies for National Renewal* (London: IPPR/Vintage, 1994).
2. Stuart White, *Rethinking the Strategy of Equality: A Critical Appraisal of the Borrie Commission on Social Justice* (IPPR Back to Basics seminar series, 1995).
3. Pam Meadows, *Work-out or Work In? Contributing to the Debate on the Future of Work* (York: Joseph Rowntree Foundation, 1996).
4. Michael Walzer, *Spheres of Justice* (Oxford: Blackwell, 1983).
5. Patricia Hewitt, 'Social Justice in a Global Economy', *Renewal*, Vol. 4, No. 2 (May 1996), pp. 11–20.
6. Gerald Holtham, 'The Common Good', *New Statesman*, 12 June 1995.
7. Stuart White, *Rethinking the Strategy of Equality*.
8. Commission on Social Justice, *Social Justice*.
9. Stephen Machin and David Wilkinson, *Employee Training: Unequal Access and Economic Performance* (Commission on Public Policy and British Business, Issue Paper No. 1, 1995).
10. See for example Gerald Holtham and Ken Mayhew, *Tackling Long-Term Unemployment* (London: IPPR, 1996).
11. Robert D. Puttnam, 'The Prosperous Community: Social Capital and Public Life', *American Prospect*, No. 13, Spring 1994, pp. 35–42.
12. Francis Fukuyama, *Trust: The Social Virtues and the Creation of Prosperity* (London: Hamish Hamilton, 1995).

Part IV

The Stakeholder Company

12 The Stakeholder Corporation
John Kay

MANY KINDS OF COMPANY

The 1985 Companies Act introduced into British law a distinction between a limited company and a PLC. The distinction has little practical significance (a PLC must have a share capital of £50,000 and may, but need not, offer its shares to the public). Many people think, mistakenly, that the distinction between a PLC and other firms corresponds to that between quoted and unquoted companies.

The reason for this distinction is that it already existed in several other European countries. The French regime is perhaps the one to express the objective most clearly. Most large French companies have the status of *Societé Anonyme*, a form of company whose governance structure is the subject of detailed statutory prescription. The artisan who trades under a corporate vehicle mainly in order to limit his personal exposure to the risks of his trade will normally operate through a SARL (*Societé à Responsabilité Limité*). A SARL is subject to minimal regulation, mostly concerned with registration. Germany maintains a similar distinction between the *Aktiengesellschaft* (AG) and the *Gesellschaft mit beschränkter Haftung* (GmbH). As in France, the structure and organisation of the AG, and also of the large GmbH, is the subject of detailed statutory prescription.

British law, by contrast, makes no real distinction between ICI and BT, on the one hand, and the incorporated local plumber or garage, on the other. Indeed, British statute law is virtually silent on how corporations are to be organised. Since the corporation is regarded as a creation of private contract, obligations on companies are mainly there to prevent abuse of the privilege of limited liability, and concern formal matters such as registration and audit. Corporate governance is a matter for the company itself to determine and to describe in its articles of association. The legal system therefore provides, and is intended to provide, no more than a mechanism for the negotiation and enforcement of these contracts. The American position is broadly similar.

These differences are not matters of accident. Nor are they just questions of law, though they are partly a product of the difference between the private law tradition of England, based around the enforcement of contract, and the administrative law general in continental Europe, where behaviour is regulated by public codes. They reflect basic differences in the ways large corporations are perceived in the countries concerned. In continental Europe, and in Japan, the corporation is an institution with personality, character, and aspirations of its own. Its objectives encompass the interests of a wide range of stakeholder groups – investors, employees, suppliers, customers and managers – but cannot be equated with any of them. The corporation is therefore naturally perceived as a social institution, with public responsibilities, and a proper public interest in defining the ways in which it is run and governed. In the Anglo-American environment, the corporation is a private rather than a public body, defined by a set of relationships between principal and agent. Shareholder-owners, too busy and too numerous to undertake the responsibility themselves, hire salaried executives to manage their affairs.

Much of the concern with corporate governance – a concern which is largely Anglo-American – arises from the tension between that Anglo-American model and the practical reality of how large corporations operate everywhere. The organic model of corporate behaviour – which gives to the corporation life independent from its shareholders or stakeholders – describes the actual behaviour of large companies and their managers far better than does the principal-agent perspective, and this is as true in Britain and the United States as it is in Japan.

Yet the near unanimous view of those who criticise the present structure of corporate governance is that reality should be made to conform to the model.[1] The principal-agent structure should be made more effective, through closer shareholder involvement and supervision. All experience suggests that this is not very likely to happen, and would not improve the functioning of corporations if it did. Perhaps the alternative approach – of adapting the model to reality rather than reality to the model – deserves equal consideration.

COMPANIES IN BRITAIN AND THE UNITED STATES

The term governance invites comparison with political structures. Most experience of governance systems is derived from comparative politics. There are obvious resemblances between the system of corporate governance we have and entrenched authoritarian political systems, such as those which prevailed in Eastern Europe before the fall of the Berlin Wall.

The governing elite is self-perpetuating, in the sense that it appoints its own members by reference to its own criteria. The process of succession is normally internal and orderly, but from time to time there are peaceful palace revolutions and occasionally externally induced *coups d'état*. The hostile bid for the corporation parallels the military takeover of a government. There is a nominal process of accountability through election of directors, but in practice it is defunct. There are no genuine alternative candidates and incumbents are re-elected with overwhelming majorities. The formal ritual of the corporation's annual general meeting parallels the meaningless elections which routinely returned Mr Brezhnev and Herr Honecker to power. The flow of information about the affairs of the organisation is managed by incumbents and, except in times of acute crisis, is uniformly favourable and optimistic in tone.

Authoritarian political structures sometimes work well. They offer opportunities to make rapid change and to impose firm leadership which more accountable systems lack. In the hands of honest leaders of determination and vision, they give opportunities for stability and long-term planning which democratic regimes often find difficult to achieve. One might cite the practical governance of Lee Kwan Yew's Singapore, although it is difficult to think of many other examples.

There is an important reason why this authoritarianism is less disastrous for companies than it has generally proved in politics. Many firms operate in competitive markets. So deficiencies in performance are more evident in corporations than in political systems, and internal and external pressures for reform and improvement build up more rapidly. Competition ultimately works for governments as well, and it was, above all, the failure of Eastern European regimes in economic competition that brought about their downfall, although the process took many years. But not all firms operate in competitive markets, and for these, such as privatised utilities, governance issues are still more acute.

For all but the most remarkable of men and women, authoritarian structures are insidiously corrupting. Leaders hang on to power too long, and many prefer to undermine those who might seek to replace them than to develop potential successors. Cults of personality develop, and are supported by sycophantic lieutenants. These are often associated with inappropriate accretion of privileges, and excessive fascination with the trappings of office. Slogans replace analysis, rallies replace debate. There is an alternation between periods of too little change and phases of instability in which there is too much. These features are today as commonplace in business as they were in politics. Authoritarian governance structures have a deservedly bad reputation.

And there is another way in which Anglo-American corporate governance curiously mirrors the Eastern Europe of the past. Both structures claimed legitimacy by reference to what was, in reality, empty rhetoric. Socialist bureaucrats purported to exercise power on behalf of the workers. They argued that their devotion to the interests of the workers was such that it did not matter that the workers were not involved in the process of government in any observable way; indeed, that to so involve them would inhibit the capacity of their leaders to promote their interests. The managers of many large British and American companies similarly defend their positions by claiming to act in the interests of the shareholders. Yet, if shareholder intervention (much of which is in fact ill-informed, frivolous or motivated by factors other than the interests of the company), seriously interferes with managerial prerogatives, it frequently encounters fierce resistance.[2]

WHO 'OWNS' THE COMPANY?

It is often said that a company is owned by its shareholders. It is, however, not very clear what people mean when they say this. At the very least, when we say 'BT is owned by its shareholders', we are using the word 'own' in a slightly different sense to the one we employ when we say 'I own my umbrella'. What do we mean by ownership? What could we mean by the ownership of a company?

Most legal theorists point to the classic exposition of the nature of ownership developed forty years ago by A.M. Honoré. Honoré noted that what we mean by ownership and property has varied across times and cultures.[3] But, he concluded, 'there is indeed a substantial similarity in the position of one who "owns" an umbrella in England, France, Russia, China. In all these countries, the owner of an umbrella may use it, stop others using it, lend it, sell it, or leave it by will. Nowhere may he use it to poke his neighbour in the ribs or knock over his vase.'

Honoré went on to explain that there was no simple definition of ownership: rather there are a series of characteristics of ownership, and if sufficient of these characteristics are identified, it is sensible to describe the resulting relationship as ownership. Honoré lists eleven such characteristics.

There is the right of possession: I may hold my umbrella in my hand, place it in my briefcase or an umbrella stand. There is the right of use – I am free to put it up whenever it is raining – or, for that matter, when it is not. There is a right to manage: I can tell the cloakroom attendant where to put it and if I lend it to you I can insist that you shake off the water before folding it up again, however irksome you may find that requirement.

I have a right to the income from it: if I rent out my umbrella to golf fanatics on wet days, I can keep the revenue. And I have a right to the capital value: if I sell it, I pocket the proceeds. I enjoy a right to security from expropriation: if you steal my umbrella, I can call on the police to pursue you, and if the government nationalises it without compensation, I can appeal to the European Commission on Human Rights. I have the power to transmit my umbrella by sale, gift or bequest to someone else. Then there is no limit of time on these rights. I am, as it were, the freeholder rather than the lessee of my umbrella. I have, Honoré argues, a duty to refrain from harmful use of my umbrella – hence the restriction on my right to poke you in the ribs.

Then there is another particular legal characteristic which distinguishes my property from yours: it can be used to obtain satisfaction of judgment against me – if I fail to pay my debts, my umbrella may be seized by bailiffs. And there is a right of residual control: while I may lend you my umbrella, and you may enjoy all these other attributes of ownership for the period of the loan, when the term of the loan comes to an end all these rights in the umbrella revert to me.

That is what we mean by owning an umbrella. If we apply these tests, do BT shareholders own BT? Begin by noting the difference between the statement 'BT shareholders own their shares in BT' and the statement 'BT shareholders own BT'. There is not much doubt that the first of these is true. They enjoy the rights of possession of their shares – even under CREST, you can still insist on holding a physical share certificate if you want one. And no one will dispute your right to the income from the shares, or to the capital value of your shares, or argue with you if you want to sell them or give them away. You may not use them harmfully – it is difficult to think of how you might – and your creditors may take them over when you fail to meet your obligations.

But none of this means that the owners of BT shares own BT – after all, investors own BT bonds, landlords own BT premises, and lessors own BT equipment, but no one would suggest that BT itself is owned by these investors, landlords or lessors. The claim that BT is owned by its shareholders implies that there is something special about their contract with the company which means that they are owners, not just of that contract, but of the company itself.

Whatever it is that is special, it does not seem to meet Honoré's tests of ownership. Does a BT shareholder have a right of possession? Not at all: if he goes to a telephone exchange, or the BT head office, he will be turned away at the door. Does she have a right of use? Only the same rights to use its services – no more, no less – as any other BT customer. And the right to manage – somewhat tenuously.

What of rights to the income from the sale of BT's services? Up to a point. The actual right is to the dividend declared by BT but, in principle, the shareholders collectively could vote to pay themselves the whole of the income. There again, the employees collectively could demand a larger share of the income, and are more likely to do so. And what of the capital value of BT? Shareholders are entitled to this only in the event of the liquidation of BT, an improbable event and one in which shareholders rarely in fact get anything back.

Shareholders do not have rights against the expropriation of BT assets: this was precisely the issue in the leading case of *Short* vs *Treasury Commissioners*, and the shareholders lost. Shareholders cannot sell, gift or bequest BT assets (as distinct from their BT shares): they have no duty to prevent BT conducting itself in a harmful or abusive manner; and BT assets cannot be used to satisfy their debts.

Of Honoré's eleven tests of ownership, only two (and these rather minor) are unequivocally satisfied by the relationship between BT and its shareholders; three are partly met; six are not fulfilled at all (see Table 12.1). We could make a better case, in fact, for saying that BT is owned by its directors. There is not much doubt that they have rights of possession and management, and the ability to decide on the disposal of its assets: theirs is the duty not to do harm, and with them lies both the right and the duty to take action if BT's assets are expropriated. What they do not have is personal rights to income and capital (although the development of options and incentive plans in certain other firms suggests that there are some directors who think they do).

Table 12.1: Rights of Ownership

Right	Me over my umbrella	BT shareholder over BT	BT shareholder over BT shares	BT directors over BT
Possession	Yes	No	Yes	Yes
Use	Yes	No	Yes	No
Management	Yes	Some	Yes	Yes
Income	Yes	Some	Yes	No
Capital	Yes	Some	Yes	No
Security	Yes	No	Yes	Some
Transmission	Yes	No	Yes	Yes
No limit of term	Yes	Yes	Yes	No
Duty not to do harm	Yes	No	Yes	Yes
Judgement liability	Yes	No	Yes	No
Residual control	Yes	Yes	Yes	Yes

There is, in fact, an even deeper problem here. What is the object whose ownership we are discussing? Take a company like Marks & Spencer. What is it? We can see the stores, and the goods on the shelves. I could buy both of them and yet not have bought Marks & Spencer. The brand name and the reputation are essential parts of the company. I could buy these too. Imagine that Woolworth's bought them, and hung signs outside its stores saying Marks & Spencer. It might do it a bit of good for a few days, but it would not last. You would come out of the shop saying that this was not really Marks & Spencer, and you would be right.

What really *is* Marks & Spencer is a set of systems and routines and a structure of organisation. These systems and routines enable what are, in the main, individually rather unexceptional people to perform, in aggregate, in very exceptional ways. The essence of the company is a structure of internal relationships among the staff, and a collection of external relationships with suppliers. It is not just that these things are the essence of Marks & Spencer. It is these things, rather than the stores or the name, which make Marks & Spencer the extremely profitable company it is.

But if this is true, it is difficult to see how the concept of ownership – analogous to ownership of an umbrella – could be relevant. What could we mean by the ownership of a set of routines, or a structure of relationships? You can benefit from the returns they generate, but that is not at all the same as owning them. If anyone did own these things, it is more likely to be the employees than the shareholders. But they do not really own them either. We are talking about things to which the concept of ownership simply does not apply, like friendship, or conservatism, or tennis. That seems at first sight disconcerting, but only because we are used to thinking in different terms. There are plenty of functioning entities that do not appear to be owned by anybody (not just friendship, conservatism or tennis), like London, the River Thames or Oxford University.

The obvious conclusion, then, is that no one owns or could own BT or Marks & Spencer. Many individuals and groups have rights and obligations around these companies – customers, shareholders, lenders, employees, directors – but none of these claims can plausibly be described as ownership. And so long as we all understand the nature of these claims, that raises no particular problems. It should hardly need to be said that the differences between my umbrella and the modern corporation are so wide-ranging that the legal and conceptual apparatus we use to deal with one is not very likely to be applicable to the other, and that the moral outrage I feel when you violate my rights over my umbrella is not relevant to my feelings about corporate governance. But this mistaken analogy has wide-ranging effects.

CORPORATE PERSONALITY AND CORPORATE BEHAVIOUR

It is easy to regard the issue of whether a corporation does or does not have a personality distinct from those of the agents who contract with it as a question best left to legal theory and a certain kind of abstruse continental European philosophy. Actually, it is central to an understanding of the competitive advantage of firms.

Objectives and styles of operation are likely to behave differently, in relation to issues such as:

- willingness to undertake industry-specific, as distinct from firm-specific, training;
- the provision of security and continuity of employment for their workers;
- the degree to which the firm should exploit its market power;
- readiness to undertake investment or development activities if, because of imperfect information, such investment or development is not expected to be reflected fully in share prices.

What then is the purpose of the corporate manager? Is it to build a good business, judged against many and imperfectly specified criteria, or is it to maximise shareholder value?

A persuasive account of the first approach is given by Solomons.[4] Rejecting any maximisation framework, he argues that business is, and ought to be, a practice[5] or a profession, and cites a medical analogy. We expect that a doctor's aspiration is to be a good doctor, not to maximise his income, and assume that a good doctor will at least weigh the interests of his patients against his own, if not put them ahead. The curious commercial implication of this is that a doctor whose primary motivation was to increase his income would not be perceived as a good doctor and would be unlikely to succeed even in maximising his income. Doctors who do not aim to maximise revenues may expect to earn more than those who do.

A superficial interpretation of this observation is to conclude that there is, in fact, no conflict between the commercial interests of the doctor and the interests of the patients, and indeed statements of this kind ('good business is profitable business') are frequently made. But, as a generalisation, this is obviously false. Doctors know very well that commercial concerns and patient care do not necessarily coincide, and this is a matter of concern to every conscientious doctor.

The underlying paradox is this. Robert Maxwell or Ivan Boesky, on qualifying as doctors, might correctly conclude that their income maximising strategy was to give their patients honest advice, even if this sometimes deprived them of revenues. The problem they would face is that there is no operational mechanism by which they can commit themselves to follow this course. The medical profession does try to provide such mechanisms – doctors may subscribe to the Hippocratic Oath and/or are supervised by the General Medical Council. But these come into play only in the most egregious cases. In the end, the uncertainties surrounding medical care, and the fact that the adjudicator can never have exactly the same information as the practitioner had on the day, mean that it is impossible to enforce disinterested behaviour by appeal to an external agency.

It follows that the good doctor, and the successful doctor, is the one who puts the interests of his patients first because that is his genuine concern rather than the one who puts his patients first because he believes that such behaviour is a good commercial strategy. And it is easy to see why: in dealing with the latter doctor, we can never be confident that this is not an occasion when he has decided that putting patients first is no longer the best commercial strategy.[6] The man who believes that honesty is the best policy is not an honest man, and it is the honest man, not the man who believes that honesty is the best policy, whom we trust.

The commercial analogy follows directly. When we trade with Marks & Spencer, we expect fair dealing and value for money. To the extent that we think about it all at all, our expectations are not based on beliefs about the policies that the Board of this company has adopted on behalf of their shareholders. We attach little, if any, weight to the commitments to customers or trading charters which many less well regarded companies display in their stores. We have these expectations of Marks & Spencer because that is the kind of company it is. It is a style of behaviour, not a policy adopted to maximise profits. And because of that, it would be difficult to implement a policy to change it. If the Board of Marks & Spencer was to decide that now was an opportune moment to cash in on the company's long-established reputation, it is very doubtful whether it could actually bring this outcome about. Key employees would leave; the probable result, in practice, is that the organisation would reject the new management style and those who sought to introduce it, and revert to its traditional modes of behaviour.

The commercial importance of corporate personality is very obvious in trust relationships, but not confined to them. When flight attendants go to British Airways' training school they are not told, as the agency model would predict, 'I am here to convey to you the shareholders' instructions that you should smile at the passengers.' They hear something on the lines of, 'British Airways can only be a successful airline through repeat business from satisfied customers, and by being a successful airline we will generate opportunities for investors, employees and passengers alike.' It is possible that the exercise is entirely cynical and that the first is the true message, but I doubt it. It is unlikely that the cynical approach would have more than a temporary effect on behaviour.

Commercial life necessitates many incomplete and implicit contracts, and we make such contracts with firms as employees, as customers, and as suppliers. If we identify ownership ultimately with Honoré's last criterion – the ability to determine the unresolved terms of such contracts – then shareholder ownership would raise subtle issues. If the governance structure of the firm allowed, or indeed required, all such incomplete terms to be resolved in favour of the shareholders, we would be reluctant to make such contracts, or indeed to do business with the firm at all.

It follows that shareholder-owned agency firms will be at a competitive disadvantage in areas where such implicit contracts are important. It is not an accident that the international competitive successes of Japanese and German companies are focused on precisely those areas of business which have these characteristics – such as the development of trust relationships with suppliers that secure reliable component quality, just-in-time inventory management, and flexible response to changing market conditions; trust relationships based on close consultation with, and consideration of, all relevant stakeholders. The achievements of British and American companies, in contrast, are more often based on factors, such as reputation, innovation, and brands, which flourish in their different corporate environments.[7]

THE TRUSTEESHIP MODEL OF CORPORATE GOVERNANCE

Thus there is an alternative to the shareholder-agency model of the corporation. It recognises the existence of corporate personality, and its economic and commercial importance. It accepts that the large public corporation is a social institution, not the creation of private contract. But if senior management are not the agents of the shareholders, what are they?

There is a well-established structure in English law to govern the behaviour of individuals or groups who control and manage assets they do not beneficially own; it is the concept of trusteeship.[8] Grossman and Hart[9] have described the central role of what they call the owner as being the determination of the residual terms of incomplete contracts. What they define is exactly the historic function of the trustee. The settler of property, unable to anticipate all the contingencies which might arise after his death, would appoint an honest man to determine what should be done in these circumstances. The concept is generalised to cover the governance of other institutions, such as Oxford University or the National Gallery.[10]

The notion that boards of directors are the trustees of the tangible and intangible assets of the corporation, rather than the agents of the shareholders, is one which the executives of most German and Japanese companies, and of many British firms, would immediately recognise. The duty of the trustee is to preserve and enhance the value of the assets under his control, and to balance fairly the various claims to the returns which these assets generate. The trusteeship model therefore differs from the agency model in two fundamental ways.

The responsibility of the trustees is to sustain the corporation's assets. This differs from the value of the corporation's shares. The difference comes not only because the stock market may value these assets incorrectly. It also arises because the assets of the corporation, for these purposes, include the skills of its employees, the expectations of customers and suppliers, and the company's reputation in the community.[11] The objective of managers as trustees therefore relate to the broader purposes of the corporation, and not simply to the financial interests of shareholders. Some British companies have seen it as entirely appropriate, in pursuit of shareholder value, to dispose entirely of an existing collection of businesses and buy a new one. This course would seem inconceivable to a Japanese manager. A new vice-chancellor of Oxford University, or trustee of the National Gallery, who suggested that the University should become an international language school or that the Trafalgar Square site would make an excellent shop and restaurant complex, would be seen as having fundamentally misunderstood the nature of his responsibilities.

The concept of corporate personality acknowledges, as the principal-agent model cannot, the path-dependent nature of the behaviour of companies. Businesses are defined by a nexus of long established trust relationships; the principal -agent model sees only a group of people who find it expedient every morning to renew their contracts with each other. Many of the ludicrous business books on the management of change see the Markovian nature of business evolution as a problem; yet for most successful companies, their history is a principal asset rather than a liability.

Thus the trusteeship model demands, as the agency model does not, the evolutionary development of the corporation around its core skills and activities because it is these skills and activities, rather than a set of financial claims, which are the essence of the company. This does not preclude diversification or divestment, but it restricts operations to areas that relate in an obvious way to the firm's distinctive capabilities. Deal making, even if profitable, becomes again a function of financial markets rather than corporate management.

The second fundamental difference between the agency model and the trusteeship model is that while the agency model expects the manager to attach priority to the current shareholder interest, the trustee has to balance the conflicting interests of current stakeholders and additionally to weigh the interests of present and future stakeholders. Thus future customers and employees, and the future interests of current suppliers, also come into account. These two distinct differences have the joint effect of materially shifting the balance of considerations in management towards long-term development of the capabilities of the business.

PROPOSALS FOR REFORM

Thus we can identify the delicate balancing of criteria which has to be achieved in a new model of corporate governance. It should give recognition and content to the trusteeship model which acknowledges corporate personality. It should allow managers to pursue multiple objectives, yet hold them responsible for their performance. It should encourage cohesion within an executive team, but be sufficiently open to outside influence to discourage introversion and ensure that success is rewarded and failure penalised. That basic objective of 'managerial freedom with accountability' is well set out in the Cadbury Report.

It is important to recognise that the quest for perfection in systems of corporate governance is a hopeless one. We have emphasised the comparison between political systems and corporate governance. It has been wisely, and memorably, said that democracy is the worst form of government ever invented, except for every other form of government invented.

The widely accepted consensus among those who have written about corporate governance in the last decade[12] is that the key requirement is to give content to the existing structure of notional accountability to shareholders. I am sceptical about this prescription. I doubt whether shareholders have either incentive or capacity to provide such monitoring. I doubt whether shareholder priority is an appropriate rule for the large corporation in any event. And I am not persuaded that the main lines of the proposed remedy – an enhanced role for non-executive directors, more extensive involvement of shareholders in major decisions, and the provision of fuller information about corporate affairs – represent a suitable monitoring mechanism. It is precisely the form of relationship which government, as controlling shareholder, traditionally enjoyed with nationalised industries, and its effect was to undermine management responsibility for corporate performance without providing stimulus to the effectiveness of corporations.

Moreover, there are dangers in an attempt to breathe artificial life into a model of accountability that has little practical reality. In the stultified authoritarian regimes of Eastern Europe, the rhetoric of popular democracy was used to provide spurious legitimacy for self-interested behaviour. The creation of supposedly independent remuneration committees by large companies in Britain and the United States has had precisely the same effect. The independence is generally a sham, and the institution has proved to be a mechanism not for restraining excess but for justifying it.

I therefore propose a new Companies Act. The central purpose of that Act would be to establish a distinction between the a PLC – the social institution with corporate personality – and the owner-managed limited company. The principal criterion would be that any firm above a certain size or with a diffuse shareholding structure would be required to register as PLC; a similar obligation might apply to companies in a particular area of activity (schools, water supply) or to very large private firms even if they had few shareholders (Barings, Littlewoods).[13]

What might such a stakeholder statute prescribe? A legal statement of corporate objects and responsibilities might be framed on the following lines:

A director of a PLC shall at all times act in the manner he considers in the exercise of his business judgement best fitted to advance the interests of the company. The interests of the company include:

- the payment of returns to shareholders and investors sufficient to remunerate past investment and encourage future investment in the company;
- the development of the skills and capabilities of employees and suppliers of the company;
- the achievement of stability and security in the company's employment and trading relationships;
- the provision of goods and services of good quality to the company's customers at fair prices; and
- the enhancement of the company's reputation for high standards of business conduct.

It is not clear that such a proposition does any more than put into statute law the present uncertain common law. It may be that uncertainty which accounts for the two contradictory reactions which the proposition engenders – sometimes even from the same people: that a stakeholder statute would bring about the end of capitalism as we know it, or that it would barely change the status quo. Both these statements cannot be true, and the reality is of course somewhere in between; there would be an effect on the behaviour, but much of the effect could simply to be legitimise what effective companies already in practice do.

The corporate objects clause described above is, intentionally, a relatively narrow one. It does not suggest that the object of companies is to maximise the public interest, whatever that means. I do not think companies have either the authority or the ability to pursue that objective. I want only to say that the proper responsibility of company directors is to build a good and successful business, one that earns good returns for its investors, has a capable and motivated workforce, enjoys a fine reputation with its customers and the community, and is regarded by its suppliers as a good, if tough, firm to do business with.

But a new companies act should have a number of other features.

- It should prescribe a governance framework for a PLC. A PLC should be required to have a board, with an independent chairman and a number (at least three) of independent directors. The definition of independence is primarily a financial one – an individual is independent if neither he nor his employer has received, or expects to receive, 'substantial'[14] remuneration from the company on whose board he sits (in salary or dividends).

- The Act should define the role and functions of the CEO (who should not also be the chairman), and possibly a small number of other senior officers of a PLC, and impose stringent requirements on the process by which they are selected. The independent directors would take the lead in this process, but they would be required to appoint a selection committee with other independent members drawn from other businesses and professional advisers (that is, not just the independent directors themselves), and would be obliged to consult employees, investors and suppliers and any relevant regulatory agencies. They would be expected to commission a report on the company's strategy and performance.

- The appointment of a CEO by this process should be for a fixed term of four years;[15] salary and any bonuses should be determined at the beginning of that period; the contract should expire after that period (it might, in exceptional circumstances, be extended) with a fixed and modest termination payment if it is not renewed; and, in any event, only one renewal of the contract of any individual should be permitted.[16]

- The power of nomination of directors – executive or independent – should rest with the independent directors, but they should be obliged to consult stakeholders before appointing new independent directors. We do not, it will be noted, propose a supervisory board on German lines, since supervision on a month by month basis is inconsistent with the objective of freedom with accountability.

Our scheme as a whole has one dominant objective: to give executive management the greatest possible freedom to develop the business over a period of years in whatever way they think fit, while holding them rigorously responsible to all the parties involved in the business for their performance in the long run.

Under these measures hostile takeover becomes virtually impossible in practice, since ownership of a majority of shares confers no right to appoint executive management. However, the four-yearly review provides a fixed and clear opportunity for those with alternative proposals for the management and direction of a company to put these forward, and such proposals could (but need not) be coupled with an offer to the firm's shareholders.

A key consequence is a fundamental change in the relationship between chief executive and company. Provided the review is real, the creation of responsibility to a constituency should have the same effect on the style and behaviour of the chief executives of large corporations as the introduction of free elections has on the style and behaviour of politicians. As for politicians, the best may not need such a review; but most do. The one-renewal rule is modelled on the one instituted for presidents of the United States. Like Lady Thatcher, Lord King and Lord Weinstock would have left office with reputations immeasurably higher if they had been confined to an eight-year term; the number of CEOs for whom more than eight years is too long outnumbers considerably the number for whom it is too short.

A further advantage of such a limitation of term would be that it would establish a pool of able and experienced candidates for the role of company chairman. There may be corporations that would fail to benefit from the services of such a person, but not many. The political analogy is instructive here too: the political leaders who thought it necessary to combine the roles of prime minister and head of state were Hitler and Idi Amin, not Winston Churchill or Ludwig Erhard.

All this is not very different from what many well-managed companies currently do – or what others would like to do. It would, nevertheless, have a profound effect on corporate behaviour. And it would also have a profound effect on our recommendations for the newly marketised economies of Eastern Europe.

NOTES

1. This is as true of those who are fundamentally critical of current arrangements (for example, W. Hutton, *The State We're In*, London: Jonathan Cape, 1994) as of those who broadly support them (Cadbury Committee Report, *Report of the Cadbury Committee on the Financial Aspect of Corporate Governance*, London: Gee, 1992); and is equally reflected in intermediate positions such as J. Charkham, *Keeping Good Company*, (Oxford: Oxford University Press, 1994), or A. Sykes, 'Proposal for a Reformed System of Corporate Governance to Achieve Internationally Competitive Long-Term Performance', in N. Dimsdale and M. Prevezer (eds), *Capital Markets and Corporate Governance,* (Oxford: Clarendon Press, 1994).

2. The hostility of General Motors' management in the 1980s to expressions of view by Ross Perot and the Californian Public Employees Retirement Scheme, the company's largest shareholders, illustrates the phenomenon very clearly. Note equally, however, that shareholder activism is mostly concerned with political rather than corporate issues.

3. A. Honoré, 'Ownership', in A.G. Guest (ed.), *Oxford Essays in Jurisprudence* (Oxford: Oxford University Press, 1961), pp. 107–47.

4. R.C. Solomons, *Ethics and Excellence* (New York: Oxford University Press, 1993).

5. A practice, in modern ethics, is 'Any coherent and complex form of socially established co-operative human activity through which goods internal to that form of activity are realised in the course of trying to achieve those standards of excellence which are appropriate to that form of activity.' A. MacIntyre, *After Virtue* (London: Duckworth, 1981). A Japanese businessman would immediately recognise the concept; Kohlberg Kravis Roberts, the ultimate purchasers of RJR Nabisco, would not. And, a reader asks, would McKinsey?

6. Paradoxes of this kind are familiar in game theory. The current version is explored in R. Franch, *Passions, After Reason* (1988), and A. Blinder, *Profit Maximisation and International Competition* (Amex Essay Prize Volume, Oxford: Oxford University Press, 1991).

7. J. Kay, *Foundations of Corporate Success* (Oxford: Oxford University Press, 1993); and J. Kay, *The Foundations of National Competitive Advantage*, Fifth ESRC Annual Lecture, ESRC, London, 1994.

8. G. Goyder (*The Just Enterprise,* London: Deutsch, 1987) explains this concept and describes some legal history.

9. S. Grossman and O. Hart, 'The Costs and Benefits of Ownership: A Theory of Vertical and Lateral Integration', *Journal of Political Economy*, 94 (August 1986), pp. 691–719.

10. The River Thames too had its conservators, whose functions have since been absorbed into the newly created regulatory agencies.

11. See the definition of a practice at note 5 above.

12. See, for example, R. Monks and N. Minow, *Power and Accountability* (London: HarperCollins, 1991); and M. Bishop, 'A Survey of Corporate Governance', *The Economist*, 1994; also Charkham and the Greenbury Report (see note 1).

13. This creates an issue, or problem, of transition. Broadly, I envisage that a company must convert to PLC once it achieves a certain size or, more usually,

its ownership becomes dispersed. This is a Rubicon: once the bridge is crossed, there is no going back.

14. Judged by generous contemporary standards.

15. For a similar proposal, although framed in the shareholder priority framework, see M. Lipton and S. Rosenblum, 'A New System of Corporate Governance: the Quinquennial Election of Directors', *University of Chicago Law Review*, 58/1 (Winter, 1991).

16. Few corporate strategies cannot be expected to produce some result within four years. Experience with political systems suggests that a seven-year term is too long (France) and a three-year term too short (Australia, New Zealand). There is a widespread consensus on four to five years.

13 Company Law and Stakeholder Governance

John Parkinson

The idea that companies should act in the interests of all their stakeholders, and not just their shareholders, is central to the wider notion of a stakeholder economy, and wider still, of a stakeholder society. Indeed, it was in theories about corporate governance and the objectives that the managers of large businesses should pursue that the language of stakeholding originated in the 1960s. Since that time a number of different varieties of stakeholder theory, with differing policy prescriptions, have been developed. This chapter will not attempt to describe those theories, but instead will defend one particular version of the stakeholder concept as it applies to the public company and will consider how corporate governance arrangements and company law might be altered to accommodate it.

It is necessary first to say more precisely what 'corporate governance' means. The term 'governance' is often used rather loosely to refer to anything to do with the running of companies, but its more technical meaning relates to the system of control over the company's directors and managers. Governance is not therefore the process of management, either in the sense of day-to-day decision making or even of strategic planning. Rather it is the system through which those involved in the company's management are held accountable for their performance, with the aim of ensuring that they adhere to the company's proper objectives. Two important questions arise in relation to this accountability. First, by what standards should management performance be judged? Put more broadly, if the purpose of governance is to secure compliance with corporate objectives, we need first to decide what those objectives should be. The answer to this question lies at the centre of the debate about stakeholding and the company. Second, what governance mechanisms should be used? The answer here depends on the answer to the first question, since not all governance arrangements are likely to be equally effective in achieving compliance with differently defined corporate goals.

This chapter will look first at the objectives that directors are currently required to fulfil and the system of governance as it stands at the moment. After that it will examine the alternative 'stakeholder' concept of the company and how effect might be given to it.

142

CURRENT OBJECTIVES OF GOVERNANCE

The objectives that companies are legally required to pursue are determined by the duties imposed on directors by company law. The present position is that a company's directors are under an obligation to operate the business in the interests of 'the company as a whole'. This expression has been interpreted by the courts to mean the interests of the shareholders, however, and implicit in companies' legislation in general and in the body of case law is the idea that companies exist in order to benefit their members – the shareholders. The supremacy of shareholder interests in the legal conception of the company is most clearly revealed in those aspects of directors' duties (echoed by the City Takeover Code) that prohibit the board from taking certain forms of action to preserve the company's independence in the face of a takeover bid. These are designed to ensure that the shareholders alone shall determine the outcome of a bid, and prevent management from frustrating an offer, whether in order to protect their own position or the interests of other groups who are likely to be affected, such as the employees or suppliers. It is true that as well as having an obligation to act in the interests of the shareholders, section 309 of the Companies Act 1985 imposes on directors a duty to 'have regard' to the interests of the employees. The precise significance of this provision is uncertain, however. The more ambitious reading suggests that it allows the directors to balance the interests of shareholders and employees, with the implication that if they consider it appropriate the directors are permitted to subordinate the interests of the shareholders to those of the employees, for example by delaying closure of an unprofitable plant. But it has also been argued that the section merely requires the directors to consider the impact of a proposed policy on the employees: while the directors must do their best to safeguard the employees' position, it does not alter the basic principle that the shareholders' interests come first.

Although giving effect to a stakeholder model of the company would require amendment of directors' duties and a number of associated technical rules, the practical importance of the legal position should not be exaggerated. Even if the duty of the directors is to act in the interests of the shareholders alone, these interests are construed as long-term interests, and in order to benefit the shareholders in the long term companies will need to cultivate positive relationships with their employees, customers, suppliers and others. Further, it is in any event extremely difficult to mount a legal attack on the exercise of management discretion other than in cases in which the directors have obtained an improper personal benefit. The duty to act in the interests of the company is a subjective one, that is, the court will not ask whether a course of conduct *was* in the interests of the company, but whether the directors honestly believed it to be so. Except in the unlikely event that there is evidence that the directors did not consider that what they were doing would benefit the shareholders, or their behaviour is completely irrational, there will, therefore, be no basis for judicial intervention. This means that a management disposed to safeguard the interests of non-shareholder groups will rarely have much to fear from the courts.

CURRENT MECHANISMS OF GOVERNANCE

As to the current mechanisms of corporate governance, the cornerstone of the system is the ability of the shareholders by majority vote to remove the directors from office, echoing the primacy afforded to the shareholders in the way the duties of the directors are formulated. The reality, however, is very different from the theory. In most public companies the shareholders' general meeting is an ineffective means of securing managerial accountability. When a company has thousands of shareholders, each with a very small percentage of the votes, there is likely to be little incentive on the part of the shareholders to intervene or even to become knowledgeable about the company's affairs. This, together with the difficulties of coordinating a campaign against the directors, means that the general meeting as an instrument of control is largely neutralised. Much is said today about the ability and willingness of institutional investors to put pressure on managers of poorly performing companies. The institutions – pension funds, insurance companies, unit trusts and investment trusts – now hold over 70 per cent of the shares in UK listed companies, and their research capabilities and the comparative ease with which a relatively small number of fund managers can cooperate in efforts to influence management suggest that they could perform a significant governance role. The evidence so far, however, indicates that while there is some institutional activity, it does not amount to a transformation of the traditional picture of shareholder non-involvement. With institutions rarely holding more than 5 per cent of the shares in a given company they are likely in many situations to regard the costs of intervention as exceeding the benefits, particularly against the background of an investment culture that favours stock market speculation rather than long-term commitment. Rather than attempt to use their voting power to remove recalcitrant managements, the institutions have preferred to await a takeover bid and then disinvest.

There are reasons to be sceptical about the effectiveness of another component of the current governance system, namely non-executive directors. Non-executives are normally part-timers who do not hold any managerial position in the company, such as finance or sales director. Their function is to provide advice and a degree of independent supervision over management. The latter responsibility has recently taken on greater prominence as a result of the recommendations of the Cadbury Committee, which require listed companies, for example, to establish audit committees made up exclusively of non-executive directors. Genuinely independent non-executives, whether as members of a unitary board or of a separate supervisory board, are undoubtedly capable of playing a very important role in governance. They could, for instance, take on the responsibility of appointing and removing the executive members of the board, thus filling the gap resulting from the ineffectiveness of the general meeting and preventing management from being self-selecting, as is currently the case. But while the Cadbury Report requires non-executives to be independent in the sense of not being members of the current management team or having a business connection with the company, the truth of the matter remains that non-executives are appointed by management. Supervisors who owe their positions to those whom they supervise cannot be expected to perform their functions effectively, and until the selection and appointment of non-executives is taken out of the hands of management their contribution to governance will remain modest.

Internal governance mechanisms, by means of shareholder voting and the appointment of non-executive directors, provide, then, only weak sources of discipline over management. To compensate, the UK corporate economy relies on a form of external governance, namely the hostile takeover bid. The theory is as follows. If a company is being operated below its true potential, shareholders, dissatisfied with the returns they are obtaining, will sell their shares. If they divest in significant numbers the price of the company's shares will fall. Observers of the market will conclude that the company's shares are trading at a discount because of the inadequacies of its current managers. This acts as a signal to one or more rival management teams who will respond by mounting a bid to buy the company's shares from their existing owners with a view to unlocking the profitability that the current management is failing to extract. Having obtained control of the company the successful bidder will replace the board with its own appointees and make the necessary changes to improve efficiency. The takeover market, or the 'market for corporate control' as it is known, is thus regarded as having benign effects, in that control of productive assets is transferred to those who can most efficiently manage them. And what is at least as important, the *threat* of takeover acts as a powerful discipline over directors, since in order to keep their jobs they must keep share prices high, and this means that they are obliged to run the company at maximum efficiency.

There are a number of problems with this theoretical account of the operation of the market for corporate control. For one thing, while some takeovers are undoubtedly a success, many do not bring about an improvement in performance. Though they make the shareholders who have sold out better off, since they are able to dispose of their shares to the bidder at a premium above the pre-bid market price, overall the evidence suggests that completed takeovers do not make a positive contribution to the economy. Second, the effectiveness of the takeover threat is exaggerated. Takeovers tend to be rather random occurrences, influenced by the economic cycle, and with many factors other than managerial efficiency – such as the desire to reduce competition or gain access to the target's markets – determining whether a bid is made. As a result poorly performing companies are not conspicuously more likely to be victims than those that are doing well, and management's fear of the consequences of failure to do well is likely to be correspondingly reduced.

So the effectiveness of takeovers as a mechanism for reallocating control of assets to those who can operate them most efficiently and for providing a source of discipline over management is suspect. It is also argued that an active takeover market has damaging side-effects. One of the main areas of concern is short-termism, that is, the neglect of investment in activities such as research and development and training, which entail short-term costs and which bring benefits only in the longer term, in order to boost current profits. It is hard to argue that British industry does not suffer from this condition, but whether the takeover market is implicated remains controversial. While other factors may be involved as well, it is not, however, implausible that the market for control creates an obsession with share price on the part of managers, which in turn pressures them to maintain a high level of dividends, draining the company of funds that might otherwise be available for investment. In the long term, of course, the shareholders and the economy as a whole are the losers.

So far the effectiveness of the existing modes of corporate governance has been examined in relation to the traditional understanding of the objective of companies – to maximise profits. It has been suggested that both internal and external forms of governance suffer from serious weaknesses in ensuring that managements comply with this goal. If we wanted to introduce a stakeholder dimension into corporate decision making it is likely that current governance arrangements would need to be reformed for that reason too. Certainly, an active takeover market does not present ideal conditions for the cultivation of long-term relationships between a company and its stakeholders, since the give-and-take that these imply involves short-term costs that pressure from the market tends to squeeze out, and where companies are liable to experience unpredictable changes in control there is an uncertainty about the future that militates against the formation of stable relationships. Nor is it obvious that increased participation in governance by institutional investors as an alternative to the market would be significantly more amenable to the stakeholder approach, given the institutions' apparent hunger for dividends. So what does the stakeholder concept of the company entail, and how might it be brought into effect?

THE STAKEHOLDER COMPANY

Some of the confusion that surrounds the stakeholder concept of the company can be dispelled if two strands that have featured in the recent debate are separated out. The first of these strands relates to the social responsibility of companies and the second to the virtues of long-term relationships. They will be taken in turn.

Social Responsibility

The law limits the ability of businesses to maximise their profits at the expense of others. Elaborate regulatory provisions are designed to ensure, for example, that consumers are not misled, that the health and safety of employees is not endangered, and that excessive damage to the natural environment is avoided. It may be noted that these restrictions often support, rather than detract from, the rationale that justifies profit maximisation, namely that it is conducive to productive and allocative efficiency. The purpose of many controls is accordingly to correct for market failures (uncompetitive market structure, inadequate information, and externalities). Others reflect society's judgement that for reasons of morality or social policy certain interests should not be overridden in the pursuit of private profit. It is often argued that compliance with legal constraints of this kind exhausts the obligation of companies to respect the interests of those affected by their activities: if society considers that the protection afforded is inadequate, it is easy enough to tighten the law. The slogan is that companies should adopt a policy of 'profit maximisation within the law', that is, they should strive to maximise profits subject to a set of externally imposed constraints. The belief that the law can achieve any desired modification of behaviour is, however, an ingenuous one. The problems include the inevitable delay in the legal response to new forms of objectionable conduct, inadequacies in the information available to standard setters and problems over arriving at a consensus in the standard-setting process, and the unsuitability of general rules as a means of solving context-specific problems. These limitations in the techniques of external regulation leave a gap that can and should be narrowed by a policy of 'self-regulation', that is, the acceptance of a sense of responsibility on the part of managers, a willingness to take account of the interests of others in formulating company policies. While management attitudes are of central importance here, there are also measures that society can take to promote greater responsibility. Requiring companies to disclose more information about the environmental consequences of their activities, for instance, or the level of consumer complaints, or prosecutions for employee health and safety offences, can play a significant part in raising standards of behaviour.

The adoption by companies of constraints on their behaviour additional to those imposed by law entails that companies should sometimes be prepared to sacrifice profits, and not only in the short run. While responsibility will often be conducive to increased profitability in the long term (for example, a company with a reputation for supplying faulty goods is unlikely to prosper), it is not true that the shareholders' interest in maximum profits and the interests of other affected groups entirely coincide. In relation to the environment, for instance, the idea that a company will incur the necessary expenditures to avoid environmental damage since it will otherwise be penalised in the various markets in which it is engaged, assumes perfect knowledge and willingness to act on it on the part of consumers and others. Limited understanding of the company's environmental impact by market participants and relative indifference towards it mean that damaging conduct will to an extent remain profitable. While responsible behaviour will sometimes entail reduced returns to shareholders, however, it should be emphasised that what is involved is the adoption of constraints on profit-seeking, not the replacement of profit-seeking with multiple, co-equal goals. There will always be room for debate about what responsibility requires in any particular circumstances, but a willingness to comply with standards of fair dealing and to avoid causing harm is not the same thing as an open-ended commitment to maximising the welfare of affected groups.

The word 'stakeholder' has not been used in this discussion of corporate responsibility. This is deliberate. The language of stakeholding in reference to corporate responsibility, while common, tends to blur the point just made, and allows the opponents of increased responsibility to invoke the spectre of rational corporate policy formation becoming impossible in the face of irreconcilable conflicts of interest. The language of stakeholding is also unnecessarily restrictive when applied to issues of ethical and social responsibility. Companies should have regard to the impact of their conduct on all the groups they affect. The employment of child labour by one of a company's overseas suppliers, for example, is an issue about which the company has a moral responsibility to act, but a supplier's employees cannot comfortably be described as stakeholders, or if they can, the term is so wide as to be deprived of useful meaning. So while advocates of the stakeholder approach and of increased corporate social responsibility are often arguing for the same thing, there are advantages in using stakeholder terminology with greater precision.

Cooperative Relationships

Turning then to the second strand in the stakeholder debate, it is suggested that it is helpful to confine the term 'stakeholder' to those who enter long-term cooperative relationships with the company. These relationships are to the mutual advantage of the parties, and have the characteristic that the entirety of the terms of the relationship cannot be readily reduced to a legally enforceable contract. Instead the creation and maintenance of the relationship depends on trust, and its existence generates legitimate expectations that each side will seek to advance the interests of the other.

On this basis employees qualify as stakeholders. Employees make investments in their employer by acquiring skills and showing commitment and adaptability. The benefits to the company from these investments are obvious, but they are likely to be forthcoming only if the employee can expect to be treated fairly in terms of pay and conditions, and above all, can look forward to a level of job security. Where employees are treated as partners in the firm and not just dispensable factors of production they are likely to cooperate with the introduction of new technology and working methods rather than fight them. Well-motivated employees are liable to respond constructively and innovatively to the challenges they face in carrying out their duties. One justification for viewing employees as stakeholders is therefore that it will lead to the more efficient functioning of enterprises. There are also ethical and social-policy justifications. Stable, fairly remunerated employment is a crucial aspect of individual well-being and as such there is a moral case for giving a high priority within the organisation to providing it. Similarly the availability of secure and properly paid jobs has significant implications for social stability. There is an important role here for macroeconomic policy and state-sponsored employment creation and preservation measures, but it is also legitimate for society to expect company decision making to reflect the public interest in the provision of appropriate employment conditions. In terms of implementation, management attitudes have an important role to play in ensuring that the employees' expectations as stakeholders in the organisation are fulfilled. It is also necessary that their status as stakeholders should be consolidated with bargaining and consultation rights.

Customers and suppliers may also be stakeholders in the company, but not necessarily so. It is not customers and suppliers as generalised groups who are stakeholders, but individual members of these groups. In many situations, for example the supply of standardised materials or goods for which the company has an infrequent need, it will often be perfectly sensible for the company to have an ordinary, arm's length relationship that is largely exhausted by the terms of the governing contract. In other cases there may be benefits to both sides in having a continuing, cooperative relationship that is based on trust rather than just legally enforceable obligations. One advantage is that the non-adversarial character of the relationship promotes the free flow of information, in effect lowering the boundaries between the organisations to allow collaboration in such areas as component design, monitoring of quality, and delivery schedules. Another positive feature of high-trust relationships is that they lessen the risks associated with transaction-specific investments. For example, a supplier of components will be reluctant to make costly investments in production processes tailored to the requirements of a particular customer unless it is confident both that the customer will continue to take the components for the lifetime of the investment, and that the customer will not opportunistically seek to alter the terms of trade once the supplier is locked into the relationship by virtue of the investment having been made. For the same reasons a customer will not wish to become dependent on a particular supplier without similar assurances.

The virtues of cooperative relationships between customers and suppliers are now widely recognised. In its report *Tomorrow's Company* the RSA Inquiry noted that while Britain had a few outstanding businesses, the average performance of UK companies is worse than that of our major competitors. Its central recommendation to improve on this position was that companies should adopt an 'inclusive' approach to business relationships along the lines just discussed. Similarly, in his influential work *Foundations of Corporate Success*, John Kay points to the 'architecture' of a company's internal and external relationships as a major source of competitive advantage. Of considerable importance also in the recognition of the value of cooperative relationships has been the study of the organisational characteristics of industry overseas, most notably in Germany and Japan. In these countries close customer–supplier (and lender) relationships are often accompanied by cross-shareholdings, and occasionally board representation (in the capacity as shareholder). These bonds are likely to be valuable in reducing opportunistic behaviour and it is unclear whether the full advantages of cooperative relationships are capable of being realised without some such means of reinforcement. On the other hand there is a danger that rigidities will result if enterprises become too closely linked, slowing down adaptation to market and technological change. The ideal would be arrangements that provide security for stakeholder expectations without permanently locking the parties together. Whether this can be realised in practice remains to be seen. In any event the measures which companies in the UK might wish to take in order to consolidate stakeholder relationships is a matter for them to decide in their own commercial interests, as is the decision whether to enter into such relationships in the first place, and not something that can or should be imposed by legal regulation. This is not to say that there is not a role for public policy: government can play a useful part in ensuring that the background conditions in which companies operate do not hinder the formation and maintenance of cooperative relations.

The essence of the stakeholder approach in terms of practical decision making is that a company must not view its stakeholders purely instrumentally, that is, it must regard their interests as having independent weight and not treat them merely as a means to the end of corporate profit. If it does, trust will be undermined and the benefits of the relationship will not be forthcoming. It follows that the company must sometimes be prepared to sacrifice profits, at least in the short term. For example, if it is to reap the advantages of having a committed supplier it must give up some freedom to switch to another supplier on purely price grounds. Similarly, satisfying a customer's urgent needs might entail short-term costs that cannot be immediately recouped, but these may be worth incurring in order to maintain the long-term health of the relationship.

Given the proposition that stakeholders should be treated as ends rather than just means to an end, it is inappropriate that the interests of shareholders, who are also stakeholders, should be regarded as overriding all others. It does not follow from this that the claims of all stakeholders are equal. Rather, what is owing to a stakeholder is an attribute of the relationship in question. A shareholder is entitled to a return on capital that reflects the risk of the investment. Employees have a legitimate claim to share in the success of the enterprise and to reasonable job security. Customers and suppliers that are parties to stakeholder relationships have a right to suppose that the company will act in accordance with the expectations thereby generated. The language used to describe these entitlements is necessarily vague since what is the appropriate course of action in any given situation cannot be reduced to a simple formula, and there will certainly be times when interests clash. Redundancies, for example, will on occasion be unavoidable, as will the termination of long-standing connections with suppliers. The point is not that stakeholder entitlements are absolute, but rather that managements should make an attempt in all good faith to balance stakeholder interests rather than routinely subordinating them to the interests of the shareholders. Companies should strive to reach constructive solutions that take seriously the interests of the different stakeholder groups.

REFORMING COMPANY LAW

What changes need to be made to company law to encourage companies to be socially responsible and to give proper regard to the interests of their stakeholders? The first is a reformulation of directors' duties. While, as mentioned earlier, these duties as they stand do not amount to a major barrier to socially responsible behaviour and the creation of cooperative relationships, it is desirable that they be brought into line with how we want directors to behave. It should be stressed that the intention is not to give an expanded role to the courts. There is nothing to be gained from subjecting the exercise of managerial discretion to a more extensive process of judicial review. This is not a task that the courts would wish to take on, or are able to perform. Rather, the main reason for reformulating directors' duties is to promote a cultural change in boardrooms, so that managers place greater weight on the development of the company's relationships and pay increased attention to the welfare of groups affected by corporate activity.

On its own, changing directors' duties is likely to have only a limited effect. A second and more substantial reform that merits serious consideration is the introduction of a two-tier board structure. Such a structure could have advantages both in improving the inadequate disciplinary framework within which management currently operates, and in facilitating a stakeholder approach. Put another way, it could tighten up management accountability, but not in such a way that makes the level of returns to shareholders the sole criterion of success.

The primary function of the second-tier or supervisory board, according to the scheme envisaged here, would be to appoint the members of the executive board. The latter should be employed on fixed-term contracts and their performance would be subject to detailed review by the supervisory board at the end of the contract period, after which the board would decide whether their employment should be renewed. There are clear advantages in using such a system as a disciplinary mechanism for controlling behaviour as compared with the market. For the latter to operate someone has to buy the company in order to get rid of management. This is hugely expensive and the cost of bringing the process into play inevitably means that poor-quality managements survive. A supervisory board is likely, furthermore, to have much more complete information about the business and thus about how management is performing than will the market, and so is capable of making better decisions about whether to remove or retain the existing management team.

There are several advantages in a supervisory board system as a means of supporting increased social responsibility and more fruitful stakeholder relationships. If it were relied on as an alternative to the market for corporate control (a two-tier board structure designed along the lines suggested here would make hostile takeovers much more difficult), managers would be free to take the business forward without the destructive consequences of a single-minded preoccupation with share price. More positively, an assessment of such matters as the company's investment programme, its research and development efforts, employee training, the health of its stakeholder relationships, and its compliance with legal and ethical norms could expressly be made part of the supervisory board's review of management performance. This would give management a specific incentive to pay regard to each of these areas. At the same time the ability of a supervisory board to carry out this function meets the argument that is often put by opponents of the stakeholder approach, that managers become unaccountable when they are set multiple objectives. The charge is that while the concept of the maximisation of shareholder value provides an easily monitored yardstick of management performance, making an overall evaluation becomes impossible where managers are required to pursue a number of different goals, because they will seek to excuse poor performance under one heading, particularly current profitability, by pointing to success under another. Or put another way, if managers are instructed to balance a set of interests, since no particular balancing is demonstrably superior to the possible alternatives, in the resulting confusion they are set free to pursue ends, probably self-serving ones, of their own choosing. But a supervisory board should be quite capable of making an appropriately discriminating evaluation of management performance. After all, it is not as though information about the financial out-turn ceases to exist or to be regarded as being of great importance. The point is that that information is judged, by persons independent of management, in the context of the other factors that make up the complex notion of corporate success.

There is nothing particularly revolutionary about adoption of a two-tier board structure in the British context. As mentioned earlier, non-executive directors, particularly after Cadbury, are required to perform some aspects of a supervisory function, and are hived-off into separate committees (the audit committee and the remuneration committee) for this purpose. In fact, the supervisory responsibilities described in the previous paragraph could be carried out by non-executive members of a single-tier board, but the functional clarity of a two-tier system seems preferable. What certainly has to change is the procedure for nominating and appointing supervisory directors, since non-executives who are selected by management would be incapable of performing the tasks envisaged above. One possibility is that the supervisory board would nominate its own members, with appointment being conditional on the approval of the shareholders in general meeting and the employees. The giving of approval on behalf of the employees could conveniently be performed by a works council (which could also be given other responsibilities that would bolster the employees' position as stakeholders). The suggestion is not, it should be noted, that any of the supervisory directors should specifically be representatives of the workforce. Rather the role of employee approval would be to prevent the appointment to the supervisory board of directors who saw their sole function as being to oblige management to maximise the returns to shareholders. In due course the position of supervisory director might develop into a profession in its own right, the importance and intrinsic interest of the work attracting high calibre candidates.

A system of governance constituted along these lines gives some hope of improving the economic performance of British industry, but at the same time within a framework that is supportive of ethical and social responsibility. While it is vital that companies should succeed in increasingly competitive markets, we also need to ensure that the costs and benefits of economic activity are fairly distributed.

FURTHER READING

M. Blair, *Ownership and Control: Rethinking Corporate Governance for the Twenty-First Century* (The Brookings Institution, 1995).

J. Kay, *Foundations of Corporate Success* (Oxford: Oxford University Press, 1993).

J. Parkinson, *Corporate Power and Responsibility* (Oxford: Oxford University Press, 1993).

Royal Society for the Arts Inquiry, *Tomorrow's Company* (1995).

14 Your Stake at Work: The TUC's Agenda[1]

Janet Williamson

Long before Tony Blair made his Singapore speech calling for a stakeholder economy, and undeterred by the yards of newspaper print that followed, trade union leaders were meeting in smoke-free rooms to discuss the topic of stakeholding and corporate governance.

This might at first seem a rather academic topic for those at the gritty heart of the struggle for workers' rights. However, it is precisely trade unions' concern for the rights of their members in the workplace which has led them into this debate. At its heart is the question: what are companies for? Do they exist simply to make money for shareholders or do they have a wider role?

Over the past decade there has been a discernible shift in the culture of corporate Britain. While once it was broadly accepted that companies had legitimate responsibilities to their workforce, to the local community and indeed to the country as a whole, this paternalist ethos has been replaced by one of selfishness and greed, where the chief executive's pay and the growth of short-term shareholder returns appear to be the only benchmarks against which companies measure their success.

The UK's system of corporate governance contributes directly to the short-termism that bedevils so many companies in Britain today. All too frequently short-termism in the boardroom translates into low standards of employment practice. Trade unions work every day within the workplace to protect the interests of their members. The corporate governance context which determines how companies are run and the short-termism it engenders have a direct impact on workplace relationships. It is the unique practical experience of being on the sharp end of the decisions taken by companies that trade unions can offer this debate.

Stakeholding is not about a return to the past. It is about forging new relationships at work and in the boardroom that enables those involved in a company to work together for its success.

THE NEED FOR CHANGE

Although there are some world-class British companies, the government's White Paper on competitiveness made it clear that there is a 'long tail' of poor and mediocre companies finding it harder and harder to compete in international markets. The UK's system of corporate governance, particularly the takeover culture and pressure for high shareholder returns, contributes to the tendency of British firms to look for immediate profits rather than long-term investment and growth.

Britain's historical problem of underinvestment has become more severe in recent years. Investment in manufacturing remains 22 per cent below the pre-recession level. Business investment as a whole has been much weaker in this recovery than in previous recoveries. Since most investment is financed from a company's internal resources, high dividend payments reduce the funds a company has available for investment. According to the Bank of England, the share of profits allocated to dividends roughly doubled in the 1980s, and continued to rise even during the recession, increasing by a further 21.5 per cent between 1990 and 1992 despite stagnant profits during this period. In 1995, profits grew by 6 per cent while dividend payments were over 30 per cent higher than in the previous year.

The impact of this on long-term research and development (R&D) has been particularly damaging: the ratio of dividends to R&D spending in the UK is 3.5 times higher than in the USA, 10 times higher than in Germany and 13 times higher than in Japan. High dividend payments are encouraged by the corporate tax system, whereby pension funds face a 33 per cent tax on profits retained in companies but only a 16.5 per cent tax on dividends. This should be reformed.

The fear of takeover creates pressure on managers to pay high dividends even when this is not justified by performance, in order to keep their share price high and avoid unwanted bids. Takeovers also absorb large amounts of company funds directly – UK firms spent over £32 billion on takeovers within the UK in 1995, exceeding the previous peak of £27 billion in 1989, and in addition spent £11 billion on overseas acquisitions. This is more than four-fifths the amount they spent on physical investment, illustrating the tendency of UK companies to expand through acquisition rather than through organic growth.

The threat of takeover is often said to be one of the few disciplines on poor management that exists in the UK. Yet research, both by academics and the government, has shown that takeovers have little or no beneficial impact on company performance. Some groups may gain – principally the shareholders in the target firm. But this is at the expense of other stakeholders, especially employees, rather than as a result of greater efficiency – the cake is being divided differently rather than being enlarged.

Apart from the tiny minority of cases referred to the Monopolies and Mergers Commission (MMC), it is the shareholders alone who have the right to determine the success or otherwise of a bid. Despite the fact that takeovers frequently have a dramatic impact upon employment levels and conditions in both the target and the bidding company, employees have no right to be consulted nor for their interests to be taken into account.

The TUC has for many years called for a wider definition of the public interest in takeover policy, embracing the effects on employment and industrial competitiveness as well as on competition. In addition, a shift in the burden of proof is required – so that any firm making a bid would be required to demonstrate that it would operate in the public interest. In all cases employees in both the bidder and target companies should be informed and consulted about a bid (this is returned to below).

OWNERSHIP AND OBLIGATIONS

The laws and practice that constitute corporate governance are based on the assumption that directors' primary duties are to their shareholders, who are the ultimate custodians of corporate responsibility and control. This view originates from an earlier era of capitalism, when there was a much more direct relationship between the individuals who provided money for investment and the companies they invested in. At that time there was a real sense of a company 'belonging' to its shareholders.

The situation now is very different. Around 60 per cent of shares in British companies are owned by institutional investors, mainly pension funds and insurance companies. These companies invest money on behalf of their many clients, and frequently own shares in not one or two but hundreds of companies, spreading their share holdings thinly in order to spread their risk. Many are passive investors, taking little active interest in the companies they invest in – indeed, it has been estimated that only 15 per cent of pension funds' votes are cast at company AGMs.[2]

This contrasts strongly with the situation in France and Germany, for example, where large companies tend to have a principal shareholder or group of shareholders who control ownership: around four-fifths have at least one shareholder holding more than 25 per cent of the equity, whereas in Britain this is the case in only one in six firms. This concentration of share ownership encourages investors to take a more committed, long-term view of the business.

One of the factors that discourages concentrated shareholdings in the UK is the Takeover Code which requires an investor who holds 30 per cent of the shares of a company to make a bid, on equal terms, for the remaining shares. This is designed to protect small shareholders, but tends to discourage the concentrations of share ownership which would encourage investors to become involved in a business. The level of the threshold should be raised to allow greater concentrations to be built up.

Encouraging shareholders to retain their shares for a longer period will lead them to take a more long-term view of their returns. This could be achieved in a number of ways: voluntary codes between investors and fund managers to look for long-term growth rather than short-term gains; making the right to exercise pre-emption rights conditional on holding shares for a minimum period; and a transaction tax on share-dealings redeemable after a fixed period.

Recently there has been an increasing recognition of the problems with the present system of corporate governance in the UK. In 1991 the Cadbury Committee sought to address issues of financial accountability following the spectacular corporate failures of Polly Peck and Maxwell. More recently, the Greenbury Committee was set up following the public outrage over executive pay. Both committees sought to address these problems by strengthening the accountability of managers to shareholders through greater transparency and controls.

The TUC believes that shareholders could have an important role to play in improving corporate governance within companies. Their role must go beyond demanding the highest dividends in the shortest possible time: improved corporate governance requires responsible and accountable shareholding. Accordingly, the TUC has produced Shareholder Voting Guidelines for trade union pension fund trustees. The Guidelines set out practical steps trustees can take to develop a voting policy for their scheme, and recommendations that aim to ensure that votes are cast in the long-term interest of beneficiaries. In addition, the TUC believes there should be a statutory requirement for all institutional shareholders to vote their shares and disclose to scheme members how they have voted.

However, these steps are not enough. Shareholders alone cannot bring about the changes in corporate governance that Britain needs; this will require the primacy that the current system affords shareholders to be challenged. Companies affect and are affected by a far wider range of groups than just shareholders – at the heart of every company is a web of stakeholder relationships, each of which is based on mutual dependence.

Cooperative relationships are more productive than adversarial ones. Working in partnership with their employees and suppliers, firms can achieve far greater efficiency than by employing low-paid and insecure workers and keeping strings of suppliers at arm's length. Cooperation with other stakeholders will always be important: a positive relationship with the local community will help firms to recruit local skills; customer satisfaction will remain the source of corporate success; and environmental responsibility has become an area of public concern which firms cannot afford to ignore.

A new approach to corporate governance is required: one which recognises that companies are not just vehicles for the maximisation of shareholder value but institutions in which the interests of different stakeholder groups are vested. Stakeholding is about investing in long-term stakeholder relationships to allow all those involved in a firm to participate in and contribute to its success.

A POLICY AGENDA: CHANGE IN THE BOARDROOM

At the heart of this debate is the question of whether companies have obligations only to their shareholders, or whether they have wider responsibilities.

Most directors believe that under existing company law directors' duties are owed only to shareholders. The TUC would support legal changes which widen the obligations of directors and require them to take into account and balance the interests of different stakeholder groups. While this on its own would be unlikely to have much impact, it would help to engender a shift in boardroom culture and underline the wider changes that stakeholding requires.

A greater diversity of corporate forms would also go some way towards enabling companies to better reflect these different requirements and priorities. There is a strong argument for a distinct corporate form for the utilities – one which would reflect their unique public function. For PLCs, the recommendations of the Cadbury and Greenbury Committees should be obligatory.

Both the Cadbury and the Greenbury Committees place considerable emphasis on the role of non-executive directors in bringing independence of judgement to company boards and in performing a monitoring function. At present, non-executive directors are drawn from a very narrow constituency – many are chief executives of other companies with similar backgrounds and interests, and the vast majority are men. Selecting non-executive directors with a wider range of skills and experience would improve their ability to fulfil the independent monitoring functions ascribed to them and could improve the quality of boardroom decision making.

A wider range of non-executive directors would also help in implementing a stakeholder approach. A pool of potential candidates should be established, with nominations coming from stakeholder representatives, including trade unions and the TUC, the CBI and National Federation of Small Businesses, the Consumers' Association and National Consumers' Council, local government and environmental organisations. This would allow company boards to boost and diversify their collective experience and would enhance their ability to consider their stakeholders' interests in decision making.

TRANSPARENCY

Disclosure of information has played an important part in the debate over corporate governance to date. Disclosure in isolation can have only limited effect, however, because the likelihood of it leading to action depends on the ability of others to use information in forums in which they have a legitimate voice. Nonetheless, transparency is a prerequisite for accountability and must increase the likelihood of change.

The type of information reported is also crucial. The Annual Reports of a great many companies concern themselves almost exclusively with information on company finances at the expense of information on employee involvement, and this despite a requirement in the Companies Act to report on such involvement.

Companies are more than just financial institutions – they are also social organisations in which significant stakeholder interests are vested. How they manage their stakeholder relationships is an important issue in its own right, but it also has important implications for the long-term success of the company. Each individual company should therefore monitor and report on its particular stakeholder relationships in the same way as each monitors and reports on its financial health.

One way of doing this is through social accounts, which are based on information gathered from the stakeholders themselves. This makes them an ideal mechanism through which to measure the social impact of firms and the stakeholder relationships within and beyond them. They must not simply be written by a PR company but should be an accurate representation of the multiplicity of stakeholder voices – so far as is possible, the stakeholders themselves should define the appropriate indicators for measuring social performance. Environmental impact must also be included.

It is important that employees, like other stakeholders, should have a say in determining what should be measured and reported in terms of their relationship with their employer. The TUC would recommend that the following be included:

- details of training and development activity and of training targets;
- the gender, and if appropriate, ethnicity profile of staff on different grades;

- the distribution of pay throughout the organisation;
- the proportion of staff on temporary contracts;
- changes in staff numbers over the previous two years, and if staff numbers have been reduced, the means by which this has occurred;
- the procedures by which the organisation consults with its employees;
- whether a trade union is recognised and if not, an explanation for this.

The value of social accounts goes beyond the production of relevant and useful information. They should also help to inculcate a change of culture and priorities and to widen the definition of 'success'. For example, widespread social accounting would help to ensure that reducing staff numbers is seen as a sign of failure rather than of success.

In the medium term the TUC would support a legal requirement on companies to report on social and environmental performance, as with financial reporting at present. However, the immediate priority should be the promotion of best practice on disclosure by the DTI and the CBI, and representatives of stakeholder groups including trade unions.

BUILDING STAKEHOLDER RELATIONSHIPS

At the heart of stakeholding is the need to build long-term relationships based on mutual trust between a company and its stakeholders. However, different stakeholder groups do not necessarily have identical stakes in the firm, which implies that each stake cannot necessarily be realised in the same way. But for all, stakeholding implies mutuality expressed in terms both of rights and of obligations: stakeholding is not a one-way ticket – it is about two-way relationships.

Suppliers. Relationships between companies are an important part of the stakeholding agenda. The efficiency of suppliers has an important impact on company competitiveness – the value of components and other goods purchased by companies are on average worth more than the value added by the final manufacturers themselves.

Increasingly, firms are recognising that rather than keeping a panel of suppliers at arm's length, it is better to develop long-term relationships with selected firms. Partnership sourcing encourages a constructive relationship between firms, facilitating collaboration to improve quality and efficiency. The DTI and CBI should actively encourage partnership sourcing and more effective intercompany communication to promote relationships of trust.

Late payment of bills has contributed to the demise of many small companies and puts considerable pressure on their financial management. Clear standards of best practice are necessary to combat this problem, and the proportion and value of bills paid over one month after receipt should be reported in annual accounts. Another key aspect of supplier relationships is the establishment of clear standards of practice expected of suppliers. This can be particularly relevant when a company is sourcing from countries which do not recognise basic human rights and where child or forced labour may be used. For example, Levi Strauss and Co., a company which has long combined strong ethical policies with commercial success, has a policy statement on 'Business Partner Terms of Engagement'. This sets out its expectations of suppliers in terms of the environment, ethical standards, health and safety, legal requirements and employment practices. These standards ensured that the company did not source from South Africa under the apartheid regime, and more recently have led to a decision not to source from China, where some employment practices would be in breach of its code.

Community.   Companies have significant local impacts; they generate employment, a sense of community and boost local economies. But they also bring noise, traffic and pollution. Companies need to work with local communities to ensure that they make a positive contribution to the area where they are based. For instance, through consultation companies can ensure that local views inform planning and decision making, while structured dialogue between companies and local communities prior to planning applications can greatly enhance the effectiveness of formal planning procedures. Local authorities could act as coordinating bodies for such initiatives, and as local elected representatives have an important role to play in promoting community interests to the business sector in their locality. This could be done by regularly bringing together employers and community representatives in forums to discuss issues of concern and mutual interest.

Customers.   Through their purchasing power customers can obviously exert influence on companies, as has been well demonstrated by the impact of the green consumer movement over the past fifteen years. Clear product information is therefore essential to allow consumers to make informed choices about their purchasing decisions. This should include a list of product ingredients, where the product was made, the method of farming used (if applicable), and an assurance that no child, prison or forced labour was used to make any part of the product. It is also important that clear lines of communication and redress should be established to ensure that individual customers can raise concerns with companies.

The environment; the silent stakeholder.   The environmental impact of a company not only affects a company's present stakeholders but also future generations for years to come. There is an important role for regulation, both national and international, to set tight universal standards for environmental practices. In addition, local consultation on planning decisions and regular published environmental audits are essential.

STAKEHOLDING IN THE WORKPLACE

In too many British workplaces, employees have little control over the most basic elements of their working lives. The hire-and-fire culture has spread across all sectors and industries. Repeated surveys have shown that both blue- and white-collar workers feel increasingly insecure. Britain is becoming a low-pay, low-skill, low-technology economy in which workers are treated as disposable assets to be used and cast away at will.

Yet ultimately, no company can succeed without motivated, committed and skilled employees. People are the key to success; and this is truer than ever in an age where information technology is putting an ever greater premium on skills and knowledge as the only basis on which firms can compete in global markets. In this new environment, developing long-term, committed employment relationships based on mutual respect and trust is the soundest base on which to build a competitive company.

Job Security

Long-term employment relationships bring many competitive advantages. Research by the OECD has shown that there is a strong link between security of employment tenure and the willingness of both employers and employees to invest in training. Employees will be more willing to work flexibly and adapt to changing work requirements if they feel secure – insecure workers are more likely to resist change. True flexibility is not attained through the ability to hire and fire, rather it requires a workforce with the skills and motivation to respond positively to change.

There is a strong contrast between the ease of redundancy in the UK and other EU countries where the law ensures that companies pursue other options before resorting to redundancy. In France and Belgium companies are obliged by law to negotiate social plans to mitigate the effects of redundancy upon the workforce. In the Netherlands, a redundancy plan has to be approved by the courts which will take account of whether there are any alternative strategies the company could pursue, while in Germany the supervisory board is unlikely to give approval to redundancies if there is a realistic alternative. These measures force companies to think of other business options such as seeking new markets or raising productivity before resorting to redundancy. Conversely, the ease of hire and fire in the UK has been highlighted by cases where a multinational company seeking to reduce its global capacity has targeted redundancies on Britain, despite the British operation being highly competitive. This arguably been the case in the closure of UK plants by Thomson CSF and Leyland Daf.

Some companies and trade unions in the UK are pushing forward best practice by negotiating job security agreements. For example in the car industry, Toyota has made a commitment to its employees that productivity improvements will not be used to shed jobs. This means that staff can engage fully with efforts to increase efficiency, secure in the knowledge they are not working themselves or others out of a job. Similarly, Rover has a job security agreement in exchange for flexibility and skill enhancement. While until recently it seemed as though they were a thing of the past, increasing numbers of employers are responding positively to job security agreements being placed on the bargaining agenda as they realise that the hire-and-fire culture of the 1980s has gone too far and that there is a strong business case for employing secure workers.

When redundancies are proposed, all employers should be required by law to consult with trade unions as early as possible in order to ensure that other options that could avoid the redundancies are pursued, and that if they do take place the process is carried out in a manner which is fair and transparent to all involved. Employers should also be required to draw up a social plan for redundant employees which would include identifying training and retraining opportunities that will assist the employee in finding new employment.

Information, Consultation and Negotiation

On 3 May 1996, 20000 Royal and Sun Alliance workers woke to hear on the radio that their companies were to merge and 5000 of the new company's jobs were to go. Not only did they have no right to be consulted; they did not even have the right to be informed. Information, consultation and negotiation lay the groundwork for working relationships of partnership and trust. All employees are entitled to basic information about the company they work for; indeed, information provision is essential if workers are to identify with the challenges and dilemmas facing the company and understand the context in which management decisions, sometimes difficult, are being taken. Companies should be required to provide regular information to employees and trade unions on finance, strategic direction, future plans and major decisions being faced.

At the heart of corporate stakeholding is the fact that the practices of companies affect all the stakeholder groups and that stakeholders should, therefore, have a right to be considered or consulted in decision making. This is particularly true for employees: there are very few decisions taken within a company that do not have an impact upon its workers. Consultation gives the employees a legitimate voice within a company, and gives the company the opportunity to benefit from its workforce's ideas and confidence.

The TUC believes that all workers should have the legal right to be consulted by their employer on major issues, which should include mergers and takeovers, investment and disinvestment decisions and issues relating to employment (although these would normally be covered in negotiations). Consultation should be with a view to agreement on both sides, and the employee view should be considered in good faith.

For meaningful consultation it is essential that workers can express their views collectively. It is not practical for all but the smallest companies to consult with their employees individually, and employees would inevitably feel constrained by the vulnerability of their situation if they were consulted in isolation from each other. In addition, while minority views should also be represented and considered, it is important to be able to identify through discussion the degree of consensus that exists on a particular issue, which is not possible without collective organisation.

Trade unions have been representing the collective interests of workers for the past 150 years, and it is in this capacity that they have a crucial role to play in supporting stakeholding in the workplace. Trade unions provide a natural mechanism through which employee voice can be effectively represented for the purposes of consultation as well as negotiation.

The right to consultation should, however, apply to all workers. In workplaces where there are no recognised trade unions, employers and employees could negotiate a mutually satisfactory consultation process, resorting to a legal process only if negotiations fail. Ninety three per cent of British people agree that there should be a right to have a union negotiate on pay, if that is what employees want. Yet in the UK, it is entirely up to the employer whether they recognise a trade union, regardless of how much support there is for the union among the workforce.

Research from Warwick University shows that 72 per cent of new trade union members cite 'support should a problem arise at work' as the primary reason for joining. Yet British workers have no right to this support. Even if they are the subject of disciplinary action or dismissal, or subjected to abuse in the workplace, workers have no right to call upon their trade union to represent them with their employer. All workers should have a right to such support, and the right to be covered by a collective agreement if that is what the majority want. It is unacceptable that an employer can deny these rights at whim.

The Distribution of Reward

The issue which has done most to bring the weakness of Britain's corporate governance system to public attention is the scandal of top pay. Of course high rewards for high performance are justified in any job. But the escalation of executive remuneration simply has not been matched by improvements in company performance (or for that matter by pay rises elsewhere in the company). It is the scale of these increases at a time of employee lay-offs and low customer satisfaction ratings which has led to widespread anger and concern.

TUC commissioned research[3] has revealed that pay differentials within companies have increased sharply between the mid-1980s and the mid-1990s. Based on pay at over 1000 companies, the salary and bonus of the highest-paid directors rose by 115 per cent over the whole period or around 10.5 per cent per annum. Average employee pay in the same companies grew by 34 per cent over the whole period or 3.1 per cent per annum. Thus top pay increases have outstripped those for ordinary employees by a factor of over three. This takes no account of any share options available to directors which can further inflate salaries considerably.

The differentials now seen in many companies cannot be justified by the differences between job characteristics. The variations in pay reflect an undervaluation of those at the bottom of the company in relation to those at the top. All staff in a company make a contribution to its performance, and while roles clearly differ, interdependence is at the heart of all working relationships. Recognising the contribution made by all staff is central to good management practice and a prerequisite for stakeholding. The TUC believes that executive pay increases should reflect those offered to other staff in the company.

Financial participation schemes can play a useful role in promoting partnership in the workplace and a sense of ownership among the workforce. It is important however that schemes are open to all workers, including part-timers and that the introduction and design is subject to consultation with the workforce and its representatives. Many schemes allow workers to share in the financial success of the company but do not give them any further role in determining that success. The schemes that fit most closely with the stakeholding agenda are Employee Share Ownership Plans (ESOPs), which provide for the collective ownership of shares and also give workers some say in company decision making through the schemes' trustees, some of whom will represent employees.

Investment in Training

One of the most important benchmarks of a stakeholder company is the extent to which it invests in the skills and development of its workforce. Investment in training is essential to boost competitiveness and create high-tech companies producing quality goods. It also enhances the ability of the workforce to work flexibly and deal with change, raises motivation and commitment and contributes to job security and employability.

Training and employee development can play a vital part in creating social partnership in the workplace. It is also an area which benefits greatly from a partnership approach. Employees working in unionised workplaces are twice as likely to be trained as those in workplaces where unions are not recognised. And the involvement of trade unions increases the commitment of employees to training and makes it more likely that their needs are met. An influential study for the Employment Department concluded that 'those managements which have shared decision making over training have been most successful in transforming workplace attitudes to training and change'.

CONCLUSION

Much of the stakeholding agenda is common sense. The most successful British firms already put into practice different aspects of stakeholding. But trailing behind is a long tail of less successful companies where standards are much lower and where there is an urgent need for change.

The emphasis on short-term shareholder returns must be replaced by long-term strategies for investment and growth and a recognition that it is through long-term, committed relationships with their stakeholders that companies will equip themselves for the competitive challenges of the global marketplace. Changes in public policy, including company law and employment law, are necessary to encourage and underpin the changes in culture and practice that stakeholding requires.

NOTES

1. The TUC set up a high-level Stakeholder Task Group in the autumn of 1995 to develop proposals for a stakeholder model of corporate governance. This chapter is based on the Group's report 'Your Stake at Work – TUC proposals for a Stakeholder Economy' produced for the 1996 Trades Union Congress.
2. ProShare, 1994.
3. M. Conyon, Centre for Corporate Strategy and Change, University of Warwick, and S. Machin, Centre for Economic Performance, LSE, April 1995.

15 Stakeholders as Shareholders: The Role of Employee Share Ownership

Andrew Pendleton

Employee share ownership has become central to the concept of 'stakeholder capitalism', even though it rated barely a mention in Will Hutton's *The State We're In*.

Providing workers with shares appears to be a relatively easy way for their stake in their employing organisation to be realised, especially as there is a raft of supportive legislation in this area in the UK. Employee share ownership is notable also for the support given to it by all of the major political parties. Indeed the Major government replied to Tony Blair's Singapore speech in February 1996 by arguing that it had pre-empted Labour's adoption of stakeholder capitalism by providing statutory supports for employee share ownership. Yet not all observers are so well-disposed to employee share schemes. The trade union movement, whilst often welcoming the additional rewards provided by them, has argued that insufficient mechanisms have been developed in most cases for worker-shareholders to acquire a real say in the running of the firm. This criticism goes to the heart of employee share schemes and is the critical issue in evaluating the capacity of these schemes to contribute to stakeholder capitalism. If workers are to acquire a real stake in their companies they must be empowered to influence the direction of the company. How to bring this about presents a profound dilemma for policy makers. If measures to enhance industrial democracy are a voluntaristic element of employee share schemes most firms will not implement them: if they are made compulsory firms will probably discontinue their use of employee share ownership.

In this chapter we describe the main employee share ownership schemes in the UK and attempt to evaluate their merits in relation to the recommendations associated with stakeholder capitalism. We argue that most types of employee share scheme can only make a limited contribution to stakeholder capitalism. We then go on to assess a new form of employee share ownership, the Employee Share Ownership Plan (ESOP), which many observers believe to embody the philosophy of stakeholder capitalism more fully. It is suggested that though this is often the case, some of the more controversial and problematic of Hutton's proposals will need to be implemented if ESOPs are to be a viable and durable form of stakeholder capitalism.

THE EXTENT OF EMPLOYEE SHARE OWNERSHIP

There is more legislative and fiscal support for employee share schemes in the UK than virtually anywhere else in Europe, and a number of schemes have been introduced by government in recent years. The first of these, Approved Deferred Share Trusts (ADST), was introduced by Jim Callaghan's Labour government in 1978 at the prompting of the Liberal Party (upon whom Labour was dependent for a Commons majority at the time). In this scheme the firm purchases its own shares using current profits. These shares are initially held in trust before distribution to employees. If, however, employees retain their shares in trust for five years they are exempt from income tax on the value of the shares as a benefit from employment. They are liable to capital gains tax instead when the shares are sold, which for most employees means that they are a tax-free gain. The second type of scheme – Save As You Earn (SAYE) share schemes – was introduced by the Thatcher government in 1980. Employees take out an option to buy shares at some point in the future but at current prices. Meanwhile they save up to pay for these shares using a SAYE savings scheme. Assuming that the shares have increased in value over the period, employees make an immediate 'paper' gain when they exercise their option. Once again, this gain is liable to capital gains rather than income tax. If, however, the shares have not increased or have even decreased in value the employee is not compelled to exercise the option. A variant of this type of scheme was introduced in 1984, the main difference being that the SAYE savings scheme is not available and the option can be restricted to employees of the firm's choosing (usually top managers). These so-called executive schemes have attracted considerable public hostility in the last couple of years because they are viewed as an integral part of the 'fat cat' culture, that is, they provide a risk-free way for top executives to pay themselves very substantial rewards. To counter this the Chancellor, Kenneth Clarke, reduced the tax benefits in the spring 1995 budget (but then subsequently restored them in the autumn budget a few months later). At the same time a new type of scheme was introduced – so-called 'general options' – which have similar mechanisms to executive schemes in mechanisms but are open to all employees. Privatisation has also boosted employee share ownership in the 1980s and 1990s since employees have been provided with shares in nearly all of the privatisation initiatives. Finally, the development of single company Personal Equity Plans (PEPs) has also provided a mechanism for employees to acquire shares in their company on tax advantageous terms (or to avoid paying capital gains tax on shares received from other employee share schemes) but involvement in these schemes has so far been limited to high earners.

Most employee share schemes in the UK are Inland Revenue-approved schemes, as these attract tax benefits to the employee. Details of the incidence of these schemes in 1994 are provided in Table 15. 1. These figures refer to schemes which are currently in operation so the total number of employees who hold shares in their employing company is understated. Altogether it seems likely that up to 10 per cent of the employed workforce own shares in their firms, which is high by European standards.

Table 15.1: The incidence of Inland Revenue approved share schemes, 1994

Type of scheme and year of introduction	Cumulative number of schemes	Employees participating in 1994	Average value of schemes started in 1994 (£)	Cost to Treasury (£ million)
ADST (1978)	1111	700000	490	80
SAYE (1980)	1257	480000	2700	120
Executive (1984)	5680	70000	25000	70
Single company PEP (1982)	630	630	2900	n/a

Source: Inland Revenue Statistics 1995.

The most striking feature of employee share schemes in the UK is that the number of executive schemes dwarfs those of all employee schemes. The number of employees in these schemes is much smaller than all-employee schemes: on average there are thirteen participants per executive scheme. These schemes have been much criticised because they provide benefits for high-earning employees at the taxpayers' expense. Although they are often justified on the grounds that they provide an incentive for top managers to perform well, the link between performance and remuneration is often fairly tenuous in practice. The popularity of these schemes illustrates the dangers of reliance on voluntaristic action at firm level to bring about desirable public policy outcomes: many companies plainly see it as more important to provide additional rewards for their top managers than the workforce as a whole, and they use facilitative legislation to achieve this end. Since these executive schemes are inimical to stakeholder capitalism – indeed they seem to encapsulate the malaise in UK business described by Hutton in *The State We're In* – we do not consider them further in the ensuing discussion.

THE APPEAL OF EMPLOYEE SHARE OWNERSHIP

Employee share ownership is so attractive to advocates of stakeholder capitalism for several reasons. The first and most important is that employee share ownership potentially allows the stake of one key group – workers – to be recognised without encountering many of the problems that critics have identified in the implementation of stakeholder capitalism. A key tenet of the stakeholder capitalist philosophy is that the various groups who have an interest in the activities of an enterprise – workers, customers, local communities, and so on – should acquire quasi-ownership rights commensurate with the extent to which their interests are impinged upon by the activities of the firm. At the same time the company benefits from the inputs of the various stakeholder groups be it the efforts of workers, or the provision of labour from the local community. Stakeholders therefore ought to be able to share in the prosperity of the firm and to be able to influence decision making in the firm. The problem is that UK company law recognises only the rights of owners in these respects. As critics of stakeholder capitalism have pointed out, it is not at all clear how the 'rights' of other stakeholders can be incorporated into company decision making. Reforms to company law would be extremely complex and possibly unworkable since there are a multitude of practical problems: How is a stakeholder defined? Does a large stakeholder have the same rights as a smaller or more transient stakeholder? Through what mechanisms are stakeholder interests to be expressed? How are differing interests of various stakeholder groups to be reconciled where they conflict? In this context it is easy to see the attraction of employee share ownership. Employee share schemes gives employee stakeholders additional rights to those they possess as workers without violating the principles of existing company law. They are therefore a relatively painless and uncontroversial way of achieving some of the principles of stakeholder capitalism.

The second attraction of employee share ownership schemes resides in the analysis by Hutton and others of UK 'short-termism' and the functioning of capital markets. In *The State We're In* it is argued that the cost of borrowing in the UK is relatively high. For this reason there is a greater reliance on equity issues (that is, shares) to fund investment than in many of our competitor nations. Yet since UK financial markets are better developed and indeed less regulated than those in many other countries, there is always the danger that share owners will sell their stake in the company to others, especially as shareholder commitment to the firms in which shares are held is said to be lower than in many of our competitors (for example, Germany and Japan). Takeovers are therefore an ever-present possibility in the UK system. To deter takeovers (and hence to maintain some degree of ownership stability) firms have to concentrate on maintaining high levels of current profits and dividends. The most important measures of corporate success therefore tend to be those relating to short-term financial performance rather than longer-term measures of product market success. As a result UK firms tend to be reluctant to invest in training and employee development. Hutton argues in *The State We're In* that a notable feature of most of the UK's most successful firms is that they are insulated from these damaging features of UK capital markets. Once again it is easy to see the attractions of transferring some of the ownership of firms to their employees. Employee share owners are likely to have a longer time-horizon than the financial institutions, they are likely to have a closer attachment to their particular firm, and they are likely to have additional objectives to those of maximising current profits, such as providing long-term job security. Furthermore, individual share owners do not have such easy access to capital markets and hence may find it costly to dispose of their ownership stakes. There is the possibility, then, that employees will retain their shares for longer than institutional investors. Finally employee share schemes could transfer some of the risk of raising capital to the employees themselves, and hence the cost of capital to the firm could be cheaper.

A third argument in favour of employee share schemes is that they facilitate the redistribution of wealth, which is viewed as desirable by advocates of stakeholder capitalism. In Germany, one of the models for stakeholder capitalism, employee share schemes were initially developed precisely for this reason. Voluntary transfers of wealth in this way are clearly likely to be less politically contentious than use of progressive taxation, and for this reason may appeal to a Labour Party anxious not to be viewed as a high-tax party.

The fourth argument in favour of employee share ownership revolves around the idea of cooperation. The problem with the current organisation and ownership of UK industry is, as shown above, its short-termism. This tends to encourage conflictual relationships between workers and management since short-term gains for one often have to be achieved at the expense of the other. In many firms wages are kept low to ensure that current profits are high. But low wages provide little encouragement for workers to work at their most productive or to be committed to the firm. Nor do they encourage workers to share relevant information about production with management. Hutton argues that there are substantial and mutual gains to be had from cooperation, such as greater information sharing. Drawing on game theory, he claims that once a firm embarks on a cooperative strategy the benefits of cooperation will multiply over time. Firms will be able to make better quality products and services, achieve higher market share, and presumably provide better rewards to the workforce. Once again it is not hard to see the attractions of employee share ownership in this context. The act of introducing a share ownership scheme can itself be seen as a cooperative gesture. Advocates of employee share schemes also argue that workers develop a sense of identification with the firm and will become more committed to its success. Employee share schemes seem likely therefore to encourage employees to work harder and more effectively, to engender cooperation and to reduce the propensity to quit to seek employment elsewhere. In a myriad of ways, then, organisational performance will be improved.

EMPLOYEE SHARE OWNERSHIP SCHEMES: THE EVIDENCE

To assess whether employee share schemes may be so conducive to the development of stakeholder capitalism empirical evidence needs to be brought to bear on several key questions. Do employee share ownership schemes actually give workers a big stake in their firms? Do they provide a vehicle for employees to secure a large proportion of ownership, to acquire significant increases in rewards, or to gain an enhanced say in company decision making? Can employee share schemes provide a degree of insulation for the firm from the operation of capital markets, as was suggested in the second rationale for share schemes mentioned above? Does employee share ownership bring about a redistribution of wealth? Is there any evidence that employee share schemes lead to more commitment, closer identification with the firm and a greater sense of cooperation? Finally, is there any compelling evidence that firms with employee share schemes perform better than those without?

Overall the findings from empirical research are not promising. The most fundamental problem is that employee share schemes do not in practice give employees much of a stake. In most cases the proportion of equity held by employees together does not exceed 5 per cent, and is smaller than the share held by many institutional investors and, in some cases, those by top managers. One factor constraining the size of schemes is that any issue of new shares to support an employee share scheme will dilute the earnings per share of existing shareholders, and hence may not be well received by them. The small proportion of equity held by employees is matched by low participation rates where participation is voluntary (that is, SAYE schemes). On average 20 per cent of eligible employees participate in SAYE schemes.[1]

A key facet of ownership is the capacity to participate in and influence decisions about the uses to which the asset is put. One of the main attractions of employee share schemes could be that they give employees additional 'voice' to that they may possess as workers. It is doubtful, however, whether employee share schemes provide this. Employee shareholders do not usually have any special status, and the main vehicle to exert influence is the conventional one of the Annual General Meeting. In this forum employee shareholders are treated as individual shareholders (rather than as a collective entity) and, since AGMs tend to be dominated by company directors and institutional shareholders, it is not easy for employee shareholders to express their views and interests. There are, however, several ways employee shareholder interests could be more effectively represented. One is for the trusts which hold employee shares collectively in some schemes (for example, deferred profit sharing) to take a more proactive role in corporate governance matters by canvassing employee opinion and by block voting (when the trust owns the shares). Another is for non-executive directors to be appointed to the board with a remit to represent employee interests. Current company law stipulates that directors are responsible to all shareholders, but some degree of employee voice in the boardroom could be secured within the existing legal framework by selecting directors known to be sympathetic to employee-shareholder interests. Unfortunately, given the engrained hostility in UK boardrooms to the notion of giving workers a greater say in key decisions, it is unlikely that improvements to employee-shareholder representation such as these will be made voluntarily. The dilemma for policy makers is that if some degree of compulsion is introduced, many firms will simply discontinue their use of share schemes.

The second major argument in favour of employee share schemes is that they provide some degree of protection from capital markets. Yet as employee share schemes constitute only a small proportion of total equity, the degree of protection is very limited indeed. A further problem is that many employee shareholders do not retain their equity holdings over the long term because the primary financial benefit of share schemes is secured by selling the shares. This tendency might be counterbalanced to some extent if employees felt a strong ownership bond with the company. However, the evidence shows that it is usually necessary for employees to have substantial opportunities for participation in decision making for this sense of ownership to be pronounced. The tendency, then, is for the employee share of ownership to shrink over time. A good case in point is the National Freight Corporation which was bought out from public ownership by its management and employees in 1982. By 1995 the employee share of ownership had shrunk to under 10 per cent. In practice, then, employee shareholdings tend to be released onto capital markets rather than providing insulation from them.

Do employee share schemes redistribute wealth? The evidence suggests that their effects in this respect are limited. It is true that employee share schemes, coupled with the public flotations of public corporations has boosted the proportion of the UK population owning shares from 10 per cent in 1979 to around 25 per cent in 1990.[2] However, the growth of equity holdings by institutional investors has been much greater so that the proportion of total equity held by private investors has fallen substantially over the same period. In 1979 around 30 per cent of total equity holdings were owned by individuals: a decade later this had fallen to about 20 per cent. Even though employee share owners may hold onto their equity for a longer time than private investors participating in privatization flotations, the evidence suggests that the redistributive potential of employee share schemes are limited.

The final argument advanced in favour of employee share schemes is that they will induce attitudinal changes amongst employees which, over time, will lead to improvements in company performance. Here again, the evidence does not provide strong support, though the impact of schemes does seem to be positive rather than negative. Participants in share schemes appear to identify more with the firm, to be more committed and to report higher levels of job satisfaction than non-participants in the same firm,[3] but the differences tend to be fairly small. There is also some evidence to suggest that the direction of causality may run in the opposite direction: those with the most favourable attitudes to the firm may be the most likely to participate in voluntary share schemes. A critical issue is obviously what aspect of share schemes may be most likely to lead to more favourable attitudes. American and UK research suggests that those with the most favourable attitudes are those who have the strongest feelings of ownership. In turn this sense of ownership is substantially determined by the extent to which employees feel that they have a say in decision making. Since most employee share schemes in the UK are not introduced to expand employees' say in the running of the firm and lead to few if any new opportunities to influence decisions, it is not surprising that most employee share schemes do not bring about substantial attitudinal change.

Do employee share schemes lead to improved corporate performance? There has been a wealth of studies on this topic in recent years, using measures such as movements in share price, and changes in profitability, turnover and productivity. The balance of the evidence suggests that firms with share schemes or profit sharing perform better, though often only slightly so, than firms without schemes. Once again, however, the direction of causality is not always clear. There is a lot of evidence to suggest that better performing firms may be more likely to introduce share schemes. It would not be surprising if share schemes did not have a major impact on performance since they often involve only a minority of employees, pass a relatively small amount of ownership to employees and lead to little if any participation in corporate decision making. In other words employee share schemes are not big or far-reaching enough to make a fundamental change to the way the firm functions. A converse problem with the evidence to date is that share schemes are often introduced more or less contemporaneously with other measures aimed at improving employee performance, so that any changes in performance may be due as much to these other, possibly unobserved, developments.

ESOPS: AN ALTERNATIVE APPROACH TO EMPLOYEE SHARE OWNERSHIP

The evidence on employee share schemes indicates that their potential to contribute to the development of 'stakeholder capitalism' is limited. However, there is another form of employee share ownership, still relatively novel in the UK, which seems to offer far more potential than the employee share schemes discussed so far. This is the Employee Share Ownership Plan (ESOP). ESOPs are notable because they offer the potential to transfer much larger proportions of equity to employees than 'conventional' share schemes and because they often provide new structures for employee involvement in corporate governance. They have therefore attracted a much greater degree of support from trade unions and the labour movement than other types of share scheme, and the trade union bank, Unity Trust, has been instrumental in the formation of a number of ESOPs. As yet there are less than a hundred ESOPs in the UK but some measure of their potential is provided by the United States, where there are over 10000 ESOPs with a coverage of about 12 per cent of the private sector workforce.

There are two variants of the ESOPs structure in the UK. The most common is the 'case-law' ESOP, so called because the structures are based on an amalgam of legal provisions, ratified for taxation benefits on a case-by-case basis by the Inland Revenue. Typically an employee benefits trust (EBT) is established to acquire equity on employees' behalf usually using a bank loan or a gift or loan from the company. Over time these shares are purchased by a profit sharing trust, set up under the provisions for ADST schemes described earlier and financed by company profits. These shares are gradually distributed to the workforce, who secure tax benefits if they retain the shares in trust for five years. Meanwhile the employee benefits trust uses the receipts from the profit sharing trust to repay the original loan. In this way employees may acquire a substantial proportion of the equity in their company at little risk or cost. The other main form of ESOPs is known as a 'statutory ESOP' as it is based on specific legislation, passed in the 1989

Budget. Here a single trust structure is used, known as an ESOT (Employee Share Ownership Trust) or QUEST (Qualifying Employee Share Trust). To secure favourable tax treatment for employees receiving shares, statutory ESOPs were required to pass all their equity to employees within seven years and to have a majority of employee trustees, elected by a majority of the entire workforce, on the ESOT. Many ESOP advocates have argued that these rules are unattractive to companies and have inhibited the spread of ESOPs.[4] This illustrates the problem of attaching conditions to share schemes stipulating provisions for employee participation in decision making. To encourage the formation of more ESOPs, the government therefore relaxed these requirements in 1995. The Major government has also supported ESOPs by providing capital gains tax relief for owners of companies selling out to ESOPs.

ESOPs have been used in a variety of contexts. In some cases firms with conventional share schemes have used ESOP structures to buy shares on the open market so that slightly larger proportions of equity can be transferred to employees. In others philanthropic family owners have used them to buy-out their share of their firm when they have wished to retire or exit. Perhaps the most notable cases, however, have been where employees have mounted buy-outs of their companies during privatisation. In the bus industry, which has been the main site of ESOP activity in the UK, over twenty firms have used ESOPs to pass ownership to employees at privatisation, to the extent that by mid-1994 around a quarter of the industry's workforce was to be found in employee-owned firms.[5] These ESOPs have usually formed part of highly leveraged buy-outs, that is, the bulk of the sale price is met by a bank loan, whilst the equity base is fairly small. To keep ownership within the firm, departing employees are usually required to sell their shares back to the employee benefits trust, though this provision is not legally enforceable.

The significance of these ESOPs is that they appear to embody the philosophy and objectives of stakeholder capitalism. In these cases the ESOP has been used to preserve employment levels, maintain employee pay and benefits, prevent asset stripping and maintain existing levels of service at privatisation. They have facilitated the passing of large proportions of equity to employees, up to 100 per cent in some recent cases. They have also developed novel structures of corporate governance. In many cases non-executive employee directors have been elected to the main company board. In one recent conversion – Mainline in South Yorkshire – consumer representatives have also been appointed to the board. It is usual for trustees to be elected by the workforce and for a sizeable proportion of the trustees, often a majority, to be drawn from the workforce. In a few cases, 'shadow boards' have also been created, whereby trade union representatives meet the directors immediately before or after board meetings.

Even though these companies seem to exemplify the stakeholder capitalism model of corporate governance, how viable a model is the ESOP? Research into ESOPs at Bradford University[6] finds a number of problems with ESOPs structures. One obvious problem is that they are administratively complex and time-consuming both to establish and operate. This acts as a disincentive for firms to establish new ESOPs and for existing ESOPs to persist with this form of ownership and governance. A second problem is that the existence of ostensibly democratic structures of corporate governance does not guarantee that employees will secure an effective say in the running of the business. If managers in ESOPs are not genuinely committed to economic and industrial democracy then ways will be found to circumvent democratic structures of decision making. In these circumstances workers will soon become cynical about employee ownership. Equally if employees appear unwilling to assume the new responsibilities of ownership, then managers may lose interest in employee involvement. The most serious problem of all, however, is that the financial structure of ESOPs provides a very strong incentive for employees to sell their shares. Dividends are rarely paid so that profits can be used to repay the original loan. The result is that employees receive little obvious financial benefit from ownership. Add to this the huge increases in share value that result as the original loan is repaid, and it is easy to see the temptation for employees to sell. It is for this reason that employee ownership in the bus industry, the flagship for ESOPs only two years or so ago, is rapidly disappearing.

If ESOPs and similar forms of employee ownership are to provide a durable model for stakeholder capitalism, policy makers, managers and trade unions will need to address three main questions: how to increase the number of ESOP start-ups and conversions, how to lengthen the lifespan of ESOPs, and how to ensure that ESOPs fulfil the promise of enhanced industrial democracy. To some extent these issues can be tackled by relatively minor and uncontentious reforms to the laws and conventions governing the current organisation, financing and operation of ESOPs. Unfortunately, as the discussion above on the propensity of workers to seek short-term gains from increases in share value implies, ESOPs are currently as much victims of the malaise in British industry identified by Hutton as alternatives to it. The logic of this is that promotion of ESOPs cannot effectively substitute for some of the more far-reaching proposals to reform the industrial and financial system made by advocates of stakeholder capitalism. Instead the viability of ESOPs as a vehicle for stakeholder capitalism will itself be dependent on these larger policy measures.

Policy statements by Labour Party front-benchers have suggested that a Blair government will make legislative changes to promote employee ownership. For instance, it has been accepted that changes to the tax regime to promote long-term collective ownership of shares in employee benefits trusts will be beneficial. Currently, the taxation benefits associated with ESOPs are only realisable if equity is distributed from employee trusts to individual workers. If it was more advantageous for employee-owned firms to hold their equity collectively, the ability of employees to realise short-term financial gains by selling their ownership stake would be constrained. It is no coincidence that the longest-established employee-owned firms, such as the John Lewis Partnership, hold their shares in trust in perpetuity. A reforming government would, however, need to go further if it believed employee ownership was a valuable form of stakeholding. Currently, the potential for employee ownership and the avenues through which it can be secured are not widely known, and policy initiatives to promote ESOPs and similar forms of employee ownership will be necessary. An Employee Ownership Development Agency should be established to undertake or finance education on employee ownership, to provide training for managers and employees in employee-owned firms, and to support the financing of ESOP start-ups and conversions. This might take the form of direct financial support, in the form of grants or loans, or provision of guarantees for loans from commercial institutions. A condition of financial assistance might be that managers and employees attend training courses on managing the employee-owned firm.

Other policy initiatives to promote employee ownership could prove to be far more contentious. One possibility is that preference could be given to firms with an employee ownership stake in the award of contracts for government, health service and local government contracts, as part of a more general programme to extend contract compliance in the contracting-out process. This echoes the price preferences given by the Major government to employee buy-outs of some bus companies in the early 1990s but is likely to attract more opposition since contractors without employee ownership will no doubt claim that such a policy constitutes an 'unfair trading practice'.

These types of reforms centre on employee-owned firms themselves and will play a valuable role in increasing the incidence of ESOPs in similar firms. However, the evidence suggests that ESOPs are the victims of a broader malaise which tends to curtail their lifespan. In particular, the capital structure of employee-owned firms reflects and suffers from wider shortcomings of the UK financial system identified by Will Hutton in *The State We're In*, such as the high cost and short-term nature of capital. This means that in most cases employees are unable to raise sufficient capital to purchase a large equity share themselves. Banks are unwilling to take the risk of lending large sums of money to employee benefits trusts to purchase substantial blocks of equity on employees' behalf. Many ESOPs therefore have high debt to equity ratios, with the bulk of external financing taking the form of loans to the company. In common with banking practices more generally these loans tend to be expensive and require rapid repayment, with the adverse consequences for long-term employee ownership noted above. To counter these problems more fundamental changes to the financial system will be necessary. As Hutton suggests, reforms to the objectives of the Bank of England, the development of new industrial banks, and preferential treatment for banks taking a stake in the companies to which they provide finance will all be necessary to encourage long-term lending behaviour.

Finally, there is the issue of industrial democracy. This poses an especially difficult dilemma for a reforming government since employee ownership in itself may be insufficient to enhance employee participation in decision making, yet a mandatory requirement for employee-owned firms to adopt specific measures would act as a disincentive for some firms to convert to employee ownership. To avoid this problem policy initiatives to increase industrial democracy more generally might be necessary. For instance, employees could be given a statutory right to elect works councils on the German model. Although ESOPs would not be alone in exercising this right, this basic institutional mechanism could provide the basis for a deeper extension of industrial democracy than is found in firms without employee ownership. A further reform centres on the issue of corporate governance. Small shareholders could be given additional rights to information and to influence decisions to those they currently hold in company law. It might be unwise to restrict these specifically to ESOPs, for the reason outlined above, so more generalised legal reforms affecting all or most companies might be necessary. All firms affected by such reforms would be provided with the basis to develop cooperative relationships between stakeholders but the conjunction of several forms of cooperation in employee-owned firms would enable this group of firms to take particular advantage of them and to secure the benefits of cooperation. The logic of these proposals is that a reforming government cannot hope to promote ESOPs as a substitute for some of the bolder reforms associated with stakeholder capitalism. For ESOPs to survive as an effective form of stakeholder capitalism these wider and more contentious policy initiatives are likely to be necessary.

NOTES

1. See N.Millward *et al.*, *Workplace Industrial Relations in Transition* (Aldershot: Dartmouth Publishing Co., 1992).
2. See P. Grout, 'Popular capitalism' in M. Bishop *et al.*, *Privatization and Economic Performance* (Oxford: Oxford University Press, 1994).
3. See L. Baddon *et al.*, *Peoples' Capitalism: A Critical Analysis of Profit-sharing and Employee Share Ownership* (London: Routledge, 1989).
4. See J. Cornford, *A Stake in the Company. Shareholding, Ownership and ESOPs* (Institute for Public Policy Research, 1990).
5. See A. Pendleton *et al.*, 'The impact of employee share ownership plans on employee participation and industrial democracy', *Human Resource Management Journal*, Vol. 5, No. 4, 1995.
6. Financed by the Economic and Social Research Council.

Part V

The Stakeholder Economy

16 Macroeconomic Policy and Stakeholder Capitalism[1]

Dan Corry

Everything that happens at the level of the individual or the firm, every decision that is made by a head teacher, a car mechanic or a bank manager takes place in a context. A key element of that context is the macroeconomic position and prospects for the region, country or wider area. If we want to build some kind of version of capitalism that can loosely be defined as inclusive or a stakeholder one then most of the action will be at the micro-level. It is about how the firm is organised, about micro-policies for dealing with poverty and other forms of exclusion be they training schemes, benefit reforms, LETs schemes or enterprise initiatives. The question is, however, whether success in pursuing these sorts of policies is linked to the kind of macroeconomic policy that one runs. This chapter looks at the links between the stakeholder concept and macroeconomic policy.

WHAT IS MACROECONOMIC POLICY?

The macroeconomy refers to the behaviour of economy-wide aggregates like unemployment, inflation, investment, savings, tax rates and contributions, exchange and interest rates and budget deficits. The term 'macroeconomic policy' can be used in two ways. In the first instance macroeconomic policy tries to alter things like unemployment, inflation, growth, the trade balance or overall investment. In general, macro-policy tools try to do this by altering demand in the economy, rather than supply. Macro-policy tools include both fiscal and monetary ones – public spending, the overall tax burden, the money supply, interest rates and the exchange rate.

It is hard to argue that the level of any of these variables – apart from unemployment – have direct links to stakeholding. One could not say for instance that a believer in stakeholding had to believe in low interest rates or tight fiscal policy *per se*. What *is* significant, however, is the way they combine. A starting point is to say that the overall stance of macroeconomic policy and the objectives that it is trying to achieve will be important and open to debate. While the average stakeholder in the street would undoubtedly argue that the aim of policy should be to create jobs and so on, economists have argued long and loud as to whether this is sensible.

185

The second meaning of macroeconomic policy concerns economic policies that have an economy-wide effect. This is a much less often used approach. But in my view a change in the tax rate or employers National Insurance Contributions, or a change in the competition policy framework, which effects everyone in the economy, is as much a macroeconomic policy as a microeconomic one. From this perspective, the question is what role national level policies can have in helping us create the right environment for a stakeholder society.

Macro-policy as Promoting Inclusiveness

A stakeholder economy and society can mean many things. But at a minimum it is clear that such a society must be one where inequality is limited, poverty is rare and where unemployment, especially long-term unemployment, is not prevalent. When these conditions are not met people will be excluded from the world of economic activity, and lack of income will constrain them from making their own decisions about their lives: they will not be being offered a real stake.

What role then does macroeconomic policy have in promoting this kind of economic inclusiveness? First, macro-policy can, in principle, play a role in ensuring that high levels of employment are secured, primarily through affecting the scale of activity in an economy. Second, macro-policy can have an influence on how that cake is divided, and in particular whether the fruits of economic growth go into the pockets of those in work or are spread more widely throughout the economy. Third, macro-policy can affect the distribution of national income between various groups, be they savers or borrowers, workers or share owners. These are direct ways in which macro-policy can help promote inclusiveness and a stakeholder society. However, there is another mechanism that macro-policy has a bearing upon that I shall argue is of greater significance.

Macro-policy: Creating the Conditions for Stakeholder Approaches

The other way that macroeconomic policy can play a role in creating a stakeholder society is by setting the conditions in which micro measures can work well. In principle at least, macro-policy can set a climate and a background within which activity by economic agents – including the government itself – are more likely to deliver jobs and fairness. Perhaps even more importantly, the right macro-policy has the potential to facilitate more inclusive economic relationships both between and within firms. It can contribute to the creation of a world where we have higher investment in both people and machines, where there is a willingness to take on new staff rather than constantly downsize; where stable relationships between firms and their suppliers begin to make sense, and where people feel happier supporting government policies which pursue some form of equality.

This approach to macro-policy almost always leads to the argument that macroeconomic policy should be aiming to deliver stability. It is only in situations where shocks and abrupt changes of conditions and of policy are not constantly occurring, that long-term relationships are likely to emerge.[2] This leaves to one side what stability we are trying to achieve. Traditionally Keynesians argued that this must be stability of demand conditions, and this clearly still has some appeal. Increasingly however, most economists argue that the best that government can achieve in the stability stakes is to keep inflation steady (and low), to stop public borrowing getting out of control, to keep interest rates stable and to keep the exchange rate from fluctuating wildly. It is important to understand why there has been such a shift. Contrary to some exciting stories, it is not a result of a sell-out to free market 'monetarists'.

WHAT CAN MACRO-POLICY ACHIEVE? THE EVOLUTION OF CENTRE-LEFT THINKING

Left of centre thinking on what exactly macroeconomic policy can and cannot achieve has changed greatly over the years.[3] Under the Conservatives since 1979, macro-policy has been aimed primarily at achieving monetary stability (that is, low inflation) so that the market can work to best advantage. Nigel Lawson, the then Chancellor of the Exchequer, spelled this out clearly in his 1984 Mais speech: 'It is the conquest of inflation and not the pursuit of growth and employment, which is or should be the objective of macroeconomic policy.'[4] This underlying concept is rejected on the left. Irrespective of many other differences of opinion, there is agreement that a centre-left macroeconomic policy must be aimed at achieving particular 'real' goals. If then one decides that the control of inflation should be a primary focus of macro- policy it is because there is a belief that this is the best way of securing full employment and growth, not because of an overwhelming dislike of inflation in itself. In the 1960s and 1970s the dominant view was that a lot could be done with macro-policy. Reflecting the prevailing views of the time (on both right and left), there was a belief that if demand in the economy was at the right level then all else would be solved.

The important insight that a market economy cannot automatically deliver appropriate levels of demand – and can get stuck in an unemployment equilibrium that only government demand policy action can rescue it from – was turned into a universal nostrum for managing an economy. Several tendencies flowed from this approach and fed into Labour thinking. Supply in the economy (of goods made by firms, of trained and educated workers, of R&D facilities) was largely ignored. Inflation was not taken too seriously, at least until it went out of control in the early and mid-1970s. And Labour was keen on fine-tuning, often adjusting macro variables to keep demand on its correct path. These were great days for economic pundits: they were less easy days for business people looking to plan ahead.

A strongly Keynesian message, as exemplified by the Alternative Economic Strategy (AES),[5] continued to dominate the Labour Party for some time. The manifesto of 1983 was still strongly influenced by this thinking, but the approach was already being undermined. The experience of the 1970s, when, contrary to conventional mainstream Keynesian thinking of the time, inflation took off but unemployment also rose, shook many. Intellectual currents – partly responding to events – played a role too. Extreme arguments said that demand management could have no effect beyond the short run (the New Classical Macroeconomics). More generally, arguments which showed that the private sector's expectations crucially affected economic outcomes indicated that trying to solve everything with demand policies was a mistake. Also important in the evolution of thinking on the left was the perceived failure of the last great attempt at Keynesianism, the failure of Mitterand's experiment with demand expansion in one country in the early 1980s. And of course the habit of losing elections reinforced the view that Labour was out of touch on how to run a modern economy.

Change began, but progress was slow and as late as 1987 policy was still fairly Keynesian in character, with an emphasis in the Manifesto on how many billions of pounds would be pumped into the economy and how quickly to reflate: 'We will reduce unemployment by one million in two years as the first instalment in beating mass unemployment ... we will pay for them by ... prudently borrowing £3bn for useful wealth generating national investment.'

However, by 1992 the policy had shifted markedly and a new philosophy took over. On the one hand this had a major supply-side focus: training, R&D, education, investment generally – together this approach was known as 'supply-side socialism'. A certain pragmatism entered thinking on the means of creating a better society. Slowly but surely markets began to have a bigger role, a trend already apparent in John Smith's time as DTI spokesperson and carried on by Bryan Gould. 'Profits', 'incentives' and 'the private sector' ceased to be terms of abuse. Public ownership was no longer as key a concern as it had been, and the 1992 manifesto only had commitments to taking the water industry (a policy dropped during the campaign) and the National Grid back under public control, while decentralisation and regionalism replaced old certainties about central planners knowing best. Efficiency became a word that Labour tried to grab back from the Tories, while the language of social cohesion was now framed in the words of fairness rather than equality. And indeed the concept of an 'enabling' state, the Kinnockite forerunner of the stakeholder state, began to emerge. Implicitly the job was not to destroy capitalism but to create a framework in which markets could work to the benefit of all.

The role of macro-policy was to create stability. By the 1992 Manifesto this was put as follows: 'Business needs sustained and balanced growth, stable exchange rates, steady and competitive interest rates and low inflation. We will deliver them.' It is put even more sharply today, as Gordon Brown recently proclaimed, 'Labour will maintain a stable macroeconomic environment based on low inflation, closer cooperation with our trading partners and sound public finances.' The primary objective with macro-policy at present therefore is to contribute to the delivery of sustained, non-inflationary growth. Against this, some on the 'strong Keynesian' wing still argue that the urgency is to get growth going then worry about whether we can sustain it when we get there. This would imply extensive, expansionary demand policy immediately.[6] Few on the left would deny that a major portion of current unemployment is due to too little aggregate demand in the economy, so that there would be real effects from expansionary policies (be they via taxes, public spending, lower interest rates, or exchange rate devaluation). Despite this, recent analyses suggest that there are a number of persuasive reasons for us to question this type of approach.

First, there is the work based around the concept of the non-accelerating inflation rate of unemployment (NAIRU), which maintains that there is a unique level of unemployment at any one point in time which is consistent with stable inflation. This concept can be thought of in terms of a struggle going on in the labour market between workers and employers. Workers are looking for as high a real wage (after inflation) as they can get, and their power and determination to get it goes up as unemployment falls. Firms set prices in relation to costs – much of which are wage costs. The outcome of this struggle can be inflation: when unemployment falls below a threshold level – the NAIRU – inflation may begin to rise and indeed accelerate, even if this particular threshold level is hard to pin down and is constantly changing. A strong version of this approach is that the NAIRU is determined by supply-side factors so that once we have reduced unemployment that far, demand policies can only produce inflation.[7] This analysis can of course be disputed. But if accepted to at least some degree it means that those advocating strong Keynesianism must be open in advocating incomes (and/or price) policies of one form or another to overcome this inflation constraint. That has big problems in itself (see below).

Second, there are severe constraints on macroeconomic policy. The increasing power of international capital both in the form of transnational firms and massive currency movements is best known. Also widely understood is the problem of trade deficits and of inflation that put limits on the degree to which macro manipulation in itself can achieve real benefits. Differences in opinion on the degree to which these forces exist and, more crucially, can be overcome legitimately exist, but all put serious question marks over macro strategies geared around strong Keynesianism.

A third set of problems is concerned with the inherent uncertainties involved in the use of active macro management. In the first place, it is often hard to tell where the economy is, let alone where it is heading, and economic forecasting is often way off. Second, different macro-policy instruments work with varying and unpredictable degrees of effectiveness at different times. Third, shocks constantly hit the system, be they unexpected changes in behaviour (people decide to save less) or 'exogenous' factors like oil-price hikes. Fourth, totally discretionary policy can be difficult to operate in practice. Once people know that you will respond to changes in economic activity in a certain way they may play a game that means that the policy does not work. For instance if firms know that if wages go up too much you will let the pound fall to keep them competitive, they will not resist the wage pressure in the first place. Fifth, we should note that it is certainly the case that a great deal of current unemployment is not just the consequence of demand deficiency. The fall in the number of jobs for unskilled male workers reflects a structural shift in demand for skills, not just a lack of aggregate demand in the economy.[8]

For all these reasons, it is probably right that the best way to operate macro-policy is – in general – to use it indirectly to help employment while directly trying to avoid the uncertainty and dislocation that oscillating policy swings can inflict on the economy. Dashes for growth always lead to the brakes going on hard further down the road. An escape from boom–slump patterns is therefore crucial to creating the right environment for a stakeholder society. This should provide the right context for employment-creating policies at a microeconomic level – which will be vital in determining how growth is divided up.

It is worth emphasising however that the view that creating a stable economy will lead to higher rates of growth and therefore the potential for more jobs, has been disputed from time to time.[9] It is certainly correct that becoming obsessive about securing stability – especially in terms of never deviating one iota from a declared inflation target – can at times be as dangerous for growth as anything else. But most of the evidence we have does suggest that a more stable economy is a faster growing one. Recent work looking at a sample of ninety-two countries found that 'countries with higher volatility have lower growth'. This also applied to analysis of twenty-four OECD countries, so was not simply driven by the inclusion of developing countries with extreme experiences.[10] Similarly, other research has found[11] that the UK's tendency to volatility and to a pattern of 'short sharp booms followed by long shallow recessions is associated with a lower trend growth rate'. One should also note the view that for the same average growth rate, theory, as well as intuition, suggests that the lower the variance of output, the higher national welfare would be.

It is clear that New Labour and centre-left thinking on macro-policy supports the view that the inclusive society we all seek cannot be directly attained through active macro-policy. The move to arguing for stable macro conditions as the prime aim of macro-policy, is therefore in the name of creating jobs. The fact that it allows long-termism to flourish is a very important byproduct. It is to some extent a policy move made from despair, a feeling that while active macro-policy very rarely gets things right, it is very good at making everything much worse. But it is none the worse for that.

Keeping a Balance: The Continuing Role of Demand Policy

Is the role of macro-policy in a stakeholding society fairly minimal then? In the first place we have seen that it is not, for keeping things stable is important and by no means easy. But in addition we must not go overboard in throwing out the judicious use of active macro-policy. Some on the left have become too obsessed by supply-side concepts and cease to see the potential power of macro-policy. First, in a recession where there are ample unused resources it is clear that aggregate demand is too low. There simply is no supply constraint – we are way above any possible NAIRU – and there is little danger of inflation taking off. In this case macro-policy can undoubtedly be very effective and should be used boldly. We must be careful however to make sure that the appropriate conditions really exist. This does not mean boosting demand the minute unemployment goes above some estimate of the NAIRU, or some other measure of the demand and supply gap. Second, to make too deep a distinction between demand and supply and macro and micro is a major mistake. For instance, in order to raise private sector investment we need to create an expectation of future demand (that is, future consumption). The proper demand policies can therefore influence supply and a split between the two may thus be misleading. Third, there is a great deal of evidence that the performance of an economy in one period has profound effects on its performance in the next period (a process known as 'hysteresis'). This means that the supply-side can be very much affected by inappropriate demand-side policies. If unemployment is allowed to rise too high due to inadequate demand, then the level of unemployment consistent with stable inflation rises. If a recession leads to capacity cutbacks, then the potential output of the economy falls. Fourth, supply-side policies take too long and are too indirect in their effects to make up a complete strategy. The Lawson boom of the 1980s showed just how quickly a surge in demand can effect employment and growth (in this case as a consequence of financial deregulation and tax cuts). Supply-side policies can never promise this and, because they act through trying to influence private sector behaviour, lack the directness of Keynesian policies, particularly public spending.

CORPORATISM, ACCORDS, AND THE INSTITUTIONS OF MACRO-POLICY

Stakeholding can be seen in a different way. The key feature of a stakeholding firm is often said to be that it is one where all interested parties have a voice in determining its decisions and direction. Is there then a case for allowing more participation by different stakeholders in the formulation and execution of macroeconomic policy?

Incomes Policies

Traditionally this approach would have led one straight to incomes policies. These are familiar from British history, having been an explicit part of the social contract in the 1970s in particular, and an implicit feature of the 'golden age' (postwar to 1973) in much of the OECD. They remain a strong element in many continental countries in the form of corporatist arrangements and have been used successfully in the shape of 'accords' in the more 'Anglo-Saxon' style economies of Australia and Ireland over recent years. The key idea behind an incomes policy is that with agreement to control the evolution of wages and prices, one can run an economy at a higher level of demand without the problem of inflation. Here then is a stakeholder institution which can assist the smooth functioning of macro-policy. It sounds ideal! Moreover there is a healthy amount of contemporary economic analysis that supports the merits of corporatist arrangements.[12] Building on the observation that a number of Scandinavian countries, along with Austria, have good employment records (in total and given their GDP growth), some economists have concluded that centralised bargaining systems tend to enable a country to achieve lower inflation for any given level of unemployment. The logic behind this is quite straightforward. Where bargaining is centralised, bargainers – be they employee or employer representatives – take notice of the likely 'overspill' impacts of their wage claims and settlements on inflation itself. There is less need to try to keep up with the last group to settle a pay claim, and less leap-frogging that gets nobody anywhere as inflation just increases to erode the wage rise.

What then are the drawbacks with this? The main problem with incomes policies is that their great days may have gone. They worked pretty well in most countries, especially when they became part of the underlying political settlement (so that the 'what to do when it ends' question was avoided). But it is clear that they are coming under pressure in many countries. The problems are great. First, they seem to be failing or being put under strain in some countries primarily because of the pressure that international competition has put on such systems. This is partly because the institutions needed strong employers and employee organisations, which have broken down with the moves to a more casualised, small-firm labour force. It also partly reflects the problem that such arrangements can be somewhat rigid in a period when flexibility is seen as the key to economic success. This mirrors the potential problems of stakeholding at the firm level, in that it may entrench existing practices and make change difficult, at least in the short run. Second, such arrangements often leave some stakeholders out. In particular it has been noticed that those not represented at the table, the outsiders like the unemployed and those out of the labour force, and the owners of smaller businesses (and businesses yet to be formed) are neglected. For instance, one can end up with excessive labour market regulations and health and safety regulation because it suits the 'insiders', the net effect being the cushioning of those who already have a stake and the further exclusion of potential 'new entrants'.

This reflects the problem of getting the balance between stakeholders right. Even if we are only considering the key economic and social partners we still have to be concerned with the relative power of each group. In the 1970s for instance, it was argued that the trade unions became too powerful in the UK and insisted on agreements that were to the detriment of the nation in the longer run. Today the opposite may be the case in many countries. Third, and most importantly for the UK, it seems unlikely that such policies can be built in countries where they have already been dismantled and bargaining has become fragmented and even personalised. Destroying institutions that allow coordination and cooperation and thereby serve the common interest is fairly easy. Putting them together is exceptionally difficult. In addition UK employer organisations are weak and the trade union movement is now fighting hard simply to ensure its survival.

Despite these problems there has been renewed interest in corporatist institutions amongst parts of the British left, mainly due to the successes of the recent Australian agreements (known together as the 'Accord') between organised labour and the Labour government 1983–96. While there is some debate as to whether they were truly corporatist (since they largely left out employers),[13] they were an example of an arrangement in which higher growth (facilitated through wage restraint) was traded off in return for better welfare provision and progressive social policies. The Accord clearly paid political as well as economic dividends, in that it provided the basis for four consecutive Labour election victories. Despite these achievements, corporatist arrangements seem to run against the grain of the structure of our economy and the British institutional set-up. They are also at variance with the direction of much new centre-left thinking which emphasises that organised labour is an interest group which should not be treated any differently to the many other groups within society.

If old style centralised wage bargaining is a non-starter, this raises the issue of whether there is any role for national or sub-national stakeholder groups, such as unions, in other institutions of macro-policy.

Other Institutions

Putting aside the specific problems of operating an incomes policy, one could argue that in a stakeholder society the key institutions should be run on stakeholder lines. Specifically, this might mean making the body that runs monetary policy, the national Central bank (or its European equivalent under EMU) more of a participative institution where the voice of relevant stakeholders is at least heard. One could also extend this to the other side of policy, namely fiscal policy and the formulation of policies both for taxation and for public spending.

Exactly what these changes to stakeholder institutions would involve is unclear. The old NEDO was a corporatist body that in its heyday discussed the key economic issues. But it was up to government whether to act on its ideas or not. Proposals from Labour to implant a 'real' unit in the Treasury are along these lines – though it is questionable whether internalising these debates within an institution such as the Treasury (whose mission after all is to maintain some type of fiscal balance) is likely to lead to real changes in policy. Similarly Labour also has proposals to introduce a new Monetary Policy Committee at the Bank of England as well as 'an expanded Court reflecting both industry wide and regional interests',[14] but again this will only be an advisory body given that in our current constitutional set-up the Chancellor has ultimate responsibility for policy on interest rates. Labour is not explicitly arguing for representatives of trade unions or of local government to be involved in any of these institutions. Overall, if there was to be real stakeholder influence in the formulation of macro-policy it is likely that it would have to occur within the context of a wider corporatist package, where for instance wage restraint is offered in return for certain tax changes or lower interest rates, or price restraint is exchanged for changes in company taxation.

Government as the Stakeholder Representative?

This debate reveals a particular problem with the idea of creating 'stakeholder' macroeconomic institutions to run a 'stakeholder' macro-policy. Where at firm level it is easy to see that giving voice is likely to lead to longer-term commitment, more trust, a greater willingness to accept change and (at least potentially) higher productivity, this is not at all clear at the macrolevel. Giving a national representative of a trade union a voice does not mean that the shop floor will accept wage restraint, particularly given the decentralised nature of union organisation in the UK. Having a CBI boss agree to move towards the better treatment of part-timers does not mean that small firm bosses necessarily deliver on this. It may also be argued that the inflexibility inherent in a stakeholder approach to macro-institutions would lead to a poorer performance in terms of the key macroeconomic objective of creating sustainable non-inflationary growth; the very goal which is a crucial precondition for a stakeholder economy.

More fundamentally the whole of idea of stakeholder representation at a macrolevel is open to question. Surely the very role of government is – at least at the national level – to make an assessment about what is best for the country. This will inevitably be an assessment of how to balance the various interests of different stakeholders. Unlike the situation at firm level, where the company board's objective is presently defined as the pursuit of one interest (shareholders), at a macrolevel we already have a body charged with worrying about the 'community' and other interested parties. On the whole then macro-institutions should be agencies charged with carrying out the instructions of government.

Accountability in such a world is formed by the elected government itself consulting stakeholders as it sees fit and then giving instructions to the appropriate agencies to carry them out, rather than having representative stakeholder institutions. This means for instance that while we may well want to make sure that stakeholder interests are represented in the decision making process which determines what the appropriate targets for monetary policy should be, we should be less concerned about their presence on the operational body that simply implements the policy. So at the Bank of England for example, putting various regional representatives on the body that decides on the timing of interest rate changes might cause difficulties because turning the precise decisions on the day-to-day operation of monetary or fiscal policy into a stakeholder dispute both displaces it from the more important issues of what the basic strategy should be, and also could mean that the detailed decisions are taken less well. Stakeholder institutions may lessen the chance of a successful stakeholder macro-policy. Of course, if one was forced to have a totally independent macro-institution that did not take its strategic decisions from an elected body – as with the Bundesbank – then there is a strong case for more active participation by stakeholders to ensure legitimacy and to reflect the balance of interests. Some would say that under EMU the UK should become a stakeholder in the setting of EU monetary policy, currently set more or less unilaterally by the Bundesbank.

In conclusion then one might say that while consultation and openness are – as ever – to be encouraged, changing the constitution of macro-institutions would probably only lead to confusion and problems. At a time when, for other reasons, we are increasingly using agencies to run monetary policy (that is, an 'independent bank') and maybe even independent agencies for aspects of fiscal policy,[15] it would be strange to suddenly turn these bodies into hot-beds of stakeholder debate.

Instead the stakeholder approach is needed at the supply-side. This means both the involvement of stakeholder groups, especially of representatives of labour and employers, in designing and possibly delivering supply-side policies, and also in improving the efficiency at the level of the firm. It may also be the case that macro-policy will itself work better if there are strong institutions that bring together specific stakeholder interest – like employer organisations or trade unions – since these minimise the possibility of individual action against the common interest and reduce the possibility of rent seeking by particular subgroups.[16]

CAN SUPPLY-SIDE APPROACHES REALLY PROMOTE INCLUSION?

Policies that increase capacity – through enhancing investment in machines or in skills – will reduce inflationary pressure for any level of unemployment and so allow us to get closer to full employment.[17] They also increase productivity, enabling output to grow faster. While stakeholders should therefore welcome measures which aim to increase capacity, we should also be aware of some caveats. First, if we achieve productivity but the benefits all feed through into higher real wages for those in jobs (as seems to be the case in the UK) then there will be little overall effect on jobs. This suggests that measures aimed at reducing unemployment will have to consider the distributional issues of the sharing out of benefits and indeed of work. Conflicts of interests between 'insiders' (those safely in jobs) and 'outsiders' (the unemployed) are widespread. If we want to help the latter we must strengthen their hand *vis-à-vis* the insiders. Some of the measures that this involves may not be natural territory for the old left.

This conflict is often spoken of in relation to the question of the minimum wage. Interestingly, for many years most UK trade union opinion was against a minimum wage. Because it would help people whether they were in trade unions or not, it was perceived to threaten their role. In a sense, they resisted a measure that was attempting to help some of the 'outsiders'. Indeed in the design of a minimum wage one must ensure that it does not cause problems for another set of outsiders, those trying to enter the labour market. Accompanying policies like reducing NICs at the lower end of the income range can help minimise this risk.[18] Another aspect of this struggle becomes clear when we look at job sharing. Paul Gregg has shown historically that as real wages increased, people worked shorter hours, thereby releasing work hours for other people.[19] In the 1980s this trend reversed for various reasons, some of which may well be related to the increased rewards of success. The key point is that the battle for full employment may not be a game – as we like to present it – where everyone wins.

Second, if we are to accept the case for macroeconomic stability this implies a degree of faith in the ability of supply-side policies to promote both inclusiveness and a growing economy. For if not, we would have to place a greater emphasis on more active macro-policy (unless it definitely would not work). So we need to look very briefly at whether these policies can work.

Training.   There is little doubt that a better skilled workforce is likely to lead to higher productivity, although it is clear that it cannot solve things on its own.[20] In addition, we know that there are growing gaps in earning power between those with and without skills and that training is skewed towards those who already have some skills.[21]

At present the debate rages as to how to rectify this situation. On the right, more use of the market is advocated. An increased role for the market is also accepted on the left though there is still a belief in the need for intervention to overcome market failures, Individual Learning Accounts (ILAs) represent one possibility in this area. While it is clear that there is much that policy can do, we should also be aware that we are dealing with a problem that has seemed intractable in the UK for many years, perhaps because its labour market is, awkwardly, half-way between that of continental Europe (where employers train a lot) and of 'free market' America (where individuals pay for themselves much more). In short, improving basic education and skills will be very important, but quick solutions are unlikely.

The corporate sector.   Ultimately, the private sector will create most of the wealth and jobs we need. Reforms often mentioned in the stakeholder context may be able to make our firms more efficient, innovative and productive. These include changes in corporate practice which promote greater workforce participation and closer relations between firms and their suppliers, along with possible changes to company law which make it clear that the maximisation of shareholder value should not be pursued to the exclusion of other stakeholder interests; indeed shareholder interests can be promoted by taking the concerns of other stakeholders seriously.

Welfare reform.   There is little doubt that the welfare system has profound implications for inclusiveness. On one hand, its generosity determines how 'included' those who have fallen on bad times are. This is largely a question of redistribution, a difficult and age-old political issue that rests at the heart of any commitment to a stakeholder society. But of particular relevance to the current debate on welfare is the realisation that the structure of the system can determine how easily people can get themselves out of unemployment and poverty, and so become independently 'included' in mainstream society. This will require intelligent reform, and examples in Australia and the USA show that real achievements can be made here.

Can supply-side policies solve long-term unemployment?   If macro-policy is aimed at holding the boat steady then supply-side policies will have to deliver. This very brief discussion suggests that sensible micro-policy can start to make inroads into key areas like long-term unemployment. More radical ideas like using variations of public sector job creation[22] or using 'green charges' to raise money for reducing taxes on labour, can also be considered. Again, it seems that long-term unemployment cannot be solved overnight, but with determination and a judicious mix of targeted policies substantial progress can be achieved.

WHAT IS OPEN TO A LABOUR GOVERNMENT ON MACRO-POLICY? CONTINUITY...

The plain fact is that there is no longer such a thing as a clear left macro-economic policy. The right emphasise the risks of inflation and downplay the risks of depressed activity due to their dogmatic belief that *laissez-faire* capitalism will result in labour-market equilibrium and no unemployment. The only policy measures required are deregulatory micro measures. The modern left takes a different view of the balance of risk, especially since their core constituents are likely to be particularly badly affected by higher unemployment. But this hardly amounts to a massive difference of principle. Furthermore, since financial markets are always looking for any sign of inflationary laxity there is no advantage in the left emphasising any different attitudes to risk that are likely to prevail.

While one should be prepared to use fiscal policy to prevent slumps, that does not imply that we can be indifferent to the ratio of public debt to national income, nor to the way we are annually adding to that debt (that is, each year's budget deficit). Indeed if our debt burden gets too big it reduces our freedom to use active fiscal policy when it is truly required. The financial markets would more willingly accommodate a temporary fiscal splurge if the debt/GDP ratio was 50 per cent, rather than 100 per cent.

Equally, while – at least in the pre-EMU world – we may want to retain the option of the exchange rate falling to make up for the UK's inability to either restrain costs or to become more productive, it is apparent that it is not a long-term solution to unemployment and slow growth. Stable exchange rates are far more likely to be useful in building the stable economy that any concept of stakeholding requires. In an unstable, fluctuating economy, long-term relationships never emerge. That is why the case for EMU should be such a strong one for those who believe in a stakeholder world.[23]

So Labour in government must follow the stability road. In fact it is vital that Labour is sensible and tough on macro-policy, focusing on the long-term achievement of stability and refusing to let spending and borrowing spiral out of control, or inflationary expectations to rise sharply. Previous Labour governments have often been tripped up on these issues, often making the error of being 'nice' early on, forcing them to tighten their policy stance near the next election. This is even more important since Labour is likely to face some difficult problems – some of them quite possibly being deliberately engineered by the Tories. For instance, public sector pay may have been held down below a sustainable rate; 'excessive' tax cuts are likely to be given pre-election; and borrowing will still be very high given the stage of the economic cycle.

... AND CHANGE

So while the left is absolutely correct not to promise any systematic difference in the stance of macro-policy, this should not mean taking on board the whole establishment consensus on macroeconomic policy. It is possible to offer different, and better, procedures and practices to those currently used.[24]

First, we should move away from inflation targets to targets for nominal GDP growth. The current system for running monetary policy gives a bias to raising interest rates before it is necessary, thus putting a strain on the economy's ability to produce jobs. Nominal GDP targets – the sum of real growth and inflation – would avoid this tendency while keeping firm control of inflation. Second, we should make sure that the setting of the targets for monetary policy remains in the hands of government so that they can ensure that monetary and fiscal policy are coordinated. There is however no particular problem with the implementation of interest rate changes being carried out by an independent Bank of England. Third, we need to switch attention from the PSBR to a better measure of the public deficit that excludes the borrowing made for investment projects that are largely self-financing (like those made by the Post Office). Such a change should enable decisions on public sector investment to be taken more sensibly and therefore contribute to a stronger economy and a fairer society. Fourth, we should reinforce the automatic stabilisers in the economy, primarily via a more progressive income tax system, so that the economic cycle becomes less pronounced.

Within that permanent framework, questions of fiscal/monetary policy mix arise as a matter of tactics at a given place and time. While aggregate demand is reasonably buoyant we can consider trying to improve its mix. At present we should err on the side of a tight fiscal stance with reasonably accommodating monetary policy to try and ensure that there is a rebalancing of aggregate demand towards exports and away from consumer spending. Unfortunately, this desirable policy mix is likely to be hard to sustain for a new Labour government. Fearing the markets, a new government may decide to be very tough on monetary policy. This then only leaves room on fiscal policy – made easier by the extra 'credibility' that the new monetary policy may generate. While there is certainly a case for an increase in public investment in education and health, which might justify some increase in the debt/GDP ratio, a real danger therefore is that a high level of state borrowing, combined with a return to tight money, will lead to problems both in the traded goods sector and in private sector investment. We must hope that the next government manages to resist these pressures. Therefore any changes we might want to make to fiscal and monetary policy must be done gradually, carefully and from a position of strength and established (and earned) credibility. Otherwise they will threaten rather than enhance the prospects of achieving stable growth.

To restate, while there are important changes that should be made in macro-institutions and policy, there is not a clear left or stakeholder macro-policy. Despite this there are a great number of crucial things that government can and should do within a wider framework of macro-stability. The stakeholder concept reveals no blinding new truths about the shaping of macro-policy but it helps define and steer us towards its key tasks. But the real action in creating a better Britain will be at the microlevel.

NOTES

1. I am grateful to Simon Milner for helpful discussions of these issues, and to Gavin Kelly for detailed comments on an earlier draft.
2. D. Corry, 'Restating the case for EMU: Perspectives From the Left', IPPR (1995).
3. D. Corry, 'Living With Capitalism: the Macroeconomic Policy Alternatives', *Renewal*, Vol. 2, No. 1 (1995).
4. Note that this is far stronger than saying that within macro-policy monetary policy is dedicated to price stability, and fiscal policy can be used to influence real things. This latter view often takes its cue from a belief that monetary policy has no real effects beyond the short run.
5. This called for 'A policy of expansion aimed at restoring full employment and raising living standards, based on a planned reflation of the economy primarily through increases in public spending' (CSE 1980). One should note however, that many on the more extreme left saw the AES as going far beyond Keynesianism – 'a break with capitalist forms of economic control'.
6. R. Berry, M. Kitson and J. Michie, 'Creating Jobs Fast', *New Economy,* Vol. 3, No. 3, 1996.

7. See for example S.Wren-Lewis, 'Can Unemployment Come Down?', *New Economy*, Vol. 1, No. 1; and W. Carlin and D. Soskice, *Macroeconomics and the Wage Bargain* (Oxford: Oxford University Press, 1994).
8. P. Gregg, 'Jobs and Justice: Why Job Creation Alone Will Not Solve Unemployment', in *Work and Welfare* (IPPR, 1993).
9. See B. Martin, 'So Steady They're Standing Still', *New Statesman*, 19 July 1996.
10. G. Ramey and V. Ramey, 'Cross Country Evidence on the Link Between Volatility and Growth', *American Economic Review*, Vol. 85, No. 5, 1995.
11. N. Oulton, 'Supply-Side Reform and UK Economic Growth: What Happened to the Miracle?', *Nation Institute Economic Review*, No. 4, 1995. Stakeholding approaches also gain support from the literature, since there is no evidence that increased equality is harmful to growth and some evidence that it is helpful. Indeed one of the avenues that this may come through is by equality leading to less instability. See D. Corry and A. Glyn, 'The Macroeconomics of Equality, Stability and Growth', in A. Glyn and D. Miliband (eds), *Paying for Inequality: the Economic Cost of Social Injustice* (Rivers Oram Press/IPPR, 1994).
12. On this see for example L. Calmfors and J. Driffill, 'Bargaining Structure, Corporatism and Macroeconomic Performance, *Economic Policy*, No. 6, 1988; and A. Henley, 'The Case for Corporatism', *New Economy*, Vol. 1, No. 2, 1995.
13. B. Callaghan, 'Australia: Wisdom of Oz', *Renewal*, Vol. 4, No. 3, 1996.
14. Speech to Manchester Business School, 1996.
15. S. Wren Lewis, 'Avoiding Fiscal Fudge', *New Economy*, Vol. 3, No. 3, 1996.
16. L. Kenworthy, *In Search of Economic Success: Balancing Competition and Co-operation* (Sage, 1995) argues further that 'macro level cooperation appears to have adverse effects on the growth of productivity, but is a very good predictor of low misery index levels (the sum of the inflation and unemployment rates). Meso (sectora) level co-operation has exactly the opposite effects whereas microlevel cooperation seems to have a beneficial impact in both areas' (p. 186).
17. J. Haskel and C. Martin, 'Will Low Skills Kill Recovery?', *New Economy*, Vol. 1, No. 3, 1994.
18. In any case the evidence is that a minimum wage will increase labour supply since it will make work worthwhile for many more people.
19. P. Gregg, 'Share and Share Alike', *New Economy*, Vol. 1, No. 1, 1995.
20. C. Greenhalgh, 'Supply-Side Puzzles', *New Economy*, Vol. 2, No. 1, 1995.
21. S. Machin and R. Wilkinson, 'Employee Training: Unequal Access and Economic Performance' (IPPR, 1995).
22. G. Holtham and K. Mayhew, 'Tackling Long Term Unemployment', (IPPR, 1996).
23. Corry, 'Restating the case for EMU'.
24. D. Corry and G. Holtham, 'Growth With Stability: Progressive Macroeconomic Policy' (IPPR, 1995).

17 It's Profitability, Stupid*
Meghnad Desai

The story tells of C.D. Deshmukh, who was the first Indian to be Governor of the Reserve Bank of India and went on to become India's Finance Minister, that when he was a schoolboy his teacher proudly showed to the visiting education inspector (an Englishman) an essay that his star pupil had written. 'Hmm', said the inspector, 'not bad at all'. The teacher said: 'Don't say not bad, the truth is, neither you nor I could have written like this.'

Reading Will Hutton's bestselling book on the political economy of Britain, one is tempted to sneer, to cavil, to dwell on minutiae and in some way to recover one's bearing after having been swept away by the sheer passionate force of the author's argument. Debating the British Disease is an old and venerated sport. There is no shortage of radical nostrums produced by politicians, active and passé, who will preface their quack remedies with a superficial diagnosis. In more rarefied regions, the New Left exploded on to the British cultural scene with Perry Anderson's brilliant analysis of the peculiarities of the English and E.P. Thompson's riposte.[1] There is the continuing revisionist history that Corelli Barnett has been offering.[2] Yet there has been nothing quite like Will Hutton's book, *The State We're In* (hereafter *TSWI*).[3]

The book combines in one single volume the diagnosis of the hundred years' disease with an excoriating critique of the Thatcher years. It reaches out to a comparative analysis of the available forms of capitalism and drives home the advantage of the cooperative corporatism of Germany, arguing its advantage on bases as abstract as cooperative game theory and solid empirical evidence of superior performance. It offers an agenda for total reform of the economy as of the polity, showing that these are intertwined. It is truly radical without being leftwing, republican without being revolutionary or even regicidal, wedded to economic efficiency without being tied to the greed and mindless rationalism of neoclassical economics. It is fun to read.

The vision is a coherent one and follows from the preceding analysis. It is not perhaps as heart-warming as Crosland's cry for socialism but it is no less passionate and, if anything, economically more finely honed. But more than that it is the link-up with the political malaise and the case for constitutional reform which is its strength. Previous radical analyses concentrated on public ownership or narrowly economic policy, with the abolition of the House of Lords (which I am all for) as the fig-leaf for

political analysis. Hutton comes at the end of the elective dictatorship of
Thatcher and is much less sanguine about the ancient liberties.

It is obvious then that there is much of merit and much to like in this book.
It will form the basis of many a teenager's lifetime vision of British problems.
But, by the same token, since the area of agreement is large, in what follows
I shall concentrate on the differences and disagreements that I have, pointing
out the areas where I think Hutton is weak or carried away by his own
rhetoric. Enough of praise; let us start the battle in earnest.

DEBATING THE BRITISH DISEASE

TSWI is at one level a contribution to the long-running debate about the British
disease. Some of the themes in this debate go back to the 1880s when there
was public concern about Britain's ability to compete with the newly indus-
trialising countries of Germany and the USA. The shortcomings of the
British educational system, especially the lack of a good apprenticeship
scheme which also imparted education, were glaring. The contempt in which
formal, vocational as well as academic, training was held by the English
(though not the Scots, Welsh or Irish), the culture of amateurism, the desire
on the part of successful industrial entrepreneurs to ape the feudal aristocracy,
the peculiar trade unions rather than industrial unions with their demarcation
disputes, the dominance of the City over industry, of the aristocracy over
the middle classes for over a century after the Reform Act, the private–state
divide in secondary education – all these have been rehearsed in previous
debates. Some have traced the cause of the malaise to the Civil War and the
restoration of the monarchy under Whig oligarchic control. Others have
concluded that the revolutionary spirit of rationalism and bourgeois capitalism
never quite took root in England. England, it seemed, had missed out on the
two modern revolutions – capitalism and democracy – by arriving at both
before their time was ripe. From here on reason was forever displaced by
convention, change by compromise, method by muddle, and theory by
vulgar pragmatism. England was the despair of modernists, the frustrator of
revolutionaries.

But it survived. No other polity in Europe, indeed in the world, has had
an uninterrupted hegemonic political elite for 350 years and, if you discount
the Civil War, an unconquered continuity for 900 years and more. Against
all odds it defeated Revolutionary and Bonapartist France, the Kaiser's
Germany and then, in its final epitome, Hitler's Germany and fascist Japan,
the last albeit with much help from the Russians and the Americans. It had

one of the largest empires and then, with only slight resistance, gave it up, with as great a nobility in its dissolution as baseness in its acquisition.[4] Britain also, unlike the other European belligerents, paid for both the wars and did not renege on any debts. This fantastic drain on its resources, which alarmed the young Keynes working at the Treasury during the First World War and was so much in contrast with the German, French or even the Japanese experience, is hardly noted.

Neither continual survival nor the sacrifice in the two wars, especially the second, when the battle was for democracy, count for much in the balance. In Britain right and left alike have turned into vices what, for an earlier generation of Anglophile Europeans, were cardinal British achievements (think of Hayek and his veneration for common law). Indeed, in this respect, the analysis of Middlemas was no less critical of the stabilising (read compromising) tendencies of the British polity. The seeming antagonism but *de facto* cooperation of the British party political system now appeared to be adversarial and the *de facto* coalitional political culture (Butskellism) was derided for not being sharply ideological enough, by the left in the 1960s and the right in the 1970s.

But everywhere the defining criterion of success became the economy; measured as GDP growth rates in 'the league tables, the rate of growth of manufacturing output (at other times employment) took prime place. Britain's standing in the league table, especially *vis-à-vis* its European neighbours, became the one criterion by which the economy, indeed the polity, was to be judged. And here is the paradox: the rate of growth of GDP which Britain has enjoyed in the postwar period has been the highest, and most sustained over time, in its historical experience. But while the earlier debate in the interwar period was concerned with the ability to retain the Empire or retain a hegemonic position in the European balance of power, the postwar discussion was entirely about growth rates of GDP. The fact that over the last 50 years per capita GDP has trebled is of little consequence. It has not been as fast as the rest of the world, and that is what hurts. It is neither the absolute improvement in the standard of living, the quality of health, or even the human development index which is the measure. It is the GDP. And, by this count, although the UK is still among the richest 20 countries, it is down in the league table.[5]

The paradox of this debate is that it was not until the 1960s, that is, after the unprecedented 15 years of full employment and GDP growth, that the debate broke out, with the young New Left complaining about decline and stagnation and then looking for the roots of this stagnation in Britain's past. The question as to why, if the institutions had been so unchanging and moribund, if the City had dominated since the 1880s, and if trade unions had been beastly since the Taff Vale judgement (and if anything were even beastlier in the 1950s), growth should be so high relative to the past, is a question never posed. It is the fact that others were growing faster that became the worry.

Thus one concern I have with Hutton, who values solidarity, cohesion and other non-economic values, is the obsession he shares with other critics of Britain's decline about relative GDP growth rates. Even if we conceded that GDP accurately measures income and that income measures welfare (which would be very neoclassical), we have to believe that welfare depends entirely on relative income *vis-à-vis* other nations and that, by this token, British society has failed to promote the welfare of its citizens. Do we really believe this? Or is the argument that welfare depends on income, yet the data on other countries show that ours could be higher if only we were different – harder-working, better educated, better governed, better provided with healthy financial institutions? We could, by achieving higher income, have things we cannot now have. But is our deprivation the result of lower relative income or of greater inequality? Is there not maldistribution between private and public goods, between current consumption and future benefits?

The decline debate which both the right and left have taken to their heart is thus based on some strange premises. Each side comes to it with a different agenda. The right, which used to be proud of the British Constitution, the continuity, the compromise, the managed slowness of change, suddenly turned against it in the 1970s and identified all the virtues as vices. The Thatcher programme, loosely connected with Peterhouse and Hayek and in some sense buttressed by Middlemas's analysis of consensual politics, decisively adopted the decline thesis and sought a programme to reverse it.

It is a blind spot of Hutton's that he is so upset by the effects of the Thatcher revolution that he sees it in purely negative terms.[6] It is true that Thatcher did not touch the City, a core cause of decline according to Hutton, but he fails to see that the reform of trade unions, which was a constant thread in the 1966, the 1970 and the 1974 governments, was tackled by Thatcher. It was not done in the way Hutton or I would approve, but it would not have happened without Thatcher. With or without Thatcher it is difficult to show that the British trade unions would have behaved as Hutton would like – as co-partners like their German counterparts. Even in Germany it took the destruction of two Reichs to change behaviour from antagonism (recall Bismarck and his war on the unions) to cooperation. In an undestroyed civil society, long habits die hard. Attitudes of sullen servility and resentful obedience, the 'us and them' on the parts of both workers and managers, the refusal of the TUC to contemplate workers' control in the later 1940s when it was possible, or even later with the Bullock report and the abandonment of control over allocation of labour, the pathetic attachment to free collective bargaining (just as much a belief in the idea of labour as a commodity as the neoclassical *laissez-faire* which Hutton deplores) on which petard Mrs Thatcher hoisted the unions after they had scuttled the last Labour government in living memory – this culture was as much part of the diagnosis of decline as was the City. But while Hutton deplores the City, he is also against the attack on trade unions. At many places in the analysis it is not clear whether Hutton sees a particular defect as a long-term one, say, persisting over 100 years, or as the recent result of Thatcherism. Thus take his telling critique of the City, that it is short-termist, that it imposes high rates of payback and hence it discourages investment in long-term projects. At one stage it would seem that this is traced back to the demise of country banks and the failure of industrial banking experiments so that by the 1880s the pattern was established. But the decline of Britain as a manufacturing nation hardly goes back that far. It is difficult to see how one would measure it, but in terms of proportion of total labour employed in industry (somewhat broader than manufacturing) the UK had a higher proportion than France, Germany, Japan, the Netherlands and the USA until 1950, and was only exceeded by Germany in 1960 and subsequently by Japan in 1984.[7] If the decline is only dated from the oil crisis when deindustrialisation became a theme, then much of the long-term analysis is beside the point.

The labelling of the City as the problem has a long and distinguished pedigree in the decline debate. Hutton recognises, however, that the City is the only world-class sector the UK has, maintaining its high position above the USA and Japan when all other British sectors have failed to do so. But having noted this, he proceeds to criticise the City for a variety of practices which in his view discourage investment and growth. Now, as I pointed out before, growth is higher than in any previous 50 years, even while the City has remained powerful. Although it can be claimed that, with different credit conditions of different financial institutions, investment and growth would have been higher, this is not convincingly demonstrated. The decline of the share of manufacturing in total output has occurred since the oil crisis and, while all OECD countries have experienced this, the UK has declined in this respect more than others. But is this because of age-old structures in the City, or is it the result of other forces which have retarded competitiveness? The City, far from being moribund, is a rapidly innovating sector; if it were not, it would not have survived global competition. So it is not as if the City fails to meet demands made upon it as long as they are profitable. The argument has to be that more investment in manufacturing will somehow result in higher returns, either directly in terms of profitability or in terms of some wider social rates of return which can compensate for lack of economic profitability. But there is no evidence for this. Manufacturing is much beloved of the left, but it is only one of several ways of producing value added and, unlike health or education or roads, it has few, if any, externalities.

The truth is that profitability in British manufacturing collapsed in the wake of the oil shock. It had been under pressure by the end of the 1960s, as Andrew Glyn and Bob Sutcliffe pointed out to their credit way back in 1970.[8] But if the rate of return on capital was between 8 per cent and 10 per cent in 1970–2, it was 3 per cent by 1974–6.[9] Though the rate of return on capital (RRC) briefly revived in the late 1970s, it did not reach the previous peak of 1972 until 1985. The Thatcher programme thus has to be seen as a successful attempt at restoring the rate of return on capital. If Thatcherism is seen as a programme for the rescue of British capitalism and the crisis of the 1970s interpreted as the collapse of profitability, it becomes easier to understand that the manufacturing sector which went under in the UK, as in many other countries, was simply unprofitable. It could have been kept in production by subsidies but at that point the priority of manufacturing (which should be a surplus-creating rather than surplus-absorbing sector) becomes arguable. It is one thing to subsidise public transport or remove health from market calculus by subsidies, but quite another to do this for manufacturing.

The City and its structure were marginal to this. Perhaps the influx of oil and the consequent overvaluation of the pound were major factors but, in a world of flexible exchange rates, it is difficult to devalue if your currency is in demand – not impossible, but difficult. One way to counter the export surplus is either to import goods (which is what happened, wiping out manufacturing which was uncompetitive) or to export capital. But Hutton does not approve of the export of capital. So his position would have led to an even bigger decimation of manufacturing than poor (!) Mrs T. managed. This overvaluation was again at the heart of the second big recession of the 1990s. Mrs Thatcher's perverse belief that a high value of the pound was a matter of national pride led her to ask for a rise in the value of the pound *vis-à-vis* the Deutschmark as the price for entry into the Exchange Rate Mechanism (ERM). Much effort was spent deploying high interest rates in order to shadow a buoyant Deutschmark. This meant that the UK reversed the depreciation of the pound following its high level in 1980 until 1985 and ended up joining the ERM at the level of DM 2.95 to the pound. The effect on output and profitability was drastic. All the gains in the rate of return on capital were reversed and a severe recession followed from which the economy is only just recovering.

None of this seems to me to require any heart-searching about the City, which can make as much money out of a strong pound as a weak one. In this respect the City is not now as it was in the 1920s when it insisted on going back on the Gold Standard. The new City has a variety of products to sell and the global market to play in. It is not as engaged in the fortunes of the UK government and as worried about them as it used to be. UK gilt business is part of its business but there are other ways of making money. In this respect the City is socially and culturally more detached from the old Establishment structure, less a part of the feudal hangover than it used to be even as recently as when Harold Wilson was in office. It is no accident that a non-knighted, non-merchant banker, non-'toff' is the Governor of the Bank of England. That is news, as is the fact that John Major is only the third non-Oxford graduate to be prime minister since the war. Indeed, his background is neither Eton nor Harrow, nor yet grammar school nor Cambridge. That is the fruit of Harold Wilson's meritocratic revolution.

The bulk of new investment which takes place every year does not take place through the City. Nearly 90 per cent of new investment takes place independently of firms issuing new equity. So if investment is low, the City accounts for only a small part of it. Hutton nowhere makes this simple empirical fact clear. Now it is possible to argue that, despite this small actual contribution, the climate and culture of the City retards investment whether or not it is raised by new equity. But again, where is the evidence? There is a high dividend pay-out ratio. If shares were held by individuals who then proceeded to blow away their dividend on frivolous consumption rather than reinvest in other financial assets, one could argue that perhaps retention of profits by corporations would be better. But the bulk of shares is not owned by individuals but by institutions who only buy other financial assets; and the individuals who own shares are by and large big holders who do not need dividends to spend on cigars, or whatever. If they are not investing in UK manufacturing it is not because they are consuming it (though UK consumption income ratio is high, but that is another story to which I shall come). It is because there are better ways of making higher profits. To compel people to invest at home on the possible but unproven hypothesis that higher investment will lead to higher returns (since then we will all be good cooperators like the Germans) is surely a signal for a massive waste of resources. Retained earnings can still be invested abroad or spent in takeovers; so dividend control is no great panacea. The problem is not high dividends but rather the low profitability of UK manufacturing and business in general.

Hutton's conviction that the City is the core of the problem does lead him to make some strange statements. He says, for example, that 'in Britain, the necessity of financing investment from retained earnings *forced wages down and fostered brutal exploitation at work*, and the formation of British trade unions and working-class attitudes to management was closely linked to this searing experience in the early factory age'.[10] Now there are several problems here. British wages rose in real terms during the Victorian era and indeed the debate about the working-class aristocracy concerned the notion that the Empire made possible higher wages in Britain than on the Continent. It all depends on what Hutton means by early factory age. But real wages rose from £47.2 per annum in 1820 to £75.2 by 1851 (in 1851 prices) for skilled workers and from £34.2 to £52.2 for all workers.[11] What is more, real wages continued to rise in Britain throughout the rest of the nineteenth century.[12] There was poverty for those out of work or not in factory work; but to argue that the financial system led to a repression of real wages is pure rhetoric. If anything, the City, and the whole apparatus of gentlemanly capitalism via the imperial connection and the insistence on free trade, brought extra benefits to British workers. This is also why, for all the peculiarities in the attitudes of British workers towards management, the class struggle never took the violent form in Britain that it did in France and Germany.

Hutton also says that 'debt is a much cheaper form of capital than issuing shares',[13] going on to imply that the failure to borrow from banks raised the cost of capital. But this is nonsense. If I issue equity then the buyer shares in the risk. If I make a loss, I do not need to pay out anything. If I borrow from a bank or issue a bond, the risk falls entirely on me and, loss or profit, I have to service the loan or the bond. The cost which has to be compared is the expected cost, allowing for the risk of bankruptcy, and not just the recorded cost. The many Third World countries who borrowed petrodollars from banks learned to regret it; had they attracted equal sums in direct equity investment, their problems would have been greatly eased.

The most telling indictment of the City's stranglehold on industry, Hutton believes, is the CBI finding that British businessmen 'aim for a nominal or real rate of return in excess of 20 per cent'. I wonder where these people are hiding, since the ICC data on RRC that the Bank of England has put together shows that in no year between 1970–92 did the RRC exceed 12 per cent and in 1992 it was only around 6 per cent to 8 per cent (see Figure 17.1). British businessmen perhaps fantasise about the rates of return they can earn, but it is astonishing that anyone should take such a finding seriously. If true, it implies that, relative to these businessmen (apparently 40 per cent of the sample) there are an awful lot, a majority, who aim for and achieve some appallingly low rates of return. But even so, why aiming for high rates of return should be a bad thing is not clear. Would Hutton prefer it if the majority had said they expected to make a loss? Would the economy be better off if all our businessmen aimed just to break even?

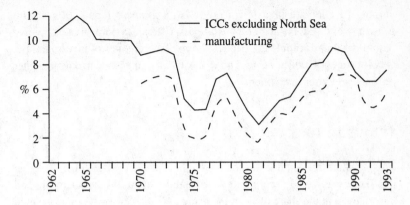

Figure 17.1: UK profitability: net rate of return on capital employed.
Source: CSO.

In short, in his indictment of the City, Hutton makes our flesh creep but does not convince those who do not have a visceral hatred of money and may possess a modicum of understanding of economics. To argue that the City pushes British industry to earn high rates of return which the latter proceeds so to do, has to be reconciled with the fact that rates of return on capital are not high relative to other countries in as much as things are comparable. What is more, historical data on RRC, as put together by the Bank of England with care and attention, fail to substantiate the story. Indeed, if British business did make 20 per cent on its capital we would all have been much better off.

What there is evidence for, and Hutton does not mention, is the peculiar diagram reproduced in the report of the Commission on Social Justice.[14] It shows a cross-section of countries and plots their rates of investment as a proportion of GDP against their rates of growth of GDP per worker. While the UK invests around 8 per cent of GDP it gets a larger than proportionate growth of output from it – nearly 2.5 per cent. The UK in this diagram lies above the line which shows that every four percentage-point-rise in share of investment after the first 5 per cent gives an extra 1 per cent rise in the growth rate of output per worker. Thus Germany is just on the line and Canada is below the line, as is Japan. This would imply that the UK gets more out of what it invests than its rivals. The diagram is unfortunately not clear about the timescale over which the data were collected, though the line is said to be a fitted statistical relationship, in which case countries above the line are more efficient than those on or below the line. The point to make, in other words, is that there is no merit in investing more if you do not get higher output. To compare investment ratios is to compare inputs; to compare growth rates of GDP is to compare outputs. Efficiency comparisons involve output per unit of input. The Soviet Union had high rates of investment but very low rates of return. There is no virtue in higher investment; only in higher returns from your investment.

THE REAL STORY

This is where Hutton has misconceived the Thatcher programme. It is true that there was savage scaling down of employment in manufacturing and indeed even in the share of manufacturing in GDP. This was not an isolated incident for the UK but was common to most OECD countries in the post-oil-shock years. In the UK the shock was more severe but this was perhaps because there was severe overmanning. The battle in newspaper printing was certainly bloody, but there was no denying that Fleet Street printing practices were outmoded and kept in existence by trade union power and indulgent press barons. If you need convincing, read Eric Hobsbawm's account of the printing industry in his *Labouring Men*, published in 1964, 20 years before reality caught up with the printers.[15] British Steel is the most cost-efficient steel-making firm in Europe today and British Airways one of the few profit-making airlines. The British experience of growth in manufacturing output being accounted for entirely by productivity growth and not necessarily involving growth of employment became the norm and was dubbed jobless growth by the UNDP's Human Development Report of 1993. Manufacturing sectors, if anything, will continue to shrink in terms of employment throughout the OECD countries, albeit at a variable pace. The shakeout in Britain came earlier and was perhaps more brutal than has been the case elsewhere, but that is all.

A telling example of this development is the British car industry. At one point in *TSWI*, Hutton compares the treatment of British Leyland (BL) with that of Mazda cars in Japan. In the British case a bail-out loan given by the UK government was frittered away on higher wages to buy industrial peace; and BL went on its way to be dismembered, with various of its parts bought out, including Rover which is now owned by BMW. In the British case the banks had (quite rightly in my view, though not in Hutton's) refused to supply $1.2 billion. Why banks should supply money without any guarantee of its wise use is beyond me. I know that they often do so, not least in the case of Third World debt, but this does not mean they should make a habit of it. The

Japanese banks took over the management of Mazda as they rescued it and the result was success.

Now, while the British did not follow the Japanese way, it was because these strategies are deeply embedded in history and culture. The car industry in Britain did not disappear. The British solution was to acquire a global car industry by inviting in foreign companies who brought better management. The British car industry is thriving. Although employment has halved since 1971 and is down to 280000 people, output, productivity and exports are up. British car workers working in Japanese-owned firms take 19 hours to produce a car, compared to 18 in Japan, 27 in the USA, 36 in Western Europe and 31 in US firms in Europe. Output from the three Japanese firms (Nissan, Toyota and Honda) plus one US-owned firm (IBC) increased from 106000 vehicles in 1990 to 540000 in 1995 and is expected to be 830000 in the year 2000. Car exports went from 339000 in 1989 to 605000 in 1991, and will be nearly 1 million in the year 2000. British labour costs per unit of output have fallen from 148 (Germany = 100) to 90 between 1984 and 1994.[16]

It is possible to say that this is not a British car industry since it is not British-owned. But the workers are British; many of the component firms are British-owned; and the exports enter British accounts. This is the nature of global capitalism. Do we want output and employment or do we care who owns capital? Since the usual complaint on the left is about exporting capital, why not welcome imports of capital? The point is that the British way of reconstructing the car industry was not the same as the German or the Japanese but was no less effective. Had we stuck to the national bourgeois path (as the Marxists used to say in the old days) there is every chance we would have no car industry.

The reason for this is one part of the British problem about which Hutton is much less eloquent. This is British management. It is well known to be class-ridden, self-indulgent, risk-averse and old-school-tie-bound. Paradoxically, British firms perform better with foreign workers than with British workers. And, obversely, foreign firms get better work out of British workers than British private or public managers do. *Tant mieux*, I say. Let us export British capital abroad along with the managers and import foreign capital and managers. This would no doubt horrify Hutton, but why should it do so unless British is defined as owned by British-born and bred capitalists, rather than as produced by British workers? The car industry story is repeated in the television manufacturing industry and the transformation of the Welsh economy is an example of this. Jobs are jobs; who cares who supplies the capital?

Thus Thatcherism did decimate the manufacturing industry, but it can claim plausibly that this retrenchment saved such manufacturing industry as Britain still has. At the time of Thatcher's election, the strategy usually tried was rescuing 'lame duck' companies, using the National Enterprise Board to give large loans to companies about to collapse, or indeed even fully nationalising loss-making companies. This had been the case during the 1964–79 period under Heath as well as Wilson and Callaghan. Deindustrialisation had been proceeding before Thatcher came to power.[17] The Left's alternative was to nationalise *x* companies where *x* was 20 or 200, depending on how far to the left you were. That strategy was based upon the notion that UK companies were strong and powerful and rich and had to be controlled by the state. The fact was that by the early 1970s UK companies were uncompetitive. Indeed, the immediate postwar years had given Britain a false competitive advantage while continental European countries were still recovering, as was Japan. But by the late 1950s and early 1960s, this advantage had eroded. Even the Americans felt the heat of German competition in the car industry when Volkswagen appeared on the scene.

This problem of micro-competitiveness was as ill-diagnosed as the question of industrial size; Wilson's setting up of the Industrial Reorganisation Corporation was meant to help create larger companies via merger in the hope that economies of scale would accrue merely thanks to largeness. But the decline in export share continued and the balance of payments constraint began to bite. Although it was not until 1984 that Britain had a balance of trade deficit on manufacturing account, deindustrialisation had been proceeding since much earlier. Of the three strategies available – Heath–Wilson, AES[18] and Thatcher – it is a moot question as to which would have led to a globally competitive manufacturing industry larger in size than the present one. All that Thatcher did was to cut subsidies off; Callaghan, had he won, would have spent North Sea Oil propping up more British Leylands at best. The AES needed a completely protected economy to bolster British manufactures.

Hutton will argue that there is a fourth way – German social partnership, which would have combined efficiency with compassion. But that was never on the cards. Even government–trade union partnership in the then much-heralded 'Social Contract' of 1975 ended in tears for the Labour government. Nor can such a fundamental institutional change be delivered in time periods shorter than decades, except in the wake of a traumatic shock such as defeat in war. The Germans, after all, developed their cohesiveness after defeat, not before. So Thatcher may have been beastly, but it is questionable whether British policy makers had a better strategy up their sleeves. The extra costs of the Thatcher era are, in my view, the result more of the inept macroeconomic policy followed than any other factor.

CAPITALISM, EMPLOYMENT, AND PROFIT

When Keynesian economics began to fail and come under attack many people, including some fine economists whom Hutton cites, mistook the problem to be one of theoretical detail about labour market behaviour. But the real cause in my view was quite other and quite obvious. Keynes was able to fashion an argument whereby, instead of the struggle between capital and labour being antagonistic, a class compromise could be worked out. Higher profits (though not higher profit rate) could be reconciled with a high level of employment. The Marxist ghost of the reserve army of labour was (temporarily as it turned out) laid to rest. The Anglo-Saxon economies which had no tradition of class compromise or social cohesion needed the Keynesian fix. And so for 25 years it worked well for both sides.

But eventually continuous full employment threatened the rate as well as the mass of profits. This was disguised as the problem of inflation and the monetarists further muddied the waters by blaming it on excess money supply and saying that it was not the fault of trade union bargaining. But the ability of governments to maintain the political equilibrium in the face of full employment, while keeping consumption stable but not too high to affect investment, was fragile. Without a viable incomes policy or a collective bargaining framework that was solidaristic this could be done, if at all, only by a stop–go policy. This affected growth and productivity. Eventually the inflationary pressures of continual full employment and free decentralised collective bargaining proved too much and in Anglo-Saxon economies the influence of monetarists displaced that of Keynesians. The data on profit rates, imperfect as they are, match perfectly. The oil price quadrupling and the collapse in profitability coincide in the early 1970s. After some struggle in the mid-1970s political leaders in the UK as well as the USA gave up the ghost. Callaghan, as much as Gerald Ford and Jimmy Carter, started as a Keynesian and ended up a wet monetarist.

Keynes had never explicitly talked about profitability, though it is implicit in his aggregate supply curve. The idea that limits to profitability may set a barrier to full employment was old Marxism and came into post-Keynesian economics via Kalecki. But at the time, in the 1970s, the left Keynesians were proud of this barrier because they thought socialism would come sooner via an intensification of the class struggle. But capitalists proved .

smarter and reneged on the social compromise implicitly entered into after the Second World War. Profitability was restored in the classic Marxian fashion by throwing out workers and making those who were there work harder, by capital migrating abroad in search of higher profits and by the once almighty state quavering before the newly internationalised/globalised capital and doing its bidding.

Now no amount of rejigging the theory of the labour market, introducing information asymmetries, or talking about the prisoner's dilemma or efficiency wages will change the pressures caused by profitability one jot. Keynes knew perfectly well that for his system to work capital mobility had to be restricted. In the Bretton Woods proposals this was allowed for. The vision of Thatcher was stark. Within weeks of her government coming to power the UK introduced full convertibility, and with globally mobile capital Keynesian policies cannot work. This is not because the neoclassical model of rationality or of labour markets is better than that of old or new Keynesians, but because capitalism works on profitability. Capitalism may generate full employment, if that is convenient, as was the case briefly and uniquely in its history for the 25 years after 1945. But the system is not meant to generate jobs; it is designed to generate and thrive on profits.

Now it would be nice, Hutton and others would say, if we could have decent capitalism which could do both. Some even think, though not many capitalists seem to agree, that profit and employment correlate positively; the German model is the exemplar of this in their view. But German economic policy was never Keynesian at any time. It was hard-line monetarist from the beginning. This was because the German economy had institutional arrangements cemented by the defeat in war and the subsequent determination of Germans to redeem themselves. They did not need the Keynesian fix. The Germans did not rely on high and stable levels of consumption to get their high levels of employment. They built a high-saving economy, and living standards in Germany, as in Japan, were far below economies with similar incomes for a long time. The Bundesbank would not tolerate high levels of employment or wage bargaining of the Anglo-Saxon variety if inflation threatened. It was by keeping the share of wages firmly in check, ownership of capital tightly concentrated and profitability guaranteed by a tough monetary policy that the Germans got where they are now. Keynesian economics is taught in German universities but German policy makers do not follow its tenets.

The globalisation of capitalism is a much debated issue, but in my view it is already here and rules out Keynesianism in one country. It is no longer valid to think of capitalism as bounded by the nation state. Countries which have high savings ratios and a hard-working but highly literate workforce will win the future economic battles. The Asian countries are already proving this. The issue is not state versus market, or neoclassical versus Keynesian economics. It is whether to work with the grain of the system based on profitability (no other system being any longer on offer) and follow policies which enhance rather than impede profitability, or go under.

CONCLUSION

Political economy is a mansion with many rooms. There is much room here for disagreements. There is much to admire in Hutton's book and I agree so much with many of the sentiments that it seems churlish to argue. But I do think he makes it sound easy for Britain to fashion a new polity along German lines. He sets up villains – the City, Thatcherism – which are not so much straw people as one-sided. Neither is all evil and to be wished away or reformed. If the world is no longer like it was in the golden age of Keynesianism, or as it is in socially cooperative and cohesive Germany, that is just too bad. You cannot travel back in time and it is not easy to shift a polity in space.

The excesses of Thatcherism were perhaps more the result of its macroeconomic short-termism – the sudden lurches from hard fiscal policies to the Lawson bonanza. If the UK could have a steady macroeconomic policy not thrown off course by short-run electoral idiocies such as bowing to the clamour for a 'feel good' factor (that is, inflation), if it could lower the level of aggregate consumption and raise the level of saving, if it could enhance the rate of return from its investments at the same time as raising the rate of investment, if it could stop subsidising the middle classes and putting punitive taxes on the poor and the unemployed, who knows, it may yet have a successful economy. It may not be Germany, but it may still be a tolerably decent place.

NOTES

* A different version of this article originally appeared in *New Political Economy*, Vol. 1, No. 1, pp. 79–95 (1996).
1. Perry Anderson's original article was 'Origins of the Present Crisis', *New Left Review*, Vol. 23 (1963), pp. 26–53. E.P. Thompson replied to this in 'The

peculiarities of the English', in Thompson (ed.), *The Poverty of Theory* (London: Merlin, 1978), pp. 35–91. Anderson returned to this theme (along with other essays) in 'The figures of descent', in Anderson (ed.), *English Questions* (London: Verso, 1992), pp. 121–92.

2. Corelli Barnett, *The Audit of War* (London: Macmillan, 1986).

3. Will Hutton, *The State We're In* (London: Jonathan Cape, 1995).

4. Like many modern British intellectuals, Hutton displays a total amnesia about the Empire; it is as if the Empire had never been there and, when there, had cost nothing and benefited nobody. The whole debate about Imperial Preference versus Free Trade which split the Liberals and Conservatives is hardly mentioned. The loss of Empire in the postwar era seems to have been a non-event though the role of sterling balances in propping up the pound was crucial at various periods through the first half of the twentieth century. The Atlee government robbed the Empire by devaluing sterling and short-changing the colonial holders of sterling balances.

5. UNDP's Human Development Index (HDI) is an alternative to GDP, designed to capture health and education as well as income, but income is heavily discounted to allow for diminishing marginal utility. The UK's rank in HDI is five above its GDP rank while Germany's HDI rank is nine below its GDP rank. Thus the UK gets more 'well-being' out of its income than Germany does.

6. See my own discussion of the British disease in 'Labour's economic policy', in J. Griffiths (ed.), *Socialism in a Cold Climate* (Allen and Unwin, 1983) and 'Is Thatcherism the cure for the British Disease?', in F. Green (ed.), *The Restructuring of the UK Economy* (Brighton: Harvester, 1989).

7. See Barry Supple, 'British economic decline since 1945', in Roderick Floud and Donald McCloskey (eds), *The Economic History of Britain Since 1700*, Vol. 3 (Cambridge: Cambridge University Press, 1995), p. 335, Table 11.10.

8. Andrew Glyn and Bob Sutcliffe, *British Capitalism, Workers and the Profit Squeeze* (Harmondsworth: Penguin, 1972).

9. The data are for industrial and commercial companies of ICCs as the Bank of England calls them. I am quoting the Bank's rate of return on capital statistics.

10. Hutton, *The State We're In*, p. 135 (emphasis added).

11. See P. Lindert, 'Unequal living standards, 1870–1914', in Floud and McCloskey, *Economic History of Britain*, Vol. 1, p. 370.

12. See M. Mackinnon, 'Living standards, 1870–1914', in *ibid.*, Vol. 2, Table 11.2, p. 272.

13. Hutton, *The State We're In*, p. 150.

14. The Report of the Commission on *Social Justice: Strategies for National Renewal* (London: Vintage, 1994).

15. Eric Hobsbawm, *Labouring Men: Studies in the History of Labour* (London: Weidenfeld and Nicolson, 1964).

16. See Garel Rhys, 'The transformation of the motor car industry in the UK', in R. Turner (ed.), *The British Economy in Transition* (London: Routledge, 1955).

17. A. Singh, 'UK Industry and the World Economy: A Case of Deindustrialisation?', *Cambridge Economic Journal*, Vol. 1 (1977), pp. 113–36.

18. The Alternative Economic Strategy (AES), as it was called in the late 1970s, wanted to erect tariff barriers so that inefficient British capitalists could make profits while employing British workers in stagnant industries.

18 Stakeholding Yes; the German Model No*

David Soskice

Whether or not 'stakeholding' is an appropriate centre-left strategy for a country like Britain, the debate about it produces the feeling that British politics is becoming serious. As Margaret Thatcher realised, serious politics requires simple, powerful ideas. Stakeholding is a strong candidate. It seems important, therefore, to put aside the temptation to talk about spin doctors and warm words, and to engage sympathetically with the concept.

The discussion so far – for instance in Tony Blair's Singapore speech or in Will Hutton's book, *The State We're In* – raises cause for concern. Labour is on the verge of power; it will govern an economy whose most fundamental traits are profoundly Anglo-Saxon: highly developed financial markets and share-based financing; deregulated labour markets; an education and training system in which companies play little part; and a company sector in which companies have highly competitive, arm's length relations with each other. Yet the main proposals for developing a stakeholder society are borrowed from a quite different system of advanced capitalism, notably from the more coordinated capitalism of northern Europe, and Germany in particular.

A central element of Labour's idea of stakeholding is to give employees a real stake in their companies through enhanced security, participation and skill development. This is a characteristic of large companies in northern European economies; it forms an attractive aspect of their type of capitalism (though do not count on benefiting to the full if you are a woman), *and* plays an important role in their competitiveness. But 'company stakeholding' works in those economies because they have a quite different institutional framework. By contrast to the liberal market capitalism of Anglo-Saxon economies like Britain and the US, the institutional framework of northern European economies underwrites several important economic relationships: companies securing long-term relations with their owners; unions and employer associations playing an important role in the *de facto* and often *de jure* regulation of labour markets; companies being closely integrated into the training system and cooperating with each other through powerful industry associations. Without this institutional framework, company stakeholding is unlikely to prosper. Thus Labour is faced with a choice: if it wants to keep company stakeholding as a central part of its strategy it must envisage institutional changes of dramatic proportions; alternatively, it needs to develop a concept of stakeholding appropriate to an Anglo-Saxon liberal market economy.

It has long been a pragmatic a legitimate practice of Britain's centre-left to borrow policies from abroad: in the 1950s and 1960s we looked to French planning; in the 1970s and 1980s to Scandinavian social democracy. Now, in the 1990s, we look to Germany and stakeholding. This approach to policy making has its attractions but it also has its problems.

For British social democrats in the institutionally bare landscape of post-Thatcherism, the Germanic northern European model opens a treasure-trove of policies: long-term financing of companies; substantial employee participation; employment security; effective training systems and so on. Moreover, Germany is undoubtedly a successful capitalist economy, which helps to counter objections from City economists and Conservative politicians. Add to that Will Hutton's heady mixture of polemic and intelligence and the attraction of policy borrowing is clear.

But there is also a very large difficulty: transplanting institutional policies from one type of system of advanced capitalism to another has seldom worked. Just as attempts to copy French planning mechanisms failed in the 1960s, so too did social contract corporatism in the 1970s. The more we understand other systems the clearer it becomes that they are institutionally interlocked: taking any one part of a system (such as company stakeholding) away from the rest of the system is unlikely to be fruitful.

STAKEHOLDING: THE GERMAN MODEL

In comparison to many American and British companies, their German counterparts provide employees with security and with systematic skill and career development in exchange for the cooperative use of those skills in the company's interest. But this depends, in at least three important ways, on a framework which would have to be constructed from scratch in Britain.

The first requirement of the company stakeholding framework is long-term financing. It is well known that German companies, large and small, benefit from the availability of long-term finance. This is critical to the security which employees enjoy. Employees would give much less credence to the idea of security if they knew that owners could suddenly demand higher returns and job cuts, or that companies could be easily sold to new owners. And companies themselves will only be interested in taking employment security seriously if they can invest in their employees – backed by patient investors.

Why could a British government not develop long-term capital? The German system's ability to provide long-term capital does not so much depend on *legislation* as on concentrated shareholding and implicit agreements among large shareholders to be 'stable shareholders'. In Germany these arrangements are coordinated by banks, which depend upon the close relations between companies (through interlocking board memberships) to help them monitor company performance. The same is true of local lending by community savings and cooperative banks: they too depend on the connections between local companies to know when problems arise.

In Britain these close and long-established links between companies seldom exist. The incentive structure encourages shareholders to sell out when trouble looms. We also have a different conception of market competition. In Germany there is a presumption that cooperation between companies will be important and should not be penalised by competition law. In Britain the underlying presumption is to encourage strong competition.

The second requirement of company stakeholding is an effective system of initial training whereby employees acquire substantial skills in the area in which the company operates. If labour markets are deregulated, as in Britain and the US, and it is easy for companies to bid skilled employees away from the companies which have trained them, the incentive to train diminishes sharply. In Germany, by contrast, labour markets are tightly regulated as far as wage determination and training is concerned, which makes poaching more difficult.

The initial training investment which companies make in employees, and which employees make in companies (by accepting low starting wages and by narrowing their future employment options) is critical to company stakeholding. Both sides must make a commitment. Again, it is difficult to see how a British government could create the institutional conditions for effective initial training without far greater changes than so far imagined. Moreover, the creation of strong employer associations in Britain seems beyond the ability of the government.

The third element of company stakeholding is participation in decision making. This is not a happy family dance in which German employees get some intrinsic pleasure from participation. It is a central part of the stakeholder bargain, and it has two aspects: from the employee's side, a big investment is made in the company in terms of the employee's skill portfolio. In return, the employee gets a conditional guarantee of employment security subject to overriding business imperatives. But the employee is not prepared to take it on trust that the company will stick to this agreement. Hence the necessity of 'work councils', elected by employees and endowed with considerable power (on overtime, redundancies, and so on) to ensure that the employer behaves appropriately. This gives the employee confidence in the stakeholder bargain and thus promotes identification with the company's success as well as restraint in the use of employee power.

Once again, the company stakeholder model depends on institutional settings. German-style works councils are far more powerful than those envisaged in the European Union's Social Chapter. They would be open to abuse by employees who had not grown up in the system and would, in any case, need to be balanced by powerful employer associations, for which there is no basis in Britain. Any attempt by Labour to move in this direction would rupture the delicate relationship which it is now developing with business.

IS GERMAN STAKEHOLDING OUT OF DATE?

Even if it *were* possible to establish the institutional framework for northern European company stakeholding, it is not clear that it would be *desirable* to do so. While northern European economies have some advantages over Anglo-Saxon ones these are not overwhelming. Here are just two reasons for scepticism about chasing after the Germanic model.

First, economies whose efficiency derives from companies being able to take a long-term perspective, often exclude women from serious careers in the private sector. This is because such companies depend on the long-term loyalty and continuous availability of employees, particularly managers. In these economies, women either care for children and elderly relatives unpaid at home (Germany, Japan), or do the same thing, paid, in the public sector (Sweden). That is the logic of these systems. By contrast, in the most developed Anglo-Saxon economy – the US – women represent over 40 per cent of private sector managers. Companies are organised on a more short-term basis and accept that able managers may leave. Well-educated women do significantly better in the US (and Britain) than in Germany, Japan or Sweden. Upwardly mobile women should be wary of proposals to develop a northern European-type labour market.

Second, while the northern European and Japanese institutional frameworks provide a comparative advantage for high-quality manufacturing, the more deregulated Anglo-Saxon frameworks have an overwhelming comparative advantage in internationally competitive services. These range from international banking (the big four German banks are in the process of moving their international banking operations from Frankfurt to London) and management consulting, to airlines and the entertainment industry. Almost all radical innovation in emergent technologies (semiconductors, biotechnology) has come from the US and to a lesser extent the UK, with virtually none from Germany. Furthermore, complex systems technology (telecommunications systems, defence systems, large aircraft production, large software systems) is another field where Anglo-Saxon economies have a comparative advantage. In none of these areas – which will be of increasing importance over the next decades – are northern European economies (or Japan) leading competitors. In all these sectors, high incentives and the ability of companies to move quickly are vital. This is why more deregulated economies perform better.

Despite all these reservations, stakeholding remains an attractive concept. Before considering what a viable strategy for stakeholding might look like in a British setting we must be clear about what stakeholding *is*, what gives it its appeal, and why it goes beyond a simple elucidation of citizens' rights.

STAKES AND CONTRACTS

Stakeholding is an implicit contract between the state and the individual citizen. The fact that it is a contract means that both sides have obligations and receive benefits. But the benefits of stakeholding for the individual stakeholder are contingent on the carrying out of associated obligations. It thus runs counter to the principle of universal entitlements to welfare benefits, for example. The universal entitlement is to the contract; the benefits only accrue to those who have carried out the relevant obligations. Also, the citizen has a choice about how much to 'invest' in the contract. Some may invest more than others. Part of the stakeholder model's attraction for the average voter (although not necessarily for the activist) is that it does not impose uniformity. It has a family connection to equality of opportunity, not to equality of outcome.

Stakeholding has other attractions, too. It implies security and inclusion. The state is underwriting the contract so you cannot be excluded so long as you have fulfilled your obligations. Stakeholding also suggests active engagement, both from the state and the individual. It is these notions – obligation, choice, security and engagement, as well as the role of the state – which give stakeholding such a potent political function for the centre-left: on the one hand it speaks to the desires and fears of the self-reliant, middle-of-the-road voters Labour needs to capture; on the other, the role of the state ties stakeholding as a political project to the centre-left, preventing its appropriation by the right.

THE UK CONTRACT: A STAKE IN THE LABOUR MARKET

So how can the concept be applied in a useful way in Britain? As we saw earlier, company stakeholding is not practical. Welfare stakeholding, as promoted by Frank Field, has an attractive ring, but when it comes to those people who cannot or will not fulfil their obligations (the unemployed, the sick), it has to fall back on a more traditional concept of entitlement. There is, however, one area where stakeholding can cut with the grain of liberal market economies and help us think in more innovative ways – the labour market.

Labour markets have become notoriously less secure for a large proportion of the population. The company can no longer guarantee employment stability and it is playing a less important role in organising individual careers. At the same time, employees' existing skills may not equip them for employment mobility. Employers now need a large proportion of their workforces to have quite high-level general, social, organisational and computing skills; specialised, company-specific technical skills can be welded on. Young people acquire these general skills by staying on at school, and increasingly by moving on to further education.

What would having a stake in the labour market, as opposed to a stake in a company, look like? And how can labour market stakeholding replace the support once provided by companies, professional bodies and trade unions? There are two elements. The first is an implicit contract that serious investment of effort by a young person at school should lead to the acquisition of the relevant general and social skills necessary for modern labour markets. For young people at schools in disadvantaged areas this may be a difficult contract to fulfil: it is one reason why it is vital for such children to be able to get out of such schools and into sixth form colleges.

But some young people from disadvantaged backgrounds may not be able to get into an environment in which appropriate general skills are acquired. If we are frank about it, those skills are the skills of being middle class. What sort of stakeholder contract can one give to a child who has no chance of developing such skills? These are the children who will fall into a low attainment/low competence trap, getting jobs without prospects at the bottom end of a deregulated labour market. We know that most 'high-quality training' policies for these young people are a cruel delusion. We also know that schemes to subsidise low-level employment in the private sector may reduce unemployment, but seldom provide ladders out. It is therefore of great importance of a government serious about stakeholding to consider *low-level public sector careers*, linked to adequate school performance. This would be a real contract for disadvantaged young people – where both they and the government would have serious obligations. Such a contract (which the private sector cannot offer) would provide security in a low level but useful public service career in exchange for hard work at school and commitment to the career.

The second element of a labour market stakeholder contract concerns the process of moving through careers for the great majority of citizens. As careers increasingly involve not just a number of different employers but also the acquisition of different skills, the traditional ways of dealing with breaks in employment through benefits and information about jobs is giving way to the need for access to education/training and counselling. It is in this area, where insecurity is rife, that imaginative stakeholding solutions are required. Any such solutions would have to reduce insecurity while preserving the sense of individual opportunity and not imposing excessive restrictions on employers. The individual learning/training account is one such idea. It puts the emphasis on the individual – through the individual's obligations to invest in his or her training in order to attract corresponding subsidies by employer and state, and through the individual's choice in how *much* to invest and where to train. But it also brings the state clearly into the picture. This would be amplified through a proper education and training counselling service, divorced from the depressing connotations of employment exchanges.

Above all, Labour must underpin the British stakeholding model with a wholehearted commitment to mass higher education. Although the present government has revolutionised higher education it is now dithering about costs. Traditionalists complain about falling standards, but almost all courses teach students – young and increasingly mature students too – the social and computing skills required by the new service economy. Even after the expansion of the past decade only one-third of young people in Britain go on to further education, compared with over half in the US. So here, at least, our model should be liberal America rather than social democratic Germany.

NOTE

* This article first appeared in the magazine *Prospect*, 1996.

19 The Global Economy

Jonathan Perraton

INTRODUCTION

Although the concept of a stakeholder economy, whether as an idea or as a characterisation of particular economies, varies between users, it typically presupposes a coherent national economy. Agents in a national stakeholder economy operate within a set of institutions and rules – formal and tacit – that lead them to develop long-term relationships with each other. The commitments these relationships entail have allowed stakeholder economies to deliver economic performance that is not merely successful but also inclusive and responsive to a wide variety of needs. The benefits of economic performance may not be distributed equally, but they do accrue to agents throughout the economy and have often been combined with social provision and environmental protection without this significantly damaging economic performance.

One of the most obvious features of the past twenty-five years has been the massive increase in international economic flows which have engendered a qualitative shift in the nature of economic activity. It is not simply that international economic activity has grown rapidly – crucially it has led to a shift from national to global markets for goods and services, finance and technology and, related to this, a shift to international organisation of production by firms; the process, in other words, often referred to as globalisation.[1] This raises two questions for the stakeholding project. First, is a national stakeholder economy still possible in this global economy? Second, what new or modified international rules and institutions might facilitate the operation of stakeholding relationships in the global economy?

In this chapter I argue that globalisation has fundamentally altered relationships within national economies. Since agents can shift their money and production abroad relatively easily and source from overseas suppliers, it is consequently much harder to tie them in to long-term stakeholding arrangements within a national economy. At the same time, the relations between agents on which stakeholder arrangements were constructed – or are proposed to be constructed – have become stretched internationally. Agents are now enmeshed internationally, economic performance is determined in a global context and many of the wider problems stakeholding seeks to address are international in scope (such as the environment). For stakeholding to be effective the long-term relations on which it is based need to be developed internationally, even globally. This is obviously a huge task and this chapter only advances some modest proposals. Moreover, I argue that international stakeholding will only emerge at different levels through continuous negotiation. For this reason, rather than advocating a specific set of rules to govern international activity I argue that stakeholding requires an international framework within which stakeholding arrangements can be negotiated and encouraged to develop at various levels.

THE IMPACT OF GLOBALISATION

The bare facts of globalisation are extraordinary. Trade rose faster than output through the postwar period: from the isolated national economies of the 1950s, the industrialised countries now typically export around a third of their private national output. Falling barriers have transformed national markets for goods and, increasingly, services into global ones so that a still larger proportion of national output is in direct competition with foreign producers. Where once production processes were largely self-contained within national boundaries – indeed often within individual plants – they are now often broken down into stages and dispersed internationally. Trade in intermediates has grown commensurably.

International finance was negligible in the 1960s, but since the 1970s on a conservative estimate it has grown three times faster than output. In some international financial markets activity is now at astronomical levels, notably the foreign exchange markets where turnover is around a trillion dollars per day, roughly 50 times the level of world trade. Countries now face a highly liquid global market which determines interest rates and exchange rates. The international trading of a wide range of instruments has transformed other financial and capital markets from national to global ones.

Multinational corporations have grown to sizes that rival many nations economically. They now account for up to a third of world output and 70 per cent of world trade, with around a quarter of world trade being between branches of the same company. They have both created global competition and been subject to it, evolving a range of strategies to meet global challenges and opportunities.

There are two responses by stakeholding's proponents to these developments, neither of them ultimately tenable. The first is simply to assert that globalisation is a much exaggerated claim and that little has really changed,[2] but this argument is based on refuting wild claims made in the sort of management literature sold at airport bookshops. The second argument claims that if stakeholding can organise a successful economy it will still thrive today, that the world economy is indifferent to forms of economic organisation and governance provided that they are effective. This argument has some validity. Significant levels of international flows have been compatible with stakeholder economies. Economies like the former West Germany, Austria and the Scandinavian countries all had relatively high trade ratios in the postwar period and relied on a successful export sector as a key source of growth for the economy. Selling to world markets was compatible with the general principles of stakeholding and more specific measures such as a developed welfare state and strong environmental protection. There is no strong evidence that an extensive welfare state led to poor export performance,[3] nor are there strong theoretical grounds for expecting this. Multinationals dominate some stakeholding countries like Sweden, companies moreover with extensive overseas operations rather than essentially national concerns with a few foreign investments.

Although this suggests that globalisation does not undermine the basis for national stakeholder economies, I argue below that it glosses over not just the magnitude of recent changes from globalisation, but also the nature of the difference globalisation makes. Before considering trade and multinationals, I consider the impact of global finance, which *is* widely considered to have undermined the basis for national stakeholder economies.

Is International Finance the Real Problem?

Since trade and the operations of multinationals appear to have been compatible with stakeholding, the conclusion often drawn from the difficulty of maintaining stakeholding arrangements in the 1980s and 1990s is that it is international finance that undermines stakeholding arrangements, not international economic activity generally.[4] Trade and international production are seen as efficient ways of organising the production of goods and services allowing countries to maximise their output through specialisation. International finance, by contrast, is seen as having grown to levels far in excess of those required to service the real economy. It is not simply that its speculative activities can seriously distort the values of key variables in the economy, important though this is. International finance provides both the incentive of exit opportunities for making money outside of the national stakeholder economy and pressure on investors to channel resources into liquid short-term projects, rather than the long-term investment that underwrites a stakeholder economy. The short-termism of the financial markets and their lack of commitment are the very antithesis of stakeholding, a recurrent theme of Will Hutton's work. The nature of global financial markets produces a qualitative change not just in the conduct of individual firms, but also in national economic policy. A particular policy may induce a negative response from business, but the effect of this on investment is likely to be marginal, whereas an adverse reaction to a policy package by the financial markets can induce a sudden and massive response.

I argue below that this view is still too sanguine about the effects of trade and multinational production, but this should not detract from its case here. The best-laid plans of stakeholding men and women can be fatally undermined if speculation drives the exchange rate to uncompetitive levels. International financial markets have periodically sustained plainly unsustainable policies – for example, the 1991–4 capital inflows to Mexico and Britain's sojourn in the ERM – before suddenly and dramatically turning against them. The very uncertainty generated by these markets is a key problem: not only have they significantly altered the costs of pursuing particular policies, they have done so in a manner that is unpredictable, penalising certain policies at some times in some countries but not in others at other times. The instability in economic variables generated by financial speculation does not help long-term planning, even if the impact of this is still in question. Financial activity has presented non-financial enterprises with tempting opportunities for money making, whilst – as Proctor and Gamble's losses from dealing in derivatives showed – sometimes leading to heavy losses.

Stakeholder arrangements developed in certain economies during the postwar period of low international financial flows and extensive controls on them. Not only did this permit a substantial degree of autonomy in national macroeconomic policy, however important that may have been for stakeholding, in some cases regulation of national financial systems played an important role in directing them towards providing long-term industrial finance. Certain East Asian boom economies provide an important example of this – although these are not identikit stakeholding economies, they have been constructed on the basis of extensive cooperation at various levels of the economy, and government direction of the financial system towards industrial investment appears to have played a crucial role in generating their rapid growth.[5]

The instability of global finance can create serious problems for national economic management generally, but for stakeholding it is further and crucially damaging by undermining the basis for relations of long-term commitment in the national economy. This is a recurrent theme in the stakeholding literature, but it is less clear what they propose to do about it. I suggest below that only piecemeal measures are possible at the moment and financial globalisation is likely to remain an important constraint on developing stakeholding arrangements.

The Difference Trade and Multinationals Make

Both stakeholding theory and the practice of economies suggest that patterns of long-term commitment in a national economy can generate a sustainable economic performance. This is usually based on a vision of separate, self-contained national economies competing against each other. In this concept the national economy generates the sources of relative advantage domestically that determine which products the country specialises in producing. This determines her trade position, it may attract foreign multinationals and home multinationals have usually grown out of this environment and remain deeply embedded in it. Thus, although countries operate in a global economy, their performance in that economy is determined nationally and the benefits from it largely accrue domestically: an economy can realise the benefits of specialisation whilst retaining stakeholding arrangements.

This is central to the current theory of stakeholding, for such a national economy provides the basis for agents to form relationships with each other and develop stakeholding arrangements. Theorists vary in how much coercive power they believe is necessary to induce agents to construct and maintain stakeholding arrangements, but the basic point is that producing within such a national economy means that agents have to form relationships with other agents in order to operate. The more agents can derive relative advantage from elsewhere, produce abroad or source from overseas suppliers and sell to export markets, the less need they may have to form relationships with other agents in the national economy in order to operate.

There are several changes that have undermined the stakeholding vision of the national economy. Individually they do not suddenly make national stakeholding economies go from being possible to being impossible, rather in combination they make stakeholding arrangements significantly more difficult to construct and maintain, whilst increasing the costs of policies often associated with stakeholding.

Increasingly, potential sources of relative advantage do not remain within the national boundaries where they were generated and, conversely, sources of advantage may be derived from overseas: technology and management techniques flow across borders, machinery can be imported and at least some skilled labour has become internationally mobile. Multinationals can and do invest overseas expressly to tap into the innovation networks of other countries. These changes have brought many benefits as productivity has risen through the spread of best practice, and countries continue to specialise in producing the goods and services they have a relative advantage in. The point here is that we can no longer assume that the generation of specific advantages is essentially domestic with the benefits largely being realised domestically.

Trade and multinational operations have meant that firms have become increasingly enmeshed with a range of relations outside of their home country base, with both suppliers and buyers in foreign markets. Rising levels of trade, both sales of products for export and imports of intermediate goods, means that firms' networks of relationships with other agents are becoming increasingly stretched across national boundaries. Multinationals by their very nature are enmeshed in such international relations. As the networks which are central to constructing a stakeholding economy become increasingly international, where previously they were national or local, stakeholding arrangements have to be constructed at that level.

It is important to state what this does not mean. Trade is not a zero-sum Darwinian struggle in which countries suddenly become uncompetitive as a result of a particular measure. Equally, multinationals' investment in developed countries is typically not footloose, ready to shift abroad at the slightest change in conditions. As such, globalisation does not imply that wages and standards will be driven down to the lowest common denominator. It does mean that the exit options of firms increase as they are able to produce abroad and/or source from overseas suppliers. Further, although countries continue to produce in line with their relative advantage, the patterns of this can shift rapidly. For a stakeholder economy to remain inclusive it needs to be able to move labour (and other resources) from declining to expanding sectors in line with shifting relative advantage. A good example of this is the decline in low-skilled employment as a result of rising exports of manufactures by developing countries.[6] Although the other side of this has been an expansion of high-skill employment, a stakeholding economy still faces the task of rectifying the mismatch of labour if it is to remain inclusive. Although the initial response has been to claim that education and training can effect this (and these are sources of advantage that remain largely generated and realised domestically), increasingly advocates of this view are hedging it with a range of qualifications. Whether patterns of relative advantage shift more rapidly than in the past is an open question; they do, however, make maintaining an inclusive stakeholding economy more difficult.

Globalisation raises a range of problems for managing national economies. It not only increases the exit options for some agents in the economy, but also means that many of the relations upon which stakeholding was built are now international where previously they were national. This does not mean we should abandon all hope of building national (or local) stakeholding arrangements, but we should recognise the limitations of such attempts and consider the possibilities of constructing such arrangements at various international levels. I turn to this in the following section.

INTERNATIONAL GOVERNANCE AND STAKEHOLDING

So far I have made two main claims: first, that globalisation has undermined the relations within a national economy that the concept of a stakeholder economy was based upon, and, second, that agents are now enmeshed in a range of relationships that extend beyond national boundaries. Although this implies that the project of constructing a national stakeholder economy is no longer tenable, it does not necessarily mean that the idea of stakeholding has become obsolete. Firms remain embedded in networks of relationships that provide the potential for negotiating stakeholder arrangements, with the attendant benefits stakeholding theory suggests. Given the international nature of these networks of relationships, there needs to be frameworks for constructing stakeholder arrangements not just at the local and national levels, but also at the regional and global levels.

A common response amongst stakeholding's advocates is to propose a new Bretton Woods, another major international settlement to provide for the orderly conduct of international economic transactions whilst allowing countries considerable national autonomy to order their own economic affairs. (Bretton Woods was the 1944 agreement that established the major international economic institutions of the postwar period and a global system of fixed exchange rates that lasted until the early 1970s.) The genie of international finance can be put back in its bottle and we can start again. This is not just unrealistic, it is also unhelpful. Bretton Woods was a product of another time and effectively only operated for about thirteen years. The degree of international enmeshment is such that it is unrealistic to believe that earlier levels of national autonomy could simply be re-established by decree. Since many of the opportunities and problems faced by agents now are irreducibly international, new and modified international institutions are required to facilitate stakeholding arrangements. The issues raised by international enmeshment are not only more complex within each area, there is also a greater range of issues to be considered in international fora, notably the environment. This suggests the establishment of a range of international negotiations and fora, rather than one big conference to establish a new set of rules.

This raises the central problem with simply trying to create international rules. Under Bretton Woods a system of rules governed international transactions, whilst arrangements between agents within each country could be negotiated domestically. Creating stakeholding arrangements between agents internationally requires rules of conduct over certain areas, but many areas will remain contested with continued negotiations between stakeholders. National stakeholding was characterised by continued negotiation between stakeholders leading to evolving arrangements and rules; the results varied significantly between countries. The difficult task for stakeholding is to develop international institutions and frameworks that permit the negotiation and development of stakeholding arrangements at an international level. Many markets have become global, and so regulation of their operations may need to be global too, but the networks and relationships that provide the basis for stakeholding arrangements have not simply shifted from the national to the global level. Rather the stretching of economic activity internationally has meant that firms are embedded in a series of relations that no longer correspond neatly to national boundaries but are not necessarily fully global either. We would expect these relations to differ between industries, between regional areas of the globe and over time, which limits the extent to which it is appropriate to devise legal rules and highlights the urgency of developing international frameworks out of which stakeholding relations and arrangements can emerge. As such, this will not emerge from the blueprint of one author, and below I confine myself to some specific proposals that could improve the prospects for developing international relations between stakeholders.

SPECIFIC PROPOSALS

The clearest source of national autonomy in economic policy during the Bretton Woods system was from capital controls: international financial flows were small in the 1950s and 1960s, but capital controls also appear to have been effective in permitting national economic autonomy. Rather than reintroducing such controls, which would probably be evaded, Tobin has proposed taxing foreign exchange transactions at a fraction of a percentage point.[7] This would dampen down speculation that leads to excessive volatility in financial markets, and can therefore be justified on welfare economics grounds; it would be small enough not to affect international trade significantly and the revenues generated could be ear-marked for worthwhile international projects. It would have to be introduced simultaneously in the major financial centres, but if this could be arranged it would be unlikely to lead to a massive shift of business to tax havens – if margins are so low in the major financial centres that such a tax would induce business to leave it is difficult to see how business is sustained in these centres in the first place.

There is no immediate prospect of the 'Tobin Tax' being introduced, but central banks do cooperate already to agree common standards of financial regulation. There are already proposals for common capital adequacy requirements in derivatives trading; it may also be possible to introduce increased requirements for traders and other controls designed to raise the price of derivatives and/or limit access to them.[8] In general attempts to manage international finance, limiting the adverse impact it can have on other parts of the economy, will be piecemeal rather than systemic; this does not mean they will be ineffective.

Rules of conduct for international trade illustrate several of the points made above. The GATT was remarkably effective as a skeleton framework for reducing formal barriers on trade without requiring significant changes in national laws. Since then attention has shifted to issues such as trade in services and intellectual property rights. Reducing barriers to trade in these areas would imply much greater legal harmonisation. Further, trade friction between the US and Japan is partly due to the difficulties American firms have in entering Japanese marketing networks. In other words, the structure and organisation of a national economy and its laws have become issues, implying reduced national autonomy to construct national frameworks of economic rules. The newly established World Trading Organization provides a forum for negotiating the rules and framework for international trade. In the immediate future the issues raised by trade are likely to be negotiated rather than a definitive set of rules produced, the WTO allowing such negotiations to proceed rather than rules simply being imposed by the most powerful trading nations.

Regulation of industries to ensure standards, for example of working conditions and environmental practice, increasingly needs to be international. National attempts at regulation will be ineffective if they do not apply to foreign producers, and existing rules largely prevent using trade restrictions to enforce such standards. National regulations will therefore be strongly resisted as they would systematically discriminate against domestic producers. International regulation may only be possible through coordinated action by stakeholders. Moreover, such action is more likely to ensure that the costs and benefits of regulation are shared more equitably than would its enforcement by particular powers. For example, proposals for international labour standards[9] are often attacked by developing country governments as disguised advanced country protectionism, but trade unions in developing countries often support them. International stakeholding relations might enable measures to be negotiated that would ensure growing prosperity in developing countries together with the establishment of certain basic standards. Similarly, using trade measures for environmental purposes may well be crude and inefficient with negative side-effects compared to establishing a global system of environmental property rights; this merely highlights the absence of such a system. Rather than using trade measures for environmental protection, there needs to be negotiation towards an international framework of regulation and taxation designed to bring prices into line with social costs: if 'polluter pays' principles are to operate they need to do so globally. There may be a case for distinguishing between negotiating standards and negotiating common global standards: certain basic global standards might be agreed with other standards being allowed to vary between countries according to their stage of development.

Whilst certain measures may need to be negotiated globally if at all, others can still be enforced at the regional, national or even local levels – for example, minimum wages in the US and those proposed in Britain largely affect workers in sectors that do not trade internationally. The Social Chapter of the EU is encouraging in this respect. Although its provisions thus far are minimal, its format allows for negotiations over labour and social issues amongst countries with high levels of mutual trade. In other words, it provides a framework within which stakeholding relations can emerge and negotiations proceed at an international level.

Past attempts to devise a global framework for regulating multinationals have failed through lack of agreement; neither is it clear that global institutions possess the power to impose such a framework. Multinationals can still be brought into stakeholding relations but they have to produce somewhere and they do incur costs in shifting production. They have frequently proved amenable to pressure on standards in both home and host countries, particularly when such pressure has been applied simultaneously in different countries, and so international organisation and coordination of stakeholders can draw them into stakeholding relations. Raising the issue of standards in international fora itself may put pressure on multinationals.

Governments should negotiate to limit their use of incentives to attract foreign investment. Both theory and evidence indicate that competition amongst local and national governments to attract such investment is ultimately self-defeating and cannot be justified on welfare economics grounds. However, without international agreements to limit it such competition is almost bound to occur. The EU already places some limits on this through its competition policy, but these could be strengthened and replicated at other international levels. It is clearly antithetical to stakeholding if countries are involved in a beauty contest with each other to attract investment from multinationals.

Organisation of International Governance

At present global political institutions have little real power. The most effective international political institutions are regional, and these are largely within the EU. As stressed earlier the task of constructing stakeholding relations internationally is not simply one of devising global institutions and rules but of permitting a range of international arrangements to emerge. As such, advocating the strengthening of regional institutions is consistent with the perspective taken here.

On stakeholder grounds there is an important case for democratising international institutions.[10] The contested terrain of domestic politics allows a continuous process of negotiation between agents, however imperfect and unequal. One of the strengths of stakeholder theory is that by stressing a framework of inclusive social group activity it suggests a way in which the negative aspects of interest group activity – in terms of unproductive activities – may be avoided, but the positive aspects – in terms of raising issues and pressing claims in a legitimised system of governance – may be retained. Governments cannot simply be assumed to maximise social welfare, rather it is only through stakeholder groups raising issues and pressing claims that an inclusive politics is likely to develop.

There is, further, the financing of such institutions. Without independent funding their effectiveness will remain limited and they will remain open to pressure from the largest contributors. Mendez raises the interesting idea of funding international agencies through taxation of international public goods (use of the sea, space, and so on) and bads (notably international pollution, excessive speculative financial activity) as a way of both providing independent funding and of getting international prices to reflect international social costs.[11]

CONCLUSIONS

Globalisation has fundamentally altered the nature of economic relations facing countries, and although this is relative rather than absolute it is still important enough not simply to be dismissed. It has increased the exit options open to certain agents and thereby undermined the national economic basis on which stakeholding was previously constructed. Simultaneously agents have become enmeshed in a range of relations with others abroad that provide the potential for international stakeholding arrangements. Providing the basis for international stakeholding arrangements to emerge is a key task for stakeholding's proponents, but without them it may become an idea with a great future behind it.

NOTES

1. The discussion of globalisation draws heavily on D. Goldblatt, D. Held, A. McGrew and J. Perraton, *Global Flows, Global Transformations* (Cambridge: Polity Press, 1997); and 'The globalisation of economic activity', *New Political Economy*, Vol. 2, No. 2 (1997).
2. P. Hirst and G. Thompson, *Globalization in Question* (Cambridge: Polity Press, 1996). See the works cited in note 1 for a counter-argument.
3. A. Pfaller, I. Gough and G. Therborn, *Can the Welfare State Compete?* (Basingstoke: Macmillan, 1991); I. Gough, 'Social welfare and competitiveness', *New Political Economy*, Vol. 1, No. 2 (1996), pp. 209–32.
4. For example, W. Hutton, 'Global free trade: the Keynesian angle', *New Political Economy*, Vol. 1, No. 1. (1996), pp. 102–6.
5. D. Rodrik, 'Getting intervention right: how South Korea and Taiwan grew rich', *Economic Policy*, No. 20 (1996), pp. 55–107.
6. A. Wood, *North–South Trade Employment and Inequality* (Oxford: Oxford University Press, 1994).
7. J. Tobin, 'Speculators' tax', *New Economy*, Vol. 1, No. 2 (1994), pp. 104–9.
8. R. Kelly, 'Derivatives: a growing threat to the international financial system', in J. Michie and J. Grieve Smith (eds), *Managing the Global Economy* (Oxford: Oxford University Press, 1995).
9. W. Sengenberger and F. Wilkinson, 'Globalization and labour standards', in J. Michie and J. Grieve Smith (eds), *Managing the Global Economy* (Oxford: Oxford University Press, 1995); Symposium on 'International Labour Standards and Human Rights', *New Political Economy*, Vol. 1, No. 2 (1996).
10. Cf. D. Held, *Democracy and the Global Order* (Cambridge: Polity Press, 1996), esp. ch. 11.
11. R. Mendez, *International Public Finance* (Oxford: Oxford University Press, 1992).

20 Conclusion: Stakeholder Capitalism

Gavin Kelly, Dominic Kelly
and Andrew Gamble

Stakeholder has become a key term in political debate. Almost everything it seems has a stakeholder dimension: stakeholder capitalism, stakeholder democracy, stakeholder company, stakeholder government, stakeholder community, stakeholder Europe, stakeholder society, stakeholder economy. Its use conveys a vague promise of inclusion, participation and accountability. But a term applied so liberally to so many different institutions arouses suspicion as to whether it contains anything of substance, rather like the word 'social' which was once added indiscriminately to almost every political category.

Conservative opponents of New Labour have been quick to deride the new enthusiasm for stakeholding as a step back to the past, either a return to old-style corporatism or an attempt to import foreign models of social and economic organisation into the UK. On the left, however, the idea of stakeholding has been condemned as another device to cover the retreat of New Labour from any radical commitments to change the distribution of wealth and power.

Others, including many sympathetic to the political project of New Labour, have questioned whether the idea of stakeholding offers anything beyond the ideas of citizenship and social inclusion. They suggest that the concern with stakeholding may turn out to be short-lived – a political soundbite which provides a new label but little else. The project to turn Britain into a stakeholder society has been launched just at the moment that the countries in which stakeholding has been strongest, particularly Germany, are turning away from it. Many of the ideas of stakeholding, it is said, belong to an old agenda of trying to oppose the community to the market and do not confront the realities of today's capitalism.[1]

If stakeholding were so vacuous, however, and so steeped in the past, it would not have attracted so much attention or stimulated so much controversy. Conservative intellectuals have become preoccupied with it because they sense that stakeholding could prove very popular and could give the intellectual leadership back to the left for the first time in twenty years. Stakeholding may fall short of the kind of clear strategic objectives and detailed policies which would be needed for a political project of the old kind. But nothing can provide that, and in any case that is not what stakeholding is about. What it offers, as the chapters in this book demonstrate, is a powerful organising concept for thinking about current political issues around inclusion and governance in many different institutions and contexts. It contains the seeds of a post-Thatcher, post-Labourist project for the left which has a strong individualist dimension with its emphasis upon autonomy, rights and obligations, as well as a radical critique of the institutional obstacles to the creation of a more meritocratic and just society and an efficient economy. It is the potential of stakeholding to combine an individualist agenda with an active state which makes it a novel and dynamic idea and one appropriate for the times.

STAKEHOLDING AND THE RIGHT

The idea of stakeholding has a long history in political debate and is not confined to one political perspective. Tony Blair's adoption of the term has made it part of the identity of New Labour, but it might easily have been appropriated by the right, and given a different slant. Margaret Thatcher rather than Tony Blair might have been the first political leader to proclaim a vision of a stakeholder society and a stakeholder economy.

This is because the political debate over stakeholding is not about the desirability of membership and inclusion in contemporary societies, but about the means by which they can be delivered and maintained, and this debate runs across both parties not just between them. There is acceptance that many people have only a very tenuous stake and in some cases no stake at all in their society. But there is sharp political disagreement as to the causes of this exclusion and the best ways to overcome it.

On the right, exclusion is still blamed on policies of state regulation and state provision and the power of special interests, which create a climate of economic rigidity and welfare dependency. The right stresses the importance for all individuals to hold stakes, in the form of transferable skills and property, and has promoted the latter through privatisation and council house sales under the slogan of popular capitalism. But these policies have barely touched the large number of citizens who have few transferable skills and are excluded from property ownership. State intervention is regarded as an evil which always produces inferior results, and faith is placed instead in spontaneous market forces to disperse opportunity more widely and provide all citizens with transferable skills and property stakes. But this happens very unevenly and imperfectly if at all. Existing concentrations of wealth have been reinforced rather than dispersed, and the distribution of educational opportunity remains highly stratified.

STAKEHOLDING AND THE LEFT

On the left a more vigorous debate on stakeholding has emerged, centred on the tension between the individual and the collective. Is stakeholding to be understood primarily as an attribute of individuals, the stakes which individuals have and which are specific to them, or is it something which arises from membership of an association or collective body? Is a stakeholder society one in which individuals hold stakes in the form of jobs, skills, capacities, and property; or in the form of rights of representation in collective entities like companies and nation states?

The answer is it must be both, but different conclusions follow for the meaning of stakeholding depending on which is given priority. If the stakeholder model is an individualist one, then as Robert Kuttner points out, individuals become stakeholders by paying attention to their own human capital. You are a stakeholder to the extent that you are a successful individual and acquire transferable skills. The stakeholder agenda is then how to equip each individual with the skills and capacities necessary to succeed in the highly flexible and constantly changing labour markets of modern capitalism. Being a stakeholder means having autonomy and choice, and the freedom to exit from unrewarding jobs or relationships. But there is also another central meaning of stakeholding which emphasises the collective obligations and rights conferred by membership of communities and organisations. Stakeholders collectively exercise rights of voice which establish accountability and control. To be a stakeholder is to be recognised as having an interest in the decisions and actions of particular organisations and to claim as a result the rights of consultation, information, and participation in decision making, while accepting that membership carries with it obligations. The stakeholder argument revives an earlier political discourse in which rights and obligations were linked, but does this within a democratic context of universal citizenship and inclusion.

One of the most influential recent approaches to stakeholding has been that set out by Will Hutton in his book, *The State We're In*. He argues that stakeholding is the appropriate organising concept for the contemporary left because it offers a radically different interpretation of how a capitalist economy can be run. For Hutton the stakeholder agenda must be comprehensive, covering ownership and control of companies, relationships at work, education and training, welfare, macroeconomic policy and constitutional change. The focus is on structures and economy-wide institutions. The main thrust of stakeholding is to identify the economic and social policies which can promote social inclusion for all citizens and build institutions, systems and values which allow cooperative relationships to flourish. The reform of key institutions, such as the City, the constitution, the legal basis of companies, and the labour market would allow a different model of capitalism to evolve in Britain, one which emphasises long-term relationships of trust and commitment, and gives individuals a greater chance of becoming stakeholders. Harold Perkin, Dominic Kelly and Robert Kuttner likewise see the idea of stakeholding as offering a different model for organising a capitalist society. What distinguishes the stakeholding from the free market model is that it seeks to place significant limits on the way in which markets operate in order to reduce their tendency to polarise society and to marginalise many groups within it.

The individualist approach, by contrast, which is an increasingly important strand of New Labour thinking (and is a theme in Alistair Darling's chapter), sees the priority not as changing institutions but as helping individuals. If individuals are properly endowed with skills and capacities then institutions are less likely to constrain them. Existing institutions are not the major obstacles to reform that Hutton supposes. The individualist approach therefore argues that if individuals are to acquire stakes they must first of all receive adequate training and education to obtain skills. This is the priority, rather than the large-scale reform of other UK economic institutions, which may create unnecessary conflict. Assisting individuals to acquire skills and assets and encouraging a cultural shift towards greater cooperation and consensus in companies and organisations are seen as the heart of the stakeholder approach.

PRINCIPLES

In order to understand some of the differences in the meanings attached to stakeholding the various principles and tools of stakeholding need to be clarified. Running through the discourse of stakeholding are a number of core principles, which often pull in different directions. The particular way in which writers on stakeholding combine these principles is what makes it a novel and refreshing political approach, but it does not provide ready-made answers or a painless way of resolving conflicts which can arise for instance between autonomy and reciprocity or between social justice and efficiency. In solving some problems a stakeholder approach raises others. Its value is that it provides new ways of thinking about how best to realise key principles, and how best to balance them.

1. Security

Security, the most potent idea in the political vocabulary of the 1990s, is central to stakeholding. If stakeholding cannot increase security it has little purpose. Demands for government to do more in limiting various kinds of insecurity are growing, at the same time that the complexity of the task is becoming better appreciated. The growth of insecurity in recent times, and some of the new forms it takes have attracted much attention, although how new some of them are is contested. The evidence on job insecurity, for example, does not all point one way. Labour market trends have long showed a move towards the employment of part-timers while the evidence on average job tenure is mixed.

Stakeholding accepts and builds on the basic idea of the twentieth-century welfare state that baseline security needs to be provided through the guaranteeing of a minimum standard of living for every citizen. What is distinctive about the stakeholding approach is the way in which the baseline is conceived. The emphasis is put on guaranteeing every individual a minimum endowment of capabilities and opportunities, not a particular outcome. It seeks to prepare individuals for change rather than to protect them from change. As James McCormick argues, increasing security is not about eliminating uncertainty – any such attempt would be futile. The strategy instead is to reduce the costs and increase the benefits to individuals of dealing with economic and social change, while recognising that not all individuals can be helped in this way. The numbers remaining dependent on the state can be minimised but not removed altogether.

2. Participation and Reciprocity

A second key idea in stakeholding is participation. Having a stake implies that the holder is active rather than passive, and is prepared to engage with others who share common activities and concerns. Participation can be achieved in many ways; there is not a uniform approach appropriate to all institutions. What participation requires is access to information and a culture which encourages consultation and cooperation. This can be informal or it can be embodied in legal regulation. Key issues on the stakeholding agenda are how to change the culture of companies who see no role for key stakeholders, such as employees, to participate in the decision making process; how to make government more open and responsive; and how to ensure that all organisations are accountable to their members.

Participation, however, like security is not straightforward for a stakeholding agenda. There is the dilemma of what should be done when people do not wish to participate, despite persuasion, incentives, information and education. Electors may not vote, institutional investors may carry on behaving as absentee owners and companies may refuse to consult with (or even forewarn) employees about changes in the workplace. Since stakeholding involves obligations as well as rights, does the obligation of being a stakeholder at some point turn into a formal duty and justify compulsion?

The language of stakeholding is suffused with the notion of obligation. Everyone has responsibilities, duties and commitments to each other, to themselves, to the associations of which they are members, and to the state. Coupling rights and responsibilities in this way emphasises the notion of contract. This is not a new idea, although the notion of a flexible contract with the state is novel. The more you put in, the more you receive back. The state provides a resource which can be drawn on to assist individuals in achieving their life-plans.

3. Social Justice

Offering every individual a meaningful stake requires action to address the glaring inequalities and the continuing barriers to a fully meritocratic society which exist in contemporary Britain. Income inequalities have increased, while the post-Second World War trend towards reduced inequality of wealth has been reversed. The economic status of the parents still has a large influence over the future quality and even the length of a child's life. No left-of-centre government can avoid addressing these issues, and a government committed to stakeholding least of all.

Where a stakeholding approach would differ from some left positions in the past is that it is primarily concerned with equality of opportunity, not equality of outcome. Stakeholding is about giving everyone real opportunities, not about choosing a punitive marginal rate of tax. The Social Justice Commission persuasively argued that social justice should be about *endowment* egalitarianism, solving the problems of escalating inequality before they occur rather than relying on subsequent cash payments which only relieve the symptoms and do not provide a cure for exclusion.[2]

But there are problems with this approach. As noted in the discussion of security, some people will not be able to enter into the bargain, and must be provided for in different ways; while providing the endowments – education, skills, child care, training and retraining – is not cheap (neither, of course, is the alternative). Funding these redistributive programmes depends on sustaining political support for adequate levels of taxation.

4. Autonomy

Stakeholding has a strong strand of individualism running through it, and therefore emphasises the attributes that are necessary for individuals to have control over their own lives, and the flexibility to make choices. To maintain autonomy over an entire lifecycle also means equipping individuals with particular information and skills, and ensuring that they have opportunities to acquire both property and social capital. In this way stakeholding connects individual aspirations to own property with obligations to dependants and the provision for retirement and old age. It speaks directly to the successful and the enterprising, not just to the excluded and the deprived.

But another key aspect of autonomy is that the exercise of genuine choice requires the kind of civic institutions, public culture and public ethos which can make knowledge of alternatives widely available and contribute to the development of personality. These institutions can only be created through collective action and the acceptance by individuals of obligations which go beyond the satisfaction of their immediate desires. This tension between individual autonomy and the need for a common public culture runs through the heart of the stakeholder agenda, as it does in other political philosophies such as communitarianism, social democracy and civic conservatism.

5. Economic Efficiency

A final principle of stakeholding is the importance of economic efficiency. Running through the entire agenda is the argument that stakeholding is not just about a fairer distribution of the wealth of society, but how to accumulate more (and different forms of) wealth. This can be seen in all the contexts to which stakeholding is applied. Individuals well endowed with economic and social capabilities will be more productive; companies which draw on the experience of all their stakeholders will be more efficient; while social cohesion within a nation is increasingly seen as a requirement for international competitiveness. The difficulty, however, of reconciling in practice the competing claims of economic efficiency and social justice remain, and focus in particular on the question of taxation.

TOOLS OF STAKEHOLDING

Stakes take different forms – such as human capital, financial assets, long-term relationships of trust, and political rights. To acquire and maintain these stakes individuals need tools. The most important are:

Transferable skills, which confer autonomy, flexibility and mobility. Such skills are gained both through formal training and through experience within organisations and can be employed in other contexts, and enable individuals to exercise rights in many different kinds of organisation.

Ownership rights, which empower individuals within markets and the broader civil society by enabling them to be self-reliant and enterprising. If individuals own property they are able to make choices and leave relationships which they find oppressive or unsatisfactory. If there is no possibility of exit relationships can often become authoritarian and oppressive, as in many traditional communities. Property can also be a tool for stakeholding in a different way. Some forms of property can involve obligations and duties and contribute to the development of civic virtues and responsibilities, and ownership often also confers rights of voice and representation, in companies for example.

Trust relationships, which are both the raw materials of an active civic culture and a key tool of economic development. They include social capital, the informal networks of all kinds which create trust, solidarity and commitment. Such networks include households, workplaces and local neighbourhoods. Being a stakeholder in these does not require the formal skills and rights that are required elsewhere; it is a grassroots form of inclusion. Also important are long-term economic relationships, many of which are a precondition for economic success but are difficult to specify in a formal contract. Informal (or implicit) contracts, built up within and between firms over time, provide an alternative and often more efficient means of structuring economic relationships.

Political rights, which permit the exercise of voice within organisations, through the establishment of procedures for decision making and accountability. The key tools here include decision making rules, such as voting, access to information, freedom of speech and association, and legal process.

THE CONTEXTS OF STAKEHOLDING

The tension between individual and collective stakeholding is reflected not only in the different forms which stakes can take, and in the different tools needed to acquire and maintain them, but also in the different contexts in which stakeholding is relevant. The stakes which individuals have are many and various. They overlap and at times may conflict. An audit of stakeholding reveals a diverse and constantly shifting array of commitments and interests. It is this pluralism which makes grasping what stakeholding means within a modern society so elusive, but it is also what makes it such an apt metaphor for exploring the commitments individuals have in different social contexts.

Three contexts in particular are important for understanding stakeholding. The easiest one to grasp is the microlevel where it refers to the stake which individuals have as members of workplaces, households and local neighbourhoods. Stakeholding at this level is hands-on and immediate. Relationships are personal and direct because the interests of individuals are actively and constantly engaged.

The second context is the wider communities, institutions and groups which make up civil society, such as companies, schools, trade unions, hospitals, churches, and voluntary associations and groups of all kinds. Nearly all individuals are involved as members in some associations, but the extent of membership and the depth of involvement vary markedly between them. Individuals have interests in the groups to which they belong, but these interests are not as direct and constant as they are in workplaces, households and neighbourhoods. The networks, relationships and culture which are established through the complex pattern of membership and participation make up the social capital which is a key resource for an inclusive society. A society of active stakeholders is one in which all individuals have stakes in workplaces, households, and neighbourhoods and in the wider civil society. Stakeholding is not about building up a single stake between individuals and society. It is about increasing the number of connections and commitments that individuals have.

The third context is the macrolevel, which is the most comprehensive, but also the least precise and the hardest to pin down. What does stakeholding mean when it is applied to political institutions at a national level? Still more difficult are supranational entities like the European Union or the United Nations. Individual citizens can be considered to be stakeholders in the United Kingdom or in the European Union to the extent that they have an interest in the stability of the constitutional order and the prosperity of the economy. But the means for exercising control become more diffuse the greater the scale. Once we move away from the microlevel it becomes much harder to specify what the mechanisms of stakeholding actually are. What does it mean to say that voters are stakeholders in the way in which the economy is managed? It can be argued that individuals are stakeholders in national and international bodies to the extent that they have an interest in the policies which these bodies pursue, but their relationship to these bodies is impersonal and indirect, making it very hard to establish mechanisms which allow effective participation. Nevertheless, decisions taken at this level have a major impact on the opportunities individuals have to acquire stakes. As Jonathan Perraton argues, the impact of globalisation has weakened the scope for national stakeholding and drawn attention to the need for new forms of international governance to facilitate long-term relationships.

Tensions can arise between these different levels, for example between the micro-policies which promote stakeholding at the individual level and those which promote social inclusion at the macrolevel. Underlying this is the sometimes complex relationship between stakeholding and inclusion. At the level of workplaces and households, and also at the level of the associations and organisations of civil society, to give some individuals stakes can mean excluding others. Stakeholding is at its most intelligible when it refers to particular groups who have a common interest in the success of an enterprise. But their very commitment assumes that those outside the group do not have that same commitment or interest. In any organisation, whether it is a firm, a hospital or a school, there will be varying levels of commitment. Alistair Darling argues that one of the implications is that in an organisation like a company there are primary stakeholders who take precedence over others. The degree of involvement and risk are not the same for everyone and cannot be made the same. Critics allege that a stakeholder agenda is in consequence not genuinely inclusive, and might serve the interests only of the already articulate and successful, excluding those lacking either the endowments or the capacities to acquire effective stakes.

Some suspicion of the stakeholder agenda is therefore understandable. The pluralism of a vigorous civil society only leads to social inclusion if there is opportunity for all citizens to become members of well-organised community groups, parent associations, churches, trade unions and professional bodies, and to become involved in the running of local schools and hospitals. It is why the principle of universality at a macrolevel, although the most difficult part of the stakeholder agenda, is also crucial for its ability to counteract social exclusion. The real problem for a stakeholder agenda is not extending new rights of exit and voice to those who already have job security and transferable skills, important though this is, but in providing them for those who are currently excluded and marginalised. On a national level this is most acutely represented by the homeless. What does a stakeholder agenda have to say about them? On a global level it is the problem of the contrast between the affluence of the industrialised countries and the poverty of the South, and the threats to the planet from pollution and the unchecked exploitation of its resources.

THE ROLE OF THE STATE

Translating stakeholding into policy raises issues about the role of the state. How far should government be involved in shaping relationships in civil society? This is not a simple left/right issue. Conservative measures to spread property ownership through council house sales and privatisation of nationalised industries were a notable attempt to restructure civil society in a particular direction. Strategic intervention to shape the way in which society develops has been embraced from every part of the political spectrum.

The state has always had a major role both in sustaining and in destroying social capital. Through its actions the state can encourage a vigorous civil society and create the basis for relationships of trust and commitment. States can be pluralistic and tolerant, or restrictive and prescriptive. How proactive and interventionist the state should attempt to be hinges on determining what the state does well and what it does badly. The dangers of a state that becomes too programmatic and rigid in what it prescribes are now well understood. But states do also have important strategic functions.[3] A minimalist and passive role for the state is not an option for a reforming stakeholder government. There may be little certainty any longer about what the state can achieve, but there is a similar lack of faith in the claims made for other institutional structures, particularly deregulated markets.

The realisation of individual stakeholding and social inclusion requires an active role for the state but there are major disagreements over whether a stakeholding agenda is best achieved through moral persuasion, the creation of a particular ethos and climate of opinion, or whether it also needs legislative and administrative action to provide opportunities and resources for all citizens to allow them to become active members of society and organisations. Given the extent of social exclusion that exists some state action is required, if only to break logjams and create conditions in which self-activity can develop. The difference between enabling and imposing is often a matter of perception, however, which makes the transparency and accountability of the political mechanisms through which decisions are taken so important, as Anthony Barnett emphasises.

POLICY DILEMMAS

If stakeholding is to be more than a vague aspiration towards greater participation and inclusion there has to be some indication as to how it might be translated into positive policies. Several of the contributions to this book provide some important pointers. Four particular policy agendas stand out – on welfare, on the constitution, on the company and on economic policy.

Welfare

Welfare is critical to the stakeholding agenda because it is where the rhetoric of inclusion comes up most sharply against the reality of poverty and exclusion. What does giving a stake to the poor and the homeless involve? At present the questioning of traditional modes of collectivist welfare provision has led in the direction of seeking to provide individuals directly with the resources and opportunities they need to become self-reliant.

This issue goes to the heart of the contemporary dilemma on welfare. How interventionist should the state be? Left and right are both shifting by degrees to a new model in which rights to welfare are being maintained but much stricter obligations are being enforced on the recipients to find work or undertake training. This approach may enable more individuals to become stakeholders but it may further exclude those who are unable or unwilling to take advantage of it. One of the recurring themes of the report of the Social Justice Commission, as Ruth Lister emphasises, is that the most serious form of social exclusion is exclusion from the labour market. The provision of paid work for counteracting poverty and all its associated problems is the single most important policy for promoting social inclusion. But Lister also argues for the importance of maintaining a universalist welfare state. The present bias of policy is to encourage the majority to shift to private provision for welfare, leaving targeted state welfare programmes for those unable to provide for themselves. Ensuring that individuals feel they have a stake in their own future entitlements has the benefit of promoting autonomy. The risk is however that if the majority feel that they no longer benefit from the welfare state, political support for welfare programmes declines, and the recipients of welfare become both marginalised and stigmatised.

The stakeholder approach to welfare favours providing support as an entitlement rather than through means-tested benefits. Two forms of entitlement income are a basic income and a participation income. A basic income is essentially libertarian, giving citizens the opportunity to be independent and make their own choices, being as spendthrift and feckless, or as prudent and responsible as they wish. A participation income makes the receipt of benefit dependent on conditions, such as the willingness to participate in activities which are deemed to be socially useful: training, caring, or involvement in the voluntary sector. It is much more communitarian in its approach and one which many on the centre-left seem inclined towards. This still leaves the difficult issue of what obligations a stakeholder state has towards individuals who – contrary to the expectations of the stakeholder approach – may not wish to enter into this bargain.

Constitution

A second agenda focuses on the political and constitutional arrangements which can promote a stakeholder economy and a stakeholder society and define the scope of the public realm. This is a vital reform, for as Mike Rustin argues, if stakeholding does not work here, what hopes can we have that it will work in the private sphere? Anthony Barnett and Paul Hirst draw attention to the way in which centralised and closed systems of decision making systematically exclude citizens from participation. The problem is to find procedures and institutions which can better represent the diversity of opinion and groups in a modern democracy, and reduce the power of unelected quangos. This task is made more complex because in the past demands for greater democracy were often a cloak for the interests and ambitions of a narrow political class rather than a genuine expression of wider participation.

Stakeholding implies diversity and pluralism. It does not prescribe a single model of governance. A key requirement to help maximise stakeholding is to ensure proper representation of all groups and interests. This means determining acceptable baselines for the participation and representation of particular groups. It involves issues such as the recruitment of Members of Parliament, and appointments to public bodies of all kinds, in relation to key criteria such as gender and race. In extremely divided polities such as Northern Ireland the importance of symbolic representation to ensure legitimacy and prevent the exclusion of any group from the political process has been painfully learnt. A stakeholder society too needs a symbolic politics of representation. The important principle is that all significant voices should be heard and their legitimacy recognised.

Decentralisation is also a precondition for a thriving civil society and local democracy. For active stakeholding certain institutions such as schools and hospitals play a vital role. While there are many criticisms to be made of the way the Conservatives have centralised power and stuffed quangos full of their own nominees, they were right to raise the need for reform of the governance of many institutions in civil society. Who owns them, in whose interests they are run, how they are funded, and how they can be made accountable are critical questions for stakeholding, because these are institutions in which the majority of citizens have a large personal stake at some point in their lives, and may be willing to participate in their governance. Similarly, encouraging active participation in local decision making on health, education, the planning of public space, and public order gives individuals rights of voice and creates the social capital, informal networks and long-term relationships necessary for a stakeholder society.

Again, none of this is easy and there will be problems. Giving new rights of representation to some groups may exclude others, by subordinating their interests to new majorities. The task is to achieve a balance which will always be imperfect and must be judged by the extent to which it promotes inclusion, sustains an active civil society and encourages individual stakeholding.

Companies and the Workplace

The most developed and controversial policy agenda which the stakeholder debate has promoted concerns corporate governance. There has been a lively debate on the issue of what companies are for, whose interests they do and should represent and who the relevant stakeholders actually are.

One of the key issues relates to ownership and whether the nature of ownership in the modern corporation, as John Kay argues, has become so attenuated that many of the most important functions of ownership, the stewardship of assets and the monitoring of managers, can no longer be exercised by the legal owners – the shareholders – at all. This begs the question: to whom should the controllers of modern corporations be accountable? For many advocates of stakeholding the answer must include a wider group of stakeholders than just shareholders, such as employees, suppliers, banks, local communities, and environmental groups. Others who are sympathetic to the notion of the stakeholder company recoil from the complexities and possible dangers of empowering such an array of interests.

While most participants in this debate agree that successful companies should safeguard the long-term interests of their key stakeholders, the best means of achieving this is contested. Many within business argue that they already are stakeholder companies so any government action would be damaging. Or as David Willetts puts it, if it is really the case that a stakeholder approach is superior, then surely firms will eagerly adopt it as a way of improving their competitive position. Less sanguine contributions recognise that the failings of the current structures of corporate governance, both in terms of accountability and transparency, are unlikely to be spontaneously remedied. There are a number of routes to achieving change which range from self-regulation through the adoption of codes of best practice, fiscal incentives (perhaps to encourage the adoption of voluntary codes), to wholesale changes in company law. Proponents of self-regulation argue that if change is to be meaningful it must not be imposed and therefore must come through a cultural shift in the attitudes of company managers and owners.

In contrast to this, both John Parkinson and John Kay argue that some legislation is desirable to facilitate the adoption of practices which promote forms of governance conducive to stakeholding. Accountability could be strengthened by changing the conditions of service of Chief Executive Officers or by changing the structure of company boards to ensure that there is an independent and professional group of non-executive directors to act as informed monitors. These changes aim at improving the quality of management by altering the type of incentives or degree of scrutiny that managers face. While these measures might help ensure that management is more responsive to their stakeholders, they do not imply radical shifts in the balance of power or an attempt to impose economic democracy. The potential of fiscal measures to change corporate priorities is explored by Robert Kuttner, who describes the legislation being proposed by US Democrats which would provide regulatory and fiscal advantages to companies which fulfilled certain criteria on investment in training and education, as well as making long-term commitments to their employees in their plans to avoid lay-offs, and provide health insurance and pensions.

Though the relative importance of different stakeholder groups will obviously vary between companies, most writers on corporate governance acknowledge that employees must be thought of as primary stakeholders. Their stakes in the firm can be enhanced in a number of ways. Janet Williamson proposes a number of specific measures, such as partnership arrangements on investment and redundancy, which would offer employees greater security with regard to the employment contract and their immediate workplace environment. Many on the right dismiss measures which afford employees basic rights to fair treatment as being a luxury from a bygone corporatist era which must be sacrificed if we are to attain a truly flexible labour market. This misinterprets the meaning of flexibility. A new framework for the employment contract is clearly required which recognises both the individualistic nature of many employment contracts and the insecurity that this can engender.[4]

The case for enhancing employees' stakes in their companies through the extension of employee share ownership schemes, is explored by Andrew Pendleton. In theory the widespread use of employee ownership arrangements seems the ideal vehicle for realising the aspirations of stakeholding in the workplace. It can combine rights with obligations, it gives rise to increased participation and will arguably improve economic efficiency. For all these reasons the poor record of employee ownership within the UK in facilitating stakeholder arrangements should be a matter of concern. But as Andrew

Pendleton argues, given the form that employee ownership has taken in the UK, it is hardly surprising that it has failed to change corporate culture. Designing schemes which can combine meaningful participation and governance responsibilities with the prospect of long-term financial rewards should therefore be a rewarding area for stakeholder initiatives.

Economic Policy

Is there a stakeholder agenda for conducting national economic policy with clear and distinctive economic policy objectives? Since unemployment and poverty are two of the key enemies of social and economic inclusion a stakeholder approach might be expected to endorse an active macro-policy which makes the attainment of full employment its overriding concern. But centre-left economists are divided on this question. Macroeconomic adventurism (as Paul Hirst calls it), instigated by both right and left, has long undermined the performance of the British economy. Targeting full employment at the expense of other variables may – as Dan Corry argues – only lead to the kind of reaction by the financial markets and the monetary authorities which raises rather than lowers unemployment. Part of the difficulties with active Keynesianism are, as Jonathan Perraton emphasises, reinforced by the internationalisation of economic relations which has reduced the effectiveness of national economic policies and increased the constraints on policy makers.

These considerations help explain why such an emphasis is now given to macroeconomic stability. From a stakeholding perspective this should help generate the long-term, high trust, high commitment relationships. But stability of a financial indicator such as prices is unlikely to be enough. One possibility proposed by Dan Corry along with many other economists is to target the growth rate of nominal GDP rather than the inflation rate. The other key component of economic policy will come from the supply side and here any consensus on economic policy ends. Conservatives stress deregulation as the key supply-side policy. Stakeholder economics also places a strong emphasis on the role of markets, but recognises that because in some of the most important areas of the economy markets are highly ineffective, there is a central role for the state.

Nowhere is this clearer than in relation to training. In all market economies there is a tendency to underinvest in human capital. This is particularly so in a relatively deregulated labour market such as the UK's, where companies are less prone to undertake training themselves. Consequently there is an even greater onus on the state, as David Soskice puts it, to enter into an implicit contract with citizens about lifelong training opportunities.

An active role for the state will be needed in other areas of supply-side policy too. A flexible labour market will not address deep-seated labour market problems such as long-term unemployment. Instead, as many have recently argued,[5] a combined work and welfare strategy is required which should involve policies such as a minimum wage, reduced NICs for employers, wage subsidies for employers who take on the long-term unemployed, further in-work welfare payments, and a larger role for the state as a direct employer of those who find it difficult to enter the private labour market. These types of measures represent a practical stakeholder approach to help tackle a key cause of economic exclusion.

Of the many other policy debates that stakeholding has touched, one which has received widespread attention is that of the role of the City and the existence or otherwise of financial short-termism. While the lines are clearly drawn both within (and outside) the centre-left on this issue (see Meghnad Desai's critique of Hutton in this volume and Hutton's reply),[6] there is at least the semblance of a consensus – as reflected here by John Parkinson and John Kay – on one aspect of the debate: the market for hostile takeovers. Most evidence suggests that hostile takeovers are not an efficient way of either disciplining managers or providing returns for shareholders. They also tend to have a debilitating impact on relations between stakeholder groups. This does not necessarily mean that there is no role for hostile takeovers, rather that there is a strong case for restricting the ease with which they occur. If the role of takeovers is reduced, the need for alternative mechanisms of accountability is increased, which reinforces the arguments made by Parkinson and Kay.

CONCLUSION

Within two weeks of the word 'stakeholder' being unleashed into mainstream political debate in 1996, many commentators were already pronouncing it dead or empty, and sometimes both. Some dismissed it as a misguided lurch into management speak, or the latest concoction of the political image makers. But if this was all there was to it, would it have excited so much interest and attention? What its future may be is difficult to foresee. Its use may be fleeting, a passing fashion, or it could conceivably come to denote a new era in British politics. Yet whatever the fate of the word, the ideas underlying it will endure.

These ideas reach back in time to the Enlightenment project and its universal principles of freedom, equality, solidarity and community, but they also connect with ideas which are particular concerns of the current age, the search for security and stability in a time of bewildering change, and the demands for individualism and personal autonomy. As the contributions to this book demonstrate, however, there is much debate as to the meaning of the term and the contexts in which it is best applied. Much work remains to be done on exploring its limits and its potential.

At the heart of stakeholding is the tension running through contemporary existence between the need for membership and inclusion, and the need for personal autonomy. The centre-left has for long been preoccupied more with the former than with the latter, and has put its energies into building and defending institutions of solidarity. A successful stakeholder project may have to shift the balance towards autonomy.

This particular tension is not a new one. But the need to find new ways of addressing it has rarely been greater. The legacy of social and economic exclusion from the Thatcher years is visible to all but the most myopic. But the expansion in the scope of personal autonomy during the same period also needs to be registered. If progressive politics is to become once again electorally successful it must recognise that it has to find a new approach and a new terrain, and it has to recover the intellectual leadership it once enjoyed. It has now become an orthodoxy in many left circles that there can be no reversal of many of the changes introduced by the Thatcher governments. This goes both too far and not far enough. A centre-left project with any substance would have to conduct little short of a war to reverse the damage inflicted on so many individuals during Conservative rule. But a radical stakeholder project should also pick up where Thatcher left off in terms of dismantling the institutions of deference and privilege which still disfigure British society.

Many on the left are suspicious of stakeholding because of its emphasis on the individual, and think that there is little difference between left versions of stakeholding and right versions, such as the property-owing democracy. This is mistaken. There is some common ground, for example, over the importance of the ownership of private property as a tool of stakeholding.[7] But there are also some stark differences, particularly over attitudes to social justice and the role of the state. Stakeholding demands a belief in the merits of active government. Not old-style nationalising, centralising, inflexible and unresponsive government, but government all the same. Those sympathetic to the project may disagree on how best government should act, but there is a broad acceptance that government can and must have an extensive role to play in the modern economy. At the same time it is accepted that this role will not be the one that centre-left governments have traditionally played.

The difficulties of delivering this agenda should not be underestimated, but neither should the potential rewards. Stakeholding is an inherently populist philosophy. It binds some key principles together in novel ways, it addresses central concerns of the modern electorate, and it can capture the mood of the country in a manner which in Britain the centre-left has been unable to do for a generation. The populism of the Conservatives under Thatcher was real, but it was built on weak foundations. It promised much more in terms of personal autonomy than it was able or prepared to deliver, it systematically excluded many individuals altogether, and its policies weakened the conditions necessary to sustain autonomy for many more.

Stakeholding is a long-term strategy. As James McCormick notes, we will only find out how successful it has been during the Conservative government that is elected after the fall of the next Labour government. A stakeholding government would be guided by the aim of ensuring that individuals have the personal capacities and collective institutions they need to balance security and autonomy. Success will depend on whether it is possible in what John Gray calls 'our flawed and fractured late-modern culture'[8] to find a way of reconciling them.

NOTES

1. John Lloyd, 'Stakeholding: the great debate', *New Statesman*, 12 July 1996, pp. 27–9.
2. Social Justice: Strategies for National Renewal', *The Report of the Commission on Social Justice* (London: IPPR, 1994).
3. Ash Amin, 'Beyond Associative Democracy', *New Political Economy*, Vol. I, No. 3, 1996.
4. See 'Changing Work', A Report by the Fabian Society, 1996.
5. R. Thomas, 'Strong Welfare and Flexible Labour?', *Renewal*, Vol. 3, No.1, January 1995.
6. Will Hutton, 'Reply to Desai', *New Political Economy*, Vol. 1, No. 3, (1996).
7. The importance of rethinking private property for a left political agenda is examined in Andrew Gamble and Gavin Kelly, 'The New Politics of Ownership', *New Left Review*, 220, November–December 1996. See also Geoff Mulgan and Charles Leadbeater, *Mistakeholding* (London: Demos, 1996).
8. John Gray, *After Social Democracy* (London: Demos, 1996) p. 58.

Index